I have worked in natio Islamic
faith. Not all Muslims are rist; and
in times of war and natura t Christians are the only ones wh

Erwin Lutzer has written about the limitation of Islamic influences in today's culture…and he brings a unique perspective to this
brewing storm that can tenderize the hearts of believers to pray for
and reach out to those lost in this darkening shadow. This book presents the challenges and opportunities we have to shine the light of
God's truth into souls who need the Savior.

Franklin Graham, President and CEO
Samaritan's Purse
Billy Graham Evangelistic Association

The tide of Islam is rising across the West, even as churches fall
vacant in large numbers. Will nations like England, France, and the
United States come under the sway of Islam, where the yardstick
of justice is the shariah and the cross of Christ is despised? Pastor
Lutzer offers a sober wake-up call to the church to repent, strengthen
what remains, and rise to meet the challenge of the hour. This book is
packed with practical advice about how to hold fast in spiritually challenging times.

Mark Durie, author of *The Third Choice:*
Islam, Dhimmitude and Freedom

The Cross in the Shadow of the Crescent is the most provocative
and salient monograph I have read on the subject of Christianity's
response to Islam. The Christian faith dare not ignore, except at its
own peril, this evenhanded and thought-provoking volume. Prepare
for the future—read this book!

Paige Patterson, President
Southwestern Baptist Theological Seminary
Fort Worth, Texas

Radical Islam is one of the greatest challenges ever faced by the Christian church. In his book *The Cross in the Shadow of the Crescent*, Dr. Erwin Lutzer does once again what he has done so many times before—written a book that every evangelical should read.

Dr. R. Albert Mohler Jr., President
The Southern Baptist Theological Seminary

Every generation has its crises, and its champions. Dr. Erwin Lutzer is a champion. His courageous book, *The Cross in the Shadow of the Crescent*, tackles head-on the impending crises Christianity is facing in Asia, Africa, the Middle East, Europe…and America, in light of the undeniable 1400-year phenomenon that where Islam increases, Christianity decreases…Those who want to understand the times *must* read this book. A fast, compelling read that is captivating, confrontational, yet compassionate.

William J. Federer, author of *What Every American Needs to Know about the Qur'an— A History of Islam & the United States*

Much of this book the world would rather not hear. The persecution of Christians at the hands of religious and political opponents has a long and storied past. Too many blindly believe it could not happen in America. Erwin Lutzer raises two questions all of us must answer: Why is the church so weak when our Lord and Savior is so strong? Why are churches in Europe and the United Kingdom dying out while mosques are growing in number? This book is a call for the church to wake up lest the lampstand of truth and testimony be diminished by the treachery and threats approaching through the pervasive spread of Islamist influence. As a result of this book you will be motivated to pray more and live differently.

Mark L. Bailey, President
Dallas Theological Seminary

If you do not want to hear the truth…if you want to bury your head in the sand…if you don't want to be confused with the facts and the stark realities, then don't read this book.

Michael Youssef Ph.D., author of *Blindsided*
Founder and President of *Leading the Way*

Dr. Lutzer has long researched the growing impact of Islam in relationship to Christianity. Anyone concerned with this challenge would be wise to consider—and heed—the words of counsel found in *The Cross in the Shadow of the Crescent*. Those who do so will learn important lessons from the past, stand equipped for the future, and grow in their understanding of how to communicate the truth of Christ with Muslims.

Dr. John Ankerberg, President and host
John Ankerberg Show

The Cross in the Shadow of the Crescent equips Christians with the information they need to engage in intelligent dialogue with those who are deceived about the single greatest external threat to America and Christendom: the spread of Islam. This book is must reading for every Christian who desires to push back against the tide of darkness that threatens to engulf our world.

Dr. Robert Jeffress
Pastor, First Baptist Dallas

With the growing threat of Muslim Brotherhood infiltration into all levels of the US government, now, more than ever, it is critical that Christians understand this threat from a biblical perspective and what their responsibility is in this hour. This book is a dire warning of the clear and present danger we face and how we should respond to it. It is a must-read for every Christian today!

Laurie Cardoza-Moore
President, Proclaiming Justice to the Nations; Special Envoy to the UN for the World Council of Independent Christian Churches

Every person of faith in America needs to read *The Cross in the Shadow of the Crescent*. Erwin Lutzer, one of America's finest expositors, has done the Christians of America a great service by analyzing the challenge presented by Islam and explaining the ways we can and should respond.

Richard Land, President
The Ethics & Religious Liberty Commission

This book is a wake-up call to every thinking American, and especially Christians. It is a powerful antidote to those who portray Islam as a religion of peace. Here the truth of Islam and its political agenda is set forth with heavy documentation from Islamic sources as well as intelligence reports from the public domain. This is a very honest and courageous assessment of the challenge Islam poses for the church around the world.

Don McCurry, founder of
Zwemer Institute for Muslim Studies in Pasadena
Missionary to Muslims in Pakistan for 18 years

The Cross in the Shadow of the Crescent is the fruit of long years of sobering research...It is a labor of love aimed at providing a balanced framework by which the body of Christ should embrace Muslims as people created in God's own image while firmly facing the ideology of Islam.

Raouf F. Boulos, pastor of Outreach & Evangelism
The Moody Church

The ongoing and ever-increasing conflict with radical Islam is the challenge of our time. Liberty hangs in the balance. This is a captivating must-read book.

Jay Alan Sekulow, Chief Counsel
American Center for Law and Justice

THE CROSS

IN THE SHADOW

OF THE Crescent

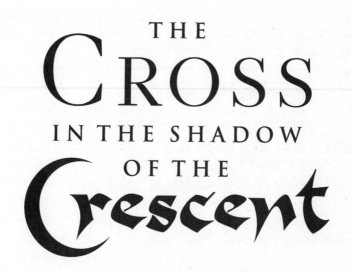

ERWIN W. LUTZER

WITH STEVE MILLER

HARVEST HOUSE PUBLISHERS
EUGENE, OREGON

Cover by Puckett, Lilburn, GA

Cover photos / illustration © Puckett; iStockphoto / raisbeckphoto; Rvs / Dreamstime

THE CROSS IN THE SHADOW OF THE CRESCENT

Copyright © 2013 by Erwin W. Lutzer
Published by Harvest House Publishers
Eugene, Oregon 97402
www.harvesthousepublishers.com

Library of Congress Cataloging-in-Publication Data
Lutzer, Erwin W.
 The cross in the shadow of the crescent / Erwin W. Lutzer ; Steve Miller, substantive editor and supportive writer.
  p. cm.
 Includes bibliographical references.
 ISBN 978-0-7369-5132-6 (pbk.)
 ISBN 978-0-7369-5133-3 (eBook)
 1. Missions to Muslims. 2. Christianity and other religions--Islam. 3. Islam--Relations--Christianity. 4. Islam--Missions. I. Miller, Steve, 1960- II. Title.
 BV2625.L88 2013
 261.2'70973--dc23

                                                                2012031799

Printed in the United States of America
        13 14 15 16 17 18 19 20 21 /BP-JH/ 10 9 8 7 6 5 4 3 2

Grateful Acknowledgments

My special thanks go to Harvest House Publishers, whose leadership believed in my initial manuscript and encouraged me to proceed toward the publication of this book. To you, Bob Hawkins, and your fine team, I owe a deep debt of gratitude. Although I have worked on this book intermittently since 2009, I could never have completed the project without the expertise of Steve Miller, whose editing and research enabled the final product to emerge in its present form. Thanks, Steve, for investing so much of your time and talent to see this book completed. God will richly reward you for your efforts.

Finally, and most importantly, thanks to the many people who have encouraged me and prayed that this, my most important book, would not only awaken the church, but be a clear call to rise to the challenges of our time. If we become all that God has promised we can be, this can be our finest hour.

Contents

Foreword

"Why another book on Islam?" It seems fashionable to begin every new book on Islam with this question. Yet this book is one that had to be written because of what it offers. In fact, I consider this one of the best books on Islam produced in the last 50 years.

At its beginning, Islam was an enigma for the visible church. Because some of its teachings are similar to Christian beliefs, some early Christians mistook Islam for a Christian sect of some sort or other. As the Middle Ages approached, more and more Christians began to recognize Islam as a separate religion. Some theologians were convinced that a Muslim could not convert to Christianity. Others detected in Islam "particles of divine light" and would eventually inspire the Vatican's "reformed" views on Islam in the 1960s.

The Protestant reformer Martin Luther, however, correctly noted that the core teachings of Islam are vehemently opposed to the core teachings of Christianity. And not until after the spread of Protestant missions endeavors in the nineteenth century did Christian theologians and missionaries acknowledge Luther's insights concerning Islam.

After 14 centuries of theological disputes, scholarly treatises, and analyses, the enigma of Islam is not yet fully solved. Seemingly, the more that is written on Islam, the greater the confusion becomes. And today, we are plagued with another extreme stance. Whereas in the past some Christian theologians thought Muslims couldn't convert to Christianity, now there are Christians—even some who profess to be within the evangelical spectrum—who don't see the need for Muslims to become Christians.

Amidst this deplorable chaos, Dr. Lutzer's book is the best help for all who desire to gain a biblical and compassionate understanding of Islam yet have been disenchanted by both books and media broadcasts that either incite fear of Islam or attempt to whitewash Islam's history and teachings. This book is different.

Dr. Lutzer offers the reader excellent information on Islam as a theological and ideological system. He points to the challenge it poses to the world, especially in the United States. He traces the history of how present-day Turkey went from Christianity to Islam, and shares how Islamic influence is spreading today in the West. Though he says his intention is not to give instruction on sharing Christ with Muslims, he nonetheless achieves this with excellence. And after having worked in ministry to Muslims for more than 30 years, I can say his pastoral heart for reaching out to Muslims is exceptional and genuine.

The Cross in the Shadow of the Crescent is highly informative, eye-opening, and alarming. Yet it is also full of great biblical hope for the church and for the transformation of Muslims from Islam to Christianity. Dr. Lutzer clearly differentiates between Islam as an anti-Christian ideology and the Muslims for whom our Lord died and who are in need of His salvation. He does not commit the mistake of declaring all Muslims to be "fanatical followers of Allah." He notes that the majority of Muslims live peacefully among us and that many of them don't even live up to the teachings of their own religion.

I was born in Pakistan to Muslim parents who became Christians, and as a minority Christian, I lived through pain, persecution, and social discrimination at the hands of Muslims. In fact, my only brother was martyred in Pakistan in 1990.

I am grateful that Dr. Lutzer has given me, and others like me, hope from the Bible. He has challenged us to be steadfast in our walk with the Lord, to trust and obey our calling to serve the Lord, and to take the gospel to Muslims, knowing that ultimate victory has already been won on the cross of Jesus. This Christ-centered, Bible-based message of salvation in Jesus' name alone is the only hope this world has. One Bible passage that has helped me to stand firm is Romans

8:35-39, where Paul reminds us not to fear death. Jesus has already won the victory, and though we may not see it now, we are assured of it. God is sovereign, and He is in control of everything.

In my years of ministry to Muslims in the United States, I have seen Christians respond to Muslims in the following ways:

1. They become paralyzed with fear and do nothing to reach out.
2. They wish Muslims would stop coming to the United States and spreading their influence.
3. They invent "creative methodologies" to reach Muslims that even Muslims mock, for they recognize this not-so-subtle "evangelism in disguise."
4. They are conciliar in their outlook and engagements.
5. They are actively engaged in ministry to Muslims.

Dr. Lutzer's book gives us hope to actively engage with Muslims. Disengagement is not an option, for American Christians in particular and the church in general. One day we will stand before the Lord and give an account of our lives lived for Him, and how we handled the opportunities entrusted to us.

In this book, you'll have the opportunity to read about how various Muslims came to Christ. Let us not be hesitant or afraid and hide within the safety of our Christian circles. The Lord is drawing Muslims to Him; let us be passionate about reaching them. They are here among us, waiting for someone to share the love and hope we have in Jesus.

Dr. Samuel Ezra Naaman
Professor, Department of World Missions,
Moody Bible Institute, Chicago

The Day the Levees Broke

The problem was not Katrina.

The problem was that the levees broke. And, as a result, millions of tons of water inundated the city of New Orleans. When it was over, the city was practically destroyed and nearly 1000 people had died. If only the levees had been strong enough to hold back the water, New Orleans might have been able to survive the catastrophe.[1]

The church in the West has already felt the first stirrings of a storm directed against it, and without question the speed of the wind and the height of the waves will intensify as time moves on. The question is whether the church will have the strength and the courage to withstand the growing onslaught. The question is whether the levees will hold.

A friend of mine who works in national security says that some Muslims view Americans as "physically weak, morally soft, and lacking in principled courage." We should be grateful for all those who are on the front lines of our security forces, for they have thwarted many a terrorist threat. However, our security forces are not designed to deal with the *spiritual* conflict that a growing secularism and Islamic presence poses in Europe and America. And while we as a church are not equipped with hidden cameras and high-tech surveillance devices to keep track of the terrorists, we do have both the resources and responsibility of working on the front lines of the religious conflict that is approaching as Islam's influence in America grows. The Scriptures teach that above and beyond the weapons of national security, we are engaged in a spiritual battle that only the church can fight. "Unless the LORD watches over the city, the guards stand watch in vain" (Psalm 127:1).

In this book, we will discover that the church will undoubtedly have to face the reality of influences that are almost entirely ignored by our national security forces. It is one thing to repel bombs and guns, but quite another to repel intimidation, lawsuits, and political correctness in all of its forms. And so our role in this coming conflict is to defend the front lines—it is to preserve the freedoms that we all too often take for granted. In brief, it is nothing less than defending and proclaiming the gospel in the face of increasing opposition.

Only the church possesses moral and spiritual resources to stand against the rising tide of secularism and false religions that are engulfing us. Very likely the next generation will be even more overwhelmed, unless the levees remain strong and unyielding. I write this book for the current generation of Christians in America, but I am more deeply concerned for the generation that will follow us. Our children and grandchildren will most assuredly fight battles that we've only heard about in other parts of the world but have never had to confront. The legal and social restrictions to prohibit us from exercising our faith are growing continuously, and the battle will only intensify in the years ahead. The day of casual Christianity is rapidly coming to a close, and the call for Christians to display courage is becoming more pressing than ever.

Today it is fashionable to say that the Islam of the terrorists is not the real Islam—that the extremists have hijacked a religion of peace and turned it into a religion of aggression and terror. However, if you take the Quran literally, you should be a militant Muslim. Anything else is to avoid its clear teachings.

Abdurrahman Wahid, the former president of Indonesia, the world's most populous Muslim country, in an essay titled "Right Islam, Wrong Islam," agrees that a literal reading of the Quran leads to what is popularly called Muslim extremism. To his credit, he is a moderate who is strongly opposed to this brand of Islam. And so he acknowledges that Muslims need to be persuaded not to take the

Quran literally. He says that extremism "rests upon a simplistic, literal and highly selective reading of the Koran and Sunna."[2] This is the bottom line: Moderate Muslims need to explain how they can be good Muslims and not obey the Quran's explicit commands.

Incredibly, in our day, secular groups such as the American Civil Liberties Union and Americans United for the Separation of Church and State are being joined by the radical Muslim community in their attacks against Christianity and the American way of life. Although these groups have very different core beliefs, they have this in common: Both are committed to using the doctrine of the separation of church and state to marginalize Christianity and attack the Judeo-Christian legal and moral foundation of this country. Ultimately, both have different visions for what America should become. But for now, they are determined to use the freedom granted us in our founding documents to diminish Christian influence and relegate Christian beliefs to the margins of society. In other words, both are equally committed to making the church weak, timid, and irrelevant.

Whether the church in America will be up to the challenge of facing these assaults remains to be seen. If we smugly believe that our churches will survive, we have to only look to history to learn that many churches in different parts of the world proved incapable of resisting similar assaults, particularly those from Islam. In this book, we will remind ourselves that thousands of churches in Asia Minor, the Middle East, and North Africa—at one time vibrant bastions of Christianity—are mosques today.

In present-day Europe, this transformation is happening right before our eyes, but the terms of battle have changed. For the most part, this has occurred through war and conquest, and that is still true in Muslim-dominated countries. But in the Western world, Islam is taking over through nonviolent means, taking advantage of the ignorance and apathy of both Europeans and Americans.

We can either see the advance of Islam in the West as a threat to the church, or we can see it as a welcome challenge—one that can be met with devotion, renewed commitment, and steadfast faithfulness. If we are willing to understand the true nature of the threat and be prepared to respond to it with the proper spiritual resources, this could be the church's finest hour.

I agree with what Tony Evans writes:

> For too long the church has operated on the defensive side of this battle. We've been reacting to the movements of hell rather than setting the pace of heaven. Jesus clearly says that the way you will know that the church is His church is that hell will be trying to stop it and hell will be failing.[3]

Evans goes on to explain that the church is designed to hold back Satan's forces being unleashed against mankind:

> The church isn't solely about choir fests, programs and luncheons...the church isn't just about feeling something, praying, clapping, singing or saying "amen," although those things are good. The church was intentionally designed to be the church, because when it is the church, even the strongest forces cannot break it down.[4]

Thankfully, there are still many tens of thousands of deeply committed believers in America, and hundreds—if not thousands—of healthy churches. Rather than predicting the demise of the American church, with God's help we can be a powerful witness to God's grace at a time when the dominoes around us are falling. After all, with our focus on the resurrected, ascended Christ, we can stand against even the most difficult attacks.

However, in my opinion, there are many in the church in America who are not sure of what the church is to be. Should we become a political voting bloc? Or should we stay out of politics altogether? Should our first concern be to avoid offending people because we want them to believe the gospel? Should we be content with doing good in our own sphere and not worry about the larger national trends that we can't seem to do much about anyway? Should we be gospel-centered? Or need-driven?

This book is not intended to answer all of these questions. Rather, it's meant to serve as a wake-up call. It is intended to help us become alert to the reality of what we are facing here in America and prepare us for the storm that is already at our doorsteps. Will we have the courage to face the onslaught, or will we die the death of a thousand appeasements? Will we be content to see the role of the church shrink until we find ourselves talking only to ourselves, hoping that the storm will pass us by and leave us alone?

I want to make this clear up front, and I will emphasize this again and again throughout this book: It is *not* my intention to stir up a fear of Islam or to incite anger toward Muslims. Not at all. As Christians, we are called to reach out to them in love.

Rather, these are my desires:

First, I hope we can learn from lessons of the past so we can stand stronger in the future. Second, I hope we would equip ourselves to meet the challenge ahead. We have no reason to fear, for our God has full control over all that happens, and He is our shelter in the storm. We can rest calmly in Him, knowing He can give us strength, wisdom, and grace for whatever is to come.

And third, my hope is that this book will contribute to a national conversation on the Western church and Islam, and that Christians will meet together to discuss how we can best share God's love, grace, and truth with the Muslim communities around us. We should not only be talking about defensive strategies but offensive strategies as well. God has given us an unprecedented opportunity to share about the gift of eternal life through Jesus Christ with those who have come to the West and would likely never hear this good news in their own countries.

This book is a journey. I do not claim to have all the answers. I do believe, however, that a powerful hurricane is on its way and we'd best be ready. We should not fear the storm that is coming, but be diligent in preparing for it.

PART I:
A DIFFERENT KIND OF INVASION

The Shadow of the Crescent

"As Islam replaces Christianity as the dominant religion in Europe, more and more churches are set to become mosques, which increasingly serve not only as religious institutions but also function as the foundational political building blocks for the establishment of separate, parallel Muslim communities in Europe that are based on Islamic Sharia law."

Soeren Kern, Gatestone Institute[1]

Chapter One

The Church of the Closed Door

Some Christians will not wake up until they go to church and discover that the door is locked and a sign has been placed on it that reads, 'This Church Is Officially Closed,'" said Frank Wright, the president of the National Religious Broadcasters association.[2] He was, of course, referring to the strong and growing anti-Christian bias exerted by many secularists, government officials, and even within the United States court system. As we know, there is a growing tide of opposition to expressions of Christianity in the so-called public square—to the point that some have even attempted to use legal means to criminalize such expressions. Our religious faith is expected to shrink until it is only a private matter that is not brought into politics, schools, or the workplace. If secularists cannot close a church, they at least want to render it powerless and irrelevant.

But there's another kind of experience Christians may soon come to face upon visiting their church. They will discover that the doors are open, but the building has been turned into a mosque. While that may seem a rather far-fetched and unlikely scenario to Christians in America, this has already been happening with increasing frequency in Europe and other parts of the world.

For example, Gatestone Institute reported this in 2012:

> The proliferation of mosques housed in former churches reflects the rise of Islam as the fastest growing religion in post-Christian Europe…The latest churches destined to become mosques are located in Germany, where the Roman Catholic Church has announced plans to close up to six churches in Duisburg, an industrial city in [the] northwestern part of the country, due to falling church attendance…

> Muslims in Duisburg are now clamoring to turn empty churches in the city into mosques, according to the Germany daily newspaper, *Der Westen*…some Protestant churches have also been converted into mosques in Germany, where the Muslim population has jumped from around 50,000 in the early 1980s to more than 4 million today.[3]

The same phenomenon is occurring in the United Kingdom, where "there are now more than 1,700 official mosques in Britain, many converted from former churches."[4]

What many people don't realize is the extent to which this has happened in centuries past. History and religious studies scholar Philip Jenkins, in an eye-opening book titled *The Lost History of Christianity*, says, "Much of what we today call the Islamic world was once Christian…In most of these cases, churches collapsed or vanished because they were unable to cope with the pressures placed upon them by hostile regimes, mainly Muslim."[5]

With regard to the spread of Islam in Europe, one of the most respected Western scholars of Islam, Bernard Lewis, says that "some have even described the present situation as the third Muslim invasion of Europe, more successful than either the first or the second."[6] As we survey what is happening there and in the United Kingdom, we need to have a wake-up call here in North America. And let's not think it cannot happen in this country. As we will see later in this book, the conditions that have led to the situation as it stands now in Europe are becoming more and more prevalent in America.

The main challenge for us as Christians is a lack of awareness. Many simply don't know what is happening. One reason is that so much of what is taking place happens under the radar. Very little media attention is given to the growing influence American-based

Muslim organizations are having on government agencies, the education system, the media, politics, the legal arena, and more. And for many of us, the impact hasn't been overt—at least, not yet. So Islamic encroachment continues quietly and largely unabated—at our peril.

THE TURNING POINT

For me, the turning point was July 2009. My wife, Rebecca, and I had the privilege of joining a group of fellow Christians on a tour of the seven churches of the book of Revelation. The trip was eye-opening. I returned home with a passionate desire to understand why the once-strong Christian presence in Turkey (Asia Minor) had essentially disappeared. I was surprised at the extent to which Islam had overcome a once-thriving Christian region. While there is a small remnant of churches in Turkey, they are overwhelmingly outnumbered by the mosques everywhere. All the towns and villages we visited were filled with tall minarets that dotted the skyline. How had all this happened?

Particularly noteworthy is the fact Jesus Himself wrote letters to seven churches located in this very region, and Revelation 2–3 preserves these letters for us. And now, the visible presence of Jesus no longer exists in these cities. In fact, it no longer exists throughout Asia Minor. Our Muslim friends tell us that the victory of Islam over Christianity in these once-Christian lands proves the superiority of Muhammad over Jesus.

Perhaps nothing symbolized my internal struggle as much as what we saw the day we stood beside the ruins of a fifth-century cathedral in the ancient city of Philadelphia. Remember, Jesus had assured this church, "These are the words of him who is holy and true, who holds the key of David. What he opens no one can shut, and what he shuts no one can open. I know your deeds. See, I have placed before you an open door that no one can shut" (Revelation 3:7-8). And yet next to the ruins of this ancient cathedral is a mosque, with a tall minaret, eclipsing the other buildings around it.

The church walls had long since caved in, but the mosque appeared in good repair and was being used as a school. Dozens of children surrounded our tour bus with their shining faces and beautiful brown eyes. They wanted to welcome us as Americans and have their pictures taken with us. Their image was indelibly burned on my mind as I realized that these precious young ones were being reared as devotees of Islam. All of them, I'm sure, will eventually hear about Jesus because He is mentioned many times in the Quran, but they will know Jesus only as a mere prophet and not as the Savior who came to rescue us from our sins.

Standing there, I realized that the One who said He could open doors that could not be shut and shut doors that no one could open—the Lord Jesus Himself—appeared to have found the door firmly shut in His face in Philadelphia. The church of the open door had become the church of the door slammed shut.

Think back to the churches to whom Jesus dictated these personal letters: Ephesus, Smyrna, Pergamum, Thyatira, Sardis, Philadelphia, and Laodicea. There are no visible churches in any of these cities today; indeed, with few exceptions, there has been no readily visible evidence of Christianity in these locales for the past 800 years.

Of course I don't mean to say that there aren't any Christians in Turkey. The 73 million people who live there are predominantly Muslim, and only .2 percent are Christian, Jewish, or of other religious backgrounds.[7] For the most part, these believers meet in secret Bible studies or cell groups far away from the prying eyes of governing authorities. And I know there are a few media ministries in the country that are sharing the gospel in that region. There are also a small number of Protestant churches in the country. According to Paul Marshall and Nina Shea of the Center for Religious Freedom, Hudson Institute, "several...are led by pastors who were formerly Muslims, [and they] have seen an increase in violence in recent years."[8]

The Turkish constitution grants freedom of religion, but that does not mean that it is always practiced. Indeed, there are virtually no clear examples in history of Christians living in Muslim-dominated lands being granted anything that even approaches equal rights. What "freedom" looks like for Christians in Muslim countries will become clearer later in this book.

While the actual churches to whom Jesus dictated His seven letters—churches that likely met in homes—probably disappeared in the early centuries AD, Christianity did flourish in the region for a time. Just as Christianity spread throughout Europe after the time of Constantine (who died in AD 337), so also Christendom came to dominate Asia Minor. Yet during the Middle Ages, all that changed drastically. Philip Jenkins notes the following:

> The statistics of decline are sobering. Look, for instance, at Asia Minor, the region that is so often mentioned throughout the New Testament: it is here that we find such historic names as Iconium and Ephesus, Galatia and Bithynia, the seven cities of the book of Revelation. Still in 1050, the region had 373 bishoprics, and the inhabitants were virtually all Christian, overwhelmingly members of the Orthodox Church. Four hundred years later, that Christian proportion had fallen to 10 or 15 percent of the population, and we can find just three bishops. According to one estimate, the number of Asian Christians fell, between 1200 and 1500, from 21 million to 3.4 million.[9]

The fact that Turkey, which was once dotted with churches, is 99.8 percent Muslim today serves as evidence that Christianity does not always prevail in the places where it is established.

This is exactly what happened in North Africa as well. At one time, this region was predominantly Christian. But all that changed with the conquest of Islam. By the twelfth century, Christianity had been largely wiped out. In his book *The Extinction of the Christian Churches in North Africa*, scholar Leonard Ralph Holme wrote that the churches "fell a victim to the resistless onslaught of the Moslem conquerors,"[10] and that it "perished so completely that the very causes of its ruin have disappeared."[11] All symbols of the Christian presence have been obliterated amid the presence of tall minarets pinpointing the location of thousands of mosques in villages, towns, and cities.

Muslims say that Jesus was great, but Muhammad was greater. He was, after all, the greatest and last of all the prophets. And they point to what happened in Asia Minor and North Africa as evidence that the crescent is more powerful than the cross.

Or is it?

JESUS AND HIS CHURCH

The book of Revelation was written in about AD 95 on the island of Patmos, to which the apostle John was exiled on account of the persecutions taking place throughout much of the Roman world. Today this island is a beautiful place to visit, with its whitewashed buildings that stand out against the deep blue waters of the Aegean Sea. The most important site here is the Cave of the Apocalypse, the place where tradition says John received his revelation from Christ. We don't know if the cave is the same one John stayed in, but it could be, for it is a natural formation with huge stones. On the ceiling of the cave are three cracks embedded in the rock, which tradition says were created when the voice of Jesus sounded forth to give John his vision.

It is generally believed that John was exiled to Patmos as punishment for his faith, for he wrote, "I, John, your brother and companion in the suffering and kingdom and patient endurance that are ours in Jesus, was on the island of Patmos *because of* the word of God and the testimony of Jesus" (Revelation 1:9). Then he went on to describe the vision he received from Jesus, who appeared with blazing glory and sovereign power.

In the vision, John saw Jesus walking amid seven candlesticks, or the churches, and in His right hand Jesus held seven stars, or "the angels of the seven churches" (Revelation 1:20—perhaps the pastors or messengers of these churches). Jesus was walking among the worshippers for whom He died. This beautiful imagery underscores the presence of Christ in His church. He is with His people in the midst of their conflicts, failures, and persecutions. He is with them to provide the help they need to serve Him despite opposition and discouragement. And He promises that those who overcome (see 2:7,11,17,26; 3:5,12,21) will be motivated to remain faithful to the end.

Just so, Jesus walks among us today. He comes to our worship services and our Bible study groups. He comes to observe, to strengthen, and to let us know that we are precious to Him. After all, He bought us with His own blood (1 Peter 1:18-19). Take a moment to visualize Jesus walking down the aisle of your church on a Sunday morning. Imagine Him both encouraging and rebuking your congregation, praising people for their faithfulness and warning them about sin.

Some churches today pay consultants to help them evaluate their strengths and weaknesses. But no human being can possibly assess the true condition of a church. Only Jesus can see what is in people's hearts. That which appears vibrant to us may be dead to Jesus. Only He can tell which churches are alive and which are dead.

For example, note what Jesus said about the church at Sardis. This church had enough energy and vitality to give the appearance of life. But when Jesus applied His stethoscope to the church, He did not find a heartbeat. "You have a reputation of being alive, but you are dead" (Revelation 3:1). If we had served on the church staff, we would likely have thought that it was a healthy congregation. Yet Jesus pronounced this church as dead. Even so, this congregation had a remnant; there were some who had not "soiled their clothes" (verse 4). There were still some strands of wheat among the many tares. But as we shall see, Jesus ultimately prevails even when regional churches fall into decline.

LESSONS WE SHOULD LEARN

My hope is this book will help us to take the pulse of our churches, and more specifically, our own lives. And as we do this, we will learn the lessons that come to us from the seven churches in Revelation 2–3. We might even be able to speculate what Jesus would say to us if He were to dictate a letter to the Western church or to us as individuals. In the process, we will consider what the future might hold for us.

If we heed the lessons to be learned from the churches in Revelation 2–3, we can make our churches stronger and persevere in the face of whatever challenges come our way. We can become an attractive witness to a watching world, pointing people to the saving grace of Jesus Christ and the hope that is found in Him alone. And we can respond wisely and with love to the Muslim community.

··

A KEY DISTINCTION

In this book, note carefully the times when I use the term *Islamists*. When I do, it's because I want to distinguish extremists from Muslims and Islam in general. When I speak of *Islamists,* I have in mind an enemy who holds to an ideology of a world ruled by Islam and the imposition of shariah law everywhere, including in America. But not all Muslims are supremacists; the vast majority of them are moderates who are glad to live peacefully within Western society.

There is some disagreement among well-qualified experts about whether it's possible to make such a distinction. Without taking sides or making this a complicated issue, I simply want to make it clear that when I use the term *Islamists,* I am deliberately focusing on the extremists only.

THE WINDS OF CHANGE

Yes, Osama bin Laden is dead. Yes, many of his co-conspirators are also dead or imprisoned. And as of this writing, there have been no successful terrorist attacks in the United States since 9/11. For all practical purposes, it seems as though the tide has turned and we're winning the war against radical Islamists who desire to punish "the Great Satan," or America. When we think of the war against terror, we think of it mostly in terms of what is happening in the Middle East in places like Afghanistan.

A Different Kind of Invasion

But this does not mean we have nothing to fear from the incursion of Islam into our country. Muslim organizations—such as CAIR (Council on American-Islamic Relations) and the OIC (Organization of Islamic Cooperation)—are still very much at work, spreading their influence through increasing immigration, building mosques and community centers, pressuring people to keep from speaking critically of Islam, making efforts to achieve political legitimacy, and even filing lawsuits intended to intimidate non-Muslims and to demand societal concessions that favor Muslims' religious practices. While these Muslim advocacy groups do much to give the appearance they are moderate, as we will learn later in this book, their founders, writings, and current commitments are anything but.

In other words, we in the West have become so focused on

terrorism itself that we have turned a blind eye to the dramatic inner transformation taking place in our midst—a transformation we don't read about in the headlines. In addition, it's easy for us to assume that it is the more moderate form of Islam that is prevailing in America because the majority of Muslims we meet go about their lives.in rather peaceful, ordinary ways. They live in our communities, have jobs, and are raising families. But when it comes to representing Islam as a whole, this segment of the Muslim population is by and large silent, and there is a reason for that, as we will soon see.

In North America, it is those who work within and through Muslim organizations such as CAIR, the OIC, and MSA (Muslim Student Association) who speak as authoritative representatives of Islam. In fact, research has shown that "many of the most prominent Muslim organizations are front groups for, or derivatives of, the Muslim Brotherhood."[12] We will learn more about the Muslim Brotherhood later in the book. For now, it's sufficient to say it is recognized as the first modern Islamic terror organization, and its writings declare that "their work in America is a kind of grand jihad in eliminating and destroying the Western civilization from within...so that it is eliminated and God's religion is made victorious over all other religions."[13] These advocacy groups, and others like them, are pushing agendas that are detrimental to the legal and religious freedoms we enjoy in America. What's more, these same groups promote strict adherence to what is known as shariah.

A POWERFUL ADVOCACY GROUP

After the United Nations, the Organization of Islamic Cooperation (OIC) is the largest inter-governmental body in the world, overseeing 57 Muslim member countries. According to the OIC's website, the organization "is the collective voice of the Muslim world."[14] In 1990, this body adopted the Cairo Declaration on Human Rights in Islam, "which officially exempted all Muslim countries from compliance with the UN Universal Declaration on Human Rights and replaced it with Islamic law (shariah)."[15] Very simply, the Cairo Declaration states that in Muslim countries, "sharia is the governing rule, and other human rights principles must yield to it."[16] And in the 1990s "when UN Special Rapporteurs criticized OIC countries for violations of international human rights standards...the rapporteurs were threatened for purportedly insulting Islam."[17]

A key objective of the OIC for the past two decades has been to persuade the UN to criminalize all criticism or perceived insults of Islam around the globe. According to a ten-year program of action produced at the Islamic Summit Conference in 2005, one of the OIC's goals is "to have the United Nations adopt an international resolution to counter Islamophobia, and call upon all States to enact laws to counter it, including deterrent punishments."[18] While the OIC claims it is doing this in the name of religious and cultural sensitivity, the real intent is obvious—to make "discussion, debate, and analysis of Islam and its various interpretations out of bounds."[19]

Understanding Why Shariah Is So Significant

What is shariah? Perhaps you've heard the term before, and you know it has something to do with Islamic law. Before we can go any further, it's vital to have a clear understanding of shariah, for it explains much of what we need to know about Islam.

One resource defines *shariah* this way:

Translated as "the path," shariah is a comprehensive legal and political framework. Though it certainly has spiritual elements, it would be a mistake to think of shariah as a 'religious' code in the Western sense because it seeks to regulate all manner of behavior in the secular sphere—economic, social, military, legal, and political.[20]

Put bluntly, because shariah encompasses all of life, it is totalitarian in nature. It dictates what Muslims can and cannot do. Every law is based on the contents of the Quran as well as the Sunna (which documents the acts and words of Muhammad and serves as a sacred source of Islamic law). These texts form the basis of all shariah.

Shariah is not optional for Muslims. For a Muslim to accept Islam and deny shariah would be similar to a Jew who claims to accept the five books of the Torah but rejects the Ten Commandments. Those Muslims who reject shariah as a way of life are viewed as not being totally devoted to their religion.

This brings us to an especially important point: Because shariah demands compliance on the part of *all* Muslims, Islamic moderates and reformers are put in a difficult position. In the eyes of Muslim supremacists or Islamists, anyone who is perceived as advocating change that questions or undermines shariah (and therefore undermines the Quran and Sunna) is considered a hypocrite, a dissenter, or an apostate who has committed a grave offense against Allah.

So when it comes to Islam's growing influence in the West, even if moderates do outnumber supremacists by far, that doesn't give us reason to breathe more easily. For the supremacists wield the positions of political and religious authority in much of the Muslim world and their front organizations here in America. It is they who have the dominant voice. Moderates are in a no-win situation because questioning the supremacists, who advocate shariah, is in a practical sense equivalent to questioning shariah itself—a punishable offense. This, of course, makes moderates reluctant to speak out.

Shariah: The Threat to America explains this further:

> The shariah adherents who comprise the supremacist camp constitute a mainstream and dynamic movement in Islam. Importantly, that characterization does not speak to the question of whether this camp is or is not representative of the "true Islam." There are over a billion Muslims in the world, and their understandings about their belief system, as well as their practices with respect to it, vary. In light of this, there may not be a single "true Islam." If there is one, we do not presume to pronounce what it holds…
>
> Regardless of what percentage of the global Islamic population adheres or otherwise defers to shariah (and some persuasive

polling indicates that percentage is high in many Islamic countries), that segment is punching well above its weight. For that reason, proponents of an expansionist shariah present a serious threat to the United States even if we assume, for argument's sake...that shariah adherent Islam is not the preponderant Muslim ideology.[21]

That explains why the many moderate Muslims who willingly integrate themselves into Western society have no real means by which to hold back their fewer and more extremist brethren who desire to Islamize the West.

The Incompatibility of Shariah with Western Society

What is it that makes shariah so dangerous to Western society? At first glance, we might think there is no harm in permitting Muslims to observe shariah within their own communities, which already happens right now in Europe and the United Kingdom. But shariah is viewed as being sacred and coming from Allah himself, which, in the adherents' eyes, makes it superior to all other law systems:

> [Muslim writers who subscribe to the supreme authority of shariah over all other laws] teach that since everything in the universe belongs to Allah, and as Muslims are the true followers of Allah and therefore his rightful representatives, the oversight of the earth—especially the exercise of political power or authority—is the responsibility of Muslims. All others are usurpers from whom Muslims must endeavour to take power.[22]

Given that perspective, we can see why Islamists who live in Western nations have persistently exerted great pressure on government authorities to grant them the right to live in full accordance with shariah.

> For these ideologues, shariah is not a private matter. Adherents see the West as an obstacle to be overcome, not a culture and civilization to be embraced, or at least tolerated. It is impossible, they maintain, for alternative legal systems and

forms of government peacefully to coexist with the end-state they seek.[23]

Once we recognize the totalitarian nature of shariah, we can see why it is said shariah cannot coexist alongside any other legal system. Sheikh Yusuf al-Qaradawi, a major legal authority in the Muslim world today, minces no words when he speaks out against integrative approaches:

> Secularism can never enjoy a general acceptance in an Islamic society. For Muslim societies, the acceptance of secularism means something totally different. As Islam is a comprehensive system of worship (Ibadah) and legislation (Shari'ah), the acceptance of secularism means abandonment of Shari'ah, a denial of the divine guidance and a rejection of Allah's injunctions...For this reason, the call for secularism among Muslims is atheism and a rejection of Islam. Its acceptance as a basis for rule in place of Shari'ah is downright apostasy.[24]

Knowing these perspectives and facts, we can easily see why the trend in the West points toward greater Islamization, and not less. Bernard Lewis is quite correct when he concludes we are witnessing "the third Muslim invasion of Europe."[25] The United Kingdom has gone far down this path as well, and in this book, we will learn more about what's happening here in America.

CLARIFYING THE NAME *ALLAH*

Allah is simply the Arabic word for "God." It is important to point out that Arabic-speaking Christians have been using the Arabic name *Allah* for centuries before Muhammad, and many Arabic-speaking Christians today still use the name *Allah* to refer to the God of the Bible (not the Quran). In this book, however, whenever I refer to "Allah," I am referring to the god of Islam.

SOME QUESTIONS TO PONDER

As my wife and I toured the seven cities where the churches in the book of Revelation once stood, here are some questions that came to our minds:

- Why did Jesus allow Islam to triumph over Christianity in such a dominating fashion?
- When a church dies, is it always the fault of the church, or are there other factors that contribute to its demise?
- Is persecution always good for the church, or does it sometimes obliterate it?
- Do Islam's widespread victories over Christianity prove Islam is superior?
- Might God use Islam to bring judgment against the Western church?
- What might American churches look like in the next 25 to 50 years?

This book serves as an open letter to Christians in the West. I write with a passion that we would wake up to the fact that our future might be in peril. Islamic influence is spreading rapidly in North America, much as it already has in the United Kingdom and the other parts of Europe, and it has drastically altered the political, cultural, legal, and religious landscape in those places. I write out of great concern for what may lie ahead.

In chapter 9 of this book, I will introduce you to experts who are in a position to know the chilling facts of Islam's designs and strategies against America. We will review evidence that our nation's leaders and policy makers are refusing to come to grips with the nature of what is happening. We will learn that the threat of terrorism is but a distraction to prevent us from recognizing the far more insidious campaign of deception and infiltration taking place in our midst. The Muslim Brotherhood and its many offspring organizations are committed to achieving increased influence through immigration, education,

Muslim community centers, mosques, political legitimacy, intimidation, lawsuits, and if necessary, terrorism. US intelligence analyst Joseph Myers described the plan as being "oriented on an 'organizational' approach, toward building and developing organizations and networks that implement 'civilizational jihad' in a gradual and efficient fashion."[26]

Does that seem unnecessarily alarmist? Not according to senior-level security and intelligence experts who have done a lot of research and study on this. Their concern is backed by hard evidence that is well documented, some of which we will survey in chapter 9.

We as a church must wake up to the reality around us and pray for this country as never before. We also have to train the next generation of Christians for what it will face as Islamists continue advancing their agenda through whatever means possible.

DIFFERENT BOOKS, DIFFERENT PURPOSES

This book has a specific purpose. My intent is not to give instruction on how to share Christ with Muslims, for there are already good resources about that. I've listed some of them in the select bibliography in the back of this book.

Also, it is important for us to recognize that there are thousands of Muslims who are converting from Islam to Christianity around the world, including in Muslim countries. Although I will make reference to these and other encouraging developments, these themes have already been more specifically addressed by other authors. In the bibliography I provide a list of resources you will find helpful for better understanding what is happening on various fronts with regard to Islam.

Be assured I deeply believe that we who are Christians have a great opportunity to show our love and compassion to the Muslims among us. I believe that God has brought Muslims to the West so that, free from the social and spiritual oppression of their own countries, they can be exposed to and examine the claims of Jesus. I urge all of us to befriend our Muslim neighbors and introduce them to the love of Christ, whether they become a "Christ follower" or not.

So, as you read this book, which exposes the many ways Islamic influence is spreading, I urge you to resist any notion that we should hate Muslims. We must *not* see them as our enemies, but rather as victims of a totalitarian and oppressive religion. We must see them as people who long for peace and happiness within their own families, and who want to do right by Allah as they understand him. We must see them as people who need not just a prophet, but a Savior to save them from their sins. Jesus made clear that hate is never an option for His people. "Love your enemies" He said, even to those who were being persecuted (Matthew 5:44).

Keep in mind that although we might be intimidated by Islam, God isn't. His purposes will continue to move ahead. And we can be confident that the future—our future—is in the hands of God, not Muhammad and his followers. Muslims cannot close a church unless Jesus gives them permission to do so. He is, after all, King of kings and Lord of lords.

DISCOVERING THE LESSONS FOR TODAY

The purpose of this book can be simply stated: It is to provide a wake-up call to the church regarding the agenda and strategies of militant Islam so that we might prepare ourselves for an uncertain future.

Fifty years ago, no one could possibly have predicted that mosques would replace large numbers of the churches of Europe. But today, Islam's growing presence in Europe—with its accompanying insistence on imposing its ways on European society—makes us realize how quickly things can change and how rapidly the Muslim agenda can advance. And similar changes are already taking place in America.

I've reduced my thoughts to seven lessons we must learn from the formerly Christian cities of Asia Minor that were conquered by Islam. I begin with the history of the church in Istanbul, which, of course, is not one of the seven cities mentioned in Revelation 2–3. But its history is a window into how a church has been turned into a mosque. If the ancient ruins of the churches in Turkey could speak, what would they say? I believe they would tell us a story that we need to hear. As philosopher George Santayana famously said, "Those who cannot remember the past are doomed to repeat it."[27]

This book is a work in progress. As long as I live, I want to grow in my understanding of what the church in America should be and do at this critical hour.

Join me on a journey that I pray will be profitable for us going forward. Many brothers and sisters in Christ have already gone ahead of us and paid a high price for their obedience to our Lord. Let us hear their history, and may we learn from their mistakes and triumphs.

Best of all, God is with us.

— The Triumph of the Cross —

A Personal Testimony

I am a Kurd who was born in Baghdad, Iraq. My grandfather was a Muslim, and my grandmother was Jewish. I hid my Jewish ancestry from my Muslim friends because I feared what they would say or do to me. As a child, I remember the Quran being read on a recorder. Every time I heard the words of the Quran my heart became sad and fearful. The god of the Quran was very angry, demanding, and controlling.

In elementary school I studied Islam, the faith my mother practiced. I first heard about Jesus when I graduated from college, and at the time I considered Him only a prophet. The next time I heard about Jesus was in July 1996 while living in Kurdistan. My husband began working as a doctor for an American organization. The wife of one of my husband's colleagues began sharing about Jesus with me. She said Jesus was more than a prophet; He was God. I was very confused and could not accept the idea that Jesus was the one true God.

Four months later, Saddam Hussein began accusing anyone involved with Americans of being spies. Fearing death or imprisonment, thousands fled Iraq, and an associate from a nongovernment organization helped me and my husband to escape. Miraculously, we were able to come to the United States. The second miracle soon followed—the same woman who had told me about Jesus in Iraq became my neighbor in America. With God, there are no coincidences.

After being in America for two years, I became very ill and saw a doctor. After performing some tests, he told me that I had tumors spreading in several areas of my body, and that I would need surgery. I returned home from this visit crying, wondering why God would withhold healing from me. But when it came time for the surgery, after the doctor prepared himself, he said it was as though someone was preventing him from moving ahead. Evidently I was healed, and I've never had relapses since.

Then I began searching for the truth of who God really is. My Muslim friends told me Islam was right, but Christians also claimed their way was right. One day I thought about a devout Muslim woman whom I knew—a woman who fasted and prayed diligently. I had noticed that her prayers had gone unanswered, and it occurred to me that perhaps she wasn't following the one true God.

I then became a Christian and accepted Jesus Christ into my heart. Jesus is my treasure; He means everything to me. I praise Him with all my heart for what He has done in my life. He traded my anger for joy and my great sadness for love and peace. All those who knew me before my conversion say they see such an incredible difference in my life. The difference is because of all that Jesus has done for me. The war within my heart is over; Jesus won.

—Amilah

Part II:
Seven Lessons for Today's Churches

The Shadow of the Crescent

"Islam is a revolutionary ideology,
a revolutionary program (agenda)
to alter the social order of the whole world,
and rebuild it in conformity with its own tenets and the ideals."
Abu Ala Maududi, Islamic scholar[1]

Chapter Two

Lesson #1:
We Cannot Take the Continued
Existence of the Church for Granted

*Yet I hold this against you: You have forsaken the love you
had at first. Consider how far you have fallen! Repent
and do the things you did at first. If you do not repent,
I will come to you and remove your lampstand
from its place (Revelation 2:4-5).*

—Jesus, written to the church at Ephesus

The Moody Church in Chicago is surely one of the most beautiful churches in America. Built in honor of the famous evangelist Dwight Lyman Moody and dedicated in 1925, this structure is a combination of Romanesque and Byzantine architecture. In fact, its architecture was inspired by Hagia Sophia (the Church of Holy Wisdom) in the city of Istanbul, Turkey.

Understandably, when I became the senior pastor of The Moody Church back in 1980, I wanted to visit Istanbul and see this historic church for myself. As I compared pictures of this great cathedral with The Moody Church, I could see the similarities with regard to the Byzantine architecture and the spacious sanctuary and seating area that characterizes both structures. But I wanted to see this famous church with my own eyes. God answered my prayers, and it has been my privilege to visit the Church of Holy Wisdom in Istanbul twice during the past few years.

The history of the Church of Holy Wisdom gives us a window into Islamists' goal of turning churches into mosques. Dedicated in the sixth century in what was then ancient Constantinople, this church was for many years the greatest one in all of Christendom— until it was turned into a mosque in 1453 after a conquest by the Ottoman Turks. The better we know the history of what happened at this church, the better we will understand what happened to the churches throughout Asia Minor when Muslim armies invaded the land.

Though the city of Istanbul is not one of the seven cities mentioned in Revelation 2–3, I write about it because what happened there on a large scale has in some ways taken place in hundreds of smaller cities and towns throughout Turkey. It is, in some respects, the most famous story of the conquest of a church, and helps us to understand what takes place when Islam takes control of a region.

The Church of Holy Wisdom was dedicated by the great emperor Justinian in AD 537, who, when giving his dedication speech, said, "Solomon, I have outdone thee!" He could not have predicted the great role this church would play in both the history of Christendom and, centuries later, in the history of Islam. Imagine a building that is 1500 years old, still standing, still beautiful, and presently as a museum is still visited by thousands of people every day!

THE COMING OF THE TURKS

This church was drastically changed in 1453 when the Ottoman Turks conquered Constantinople. For many years, the Ottoman sultans had conspired to capture this capital city of the weakening Byzantine Empire. They had made several previous attempts, and this time they accomplished their goal. First, Sultan Mehmed II isolated the city and built a fortress on the European side of the Bosphorus strait. This gave him the ability to halt all vessels to and from the Black Sea and charge exorbitant fees for passage. Those who dared to defy the power of the sultan paid a heavy price: For example, when a Venetian ship attempted to pass without stopping to pay the toll, it was sunk by cannon fire and its crew members were taken captive and executed.

Meanwhile, Emperor Constantine XI did all he could to recruit help to resist the assault that he knew was coming upon Constantinople. But thanks to disagreements of one kind or another, even the Pope was deaf to his pleas. Within the enormous walls of the city were about 50,000 people who had no other option but to hold on to their faith in God and the church. When the walls were damaged by the initial barrages of cannon fire, the men, women, and children participated in the repair work, hoping that they could delay the bloodshed they knew was coming. Rumors spread among the frightened residents that the Venetians were assembling a fleet to come and save the besieged city, but help never came.

The final assault took place shortly after midnight on May 29, 1453, when the invaders finally managed to breach the walls and enter the city. The bells of the massive church rang mournfully, and "singing hymns in Greek, Italian or Catalan, Orthodox and Catholic, men, women, children, soldiers, civilians, clergy, monks and nuns, knowing that they were going to die shortly, make peace with themselves, with God and eternity."[2]

The Byzantine emperor gave a speech to his subjects, telling them they had to be ready to face death and sacrifice themselves without fear. "They had lived in a great city and they were now going to die defending it. As for himself, he was going to die fighting for his faith, for his city and for his people."[3] Thousands crowded within the church, hoping that God would protect them there. The priests were conducting masses, and the people were singing and crying. After the emperor visited the church, he rode back to his palace to say goodbye to his household. Then he rode away into battle, and was never seen again.

The Janissaries

Among the Muslim troops who breached the walls of Constantinople were warriors who, as boys, had been captured primarily from Christian families and forced to convert to Islam. Called *janissaries* ("new warriors"), these boys were raised by Turkish parents, then enrolled into military training. They were highly skilled in the art of battle, and their responsibility was to fight wars for the sultan.

This practice of abducting young non-Muslim boys can be traced back to Orhan I, an early Ottoman ruler who reigned from 1326 to 1359. In time, these boys became a vital part of the Ottoman army and had a key role in the army's many victories. Because they had come from Christian families, that meant they were forced to fight against their own people when they fought at Constantinople.[4]

The Collapse of the City

The people of Constantinople fought bravely yet were greatly outnumbered by the troops who stormed the city. Eyewitness accounts that have survived to this day describe the horrific events of that conquest. Bands of Muslim soldiers looted all they could and killed families in their homes. Churches and convents were ransacked and nuns were raped. "Killing, raping, looting, burning, enslaving went on according to tradition. The troops had to satisfy themselves."[5]

Soldiers forced their way into the Church of Holy Wisdom and killed the worshippers. Religious icons and furnishings were either taken or destroyed. The priests performing their duties were massacred, and sometime later a superstition arose that someday these priests would come back and resume carrying out their functions in the church. Even today, tour guides point to the door where their speculated return is to take place.

When the Byzantine historian Georgius Phrantzes saw the cathedral fall, he cried, "How unfathomable and incomprehensible is thy wise judgment, O King Christ!...Who would not have mourned for you, O holy temple!"[6]

THE SUBSEQUENT HISTORY OF THE GREAT CATHEDRAL

When Sultan Mehmed II himself entered Constantinople, he was distressed by the great destruction caused by his soldiers. Upon visiting the Church of Holy Wisdom, he commanded that it be turned into a mosque. The worship of Jesus would be replaced by the worship of Allah—the Bible would be replaced by the Quran.

The Church of Holy Wisdom was just one of many churches in the city that became places of Muslim worship. A dozen of the largest churches were converted almost immediately following the conquest, and others eventually followed. All crosses were removed, holy writings were burned, and mosaics were covered over with white plaster. Within the confines of human history, Muhammad had triumphed over Jesus.

Today the Church of Holy Wisdom is a museum. Thus, people of all faiths can now visit the edifice to enjoy its remarkable architecture and fascinating history. The signs of its Muslim heritage are still very much on display. Massive dome towers stand about 180 feet in the air, and verses from the Quran adorn the walls. However, vestiges of the building's Christian origins are now evident as well. For example, some of the plaster that the Muslim conquerors had coated over the Christian mosaics has been removed. This massive building has standing room for up to 20,000 people, and it still impresses all who see it.

My personal Muslim tour guide in Istanbul made it clear that the fall of Constantinople and the conversion of the city's churches into mosques was proof of Islam's superiority over Christianity. "The triumph of Christianity over paganism indicated that Christianity was a superior religion, but the triumph of Islam over Christianity shows that Islam is superior to Christianity," he said.

This "triumph," as the Muslims call it, was evident not only by the fall of Constantinople, but also the conquest of all of the cities in what is now known as Turkey. In fact, the fall of Constantinople was but the last stage in the transformation of this region from a Christian to a Muslim territory.

CHURCHES TRANSFORMED

The story of the Church of Holy Wisdom is the story of thousands of churches throughout the Middle East, Asia, and North Africa. As Muslim armies swept their way across these lands and conquered cities and towns, churches were seized and turned into mosques.

As we learned earlier, Christianity once flourished in North Africa. But by the eighth century AD, it was virtually wiped out. One of the early church leaders there, Tertullian (c. 160–225), is famously quoted as having said that the blood of the martyrs is the seed of the church. However, his observation—at least in the case of the Middle East, Asia Minor, and North Africa—turned out to be incorrect. While it is true that the persecution of Christians in the New Testament era, ancient Rome, the Reformation period, and some other epochs and places has led the church to grow and spread, there have also been regions of the world where Christianity has died out.

As Philip Jenkins says in *The Lost History of Christianity*, "In short, the North African Church based in Carthage had at its height been one of the most powerful and influential in the whole of Christianity, yet very soon after the Muslims took Carthage in 698, that church vanished almost totally."[7] Jenkins also quotes a Catholic scholar who made this observation about the demise of the church in Algeria and Tunisia: "In this overwhelming disaster of the Arab invasion the churches of Africa were blotted out. Not that all was destroyed, but that remnant of Christian life was so small as to be a matter for erudition rather than for history."[8]

Toward the end of the tenth century, Caliph Hakim led widespread persecution against both Christians and Jews in Egypt. Some 3000 churches were destroyed or turned into mosques. Most notably, Hakim destroyed the Church of the Holy Sepulcher in Jerusalem. Toward the end of his rule, Hakim became more tolerant of people of other faiths. But some 300 years later, new waves of persecution began to sweep over Egypt. During the first half of the fourteenth century, great pressure was exerted upon Christians and Jews to convert to Islam. Monasteries were confiscated, crosses were destroyed, and churches were ransacked and many were converted into mosques. The number of Christians in Egypt diminished significantly, dropping to about a tenth of Egypt's population.

The Christians in Syria fared even worse. At the battle of Yarmuk in 636, some 50,000 Christian Byzantine soldiers were massacred. The battle raged for six days, and the Muslim victory was so decisive and complete that it ended Byzantine rule over Syria.

Time and again the Christian church in the Middle East and Asia was largely obliterated under Muslim rule. Jenkins explains, "Whole Christian communities were annihilated across central Asia, and surviving communities shrank to tiny fractions of their former size."[9] By the fourteenth century, Christianity had basically disappeared in these regions, with only a remnant of followers in pockets here and there. "The deeply rooted Christianity of Africa and Asia did not simply fade away through lack of zeal, or theological confusion: it was crushed, in a welter of warfare and persecution."[10]

THE ROLE OF THE MOSQUE

It's extremely important to recognize that the practice of turning churches into mosques has more meaning in Islam than simply providing a place for Muslims to meet for worship. Mosques are the center of authority in the Muslim community. It is at the mosque that muftis (Islamic scholars) make political declarations, interpret and expound Islamic law, and urge the faithful to fight infidels. Put another way, "mosques [are] the central point for the dissemination and application of the rulings of Islamic law (the *Shari'ah*), derived from the two primary sources, the *Qur'an* and the *Sunnah*."[11]

In light of that, we shouldn't be surprised to know that today, mosques in the West Bank and Gaza are "centers and instigators of violence against Israel, rallied on through the Friday sermons and distributing hate leaflets and materials published by Hamas and Islamic Jihad"[12] (the main Palestinian Islamist movements). Muslims in some of the leading mosques in Britain have been repeatedly caught on undercover film proclaiming hatred and violence against non-Muslims. Especially stunning was the fact one such mosque was "Regent's Park Mosque, which is supposedly committed to interfaith dialogue and moderation."[13]

Even in America this is a problem. In the summer of 2011, *Middle East Quarterly* published the results of an intensive four-year study on "sharia-adherence and the promotion of violent, jihadist literature in U.S. mosques."[14] The results? A stunning 81 percent carried jihad hate literature—with 51 percent carrying texts "rated as severely advocating violence," and 30 percent carrying texts "rated as moderately advocating violence."[15] Especially disturbing was the discovery that "mosques with this literature were not merely repositories but incubators for the messaging of this material."[16] And fully 58 percent of the mosques "invited guest imams known to promote violent *jihad*."[17]

Islam, Mosques, and Sacred Space

A mosque in a Muslim or Muslim-majority country is considered to be in the "House of Islam" (*Dar al-Islam*). That is, it's in a place under Muslim control, where both Muslim worship and shariah are the norm. But a mosque in the West is considered to be in the "house of war" (*Dar al-Harb*) or a place *not* under Muslim control—a place that is the home of infidels and unbelievers. Thus the mosque is viewed as a beachhead in enemy territory, or non-Muslim land. And the Islamic doctrine of "sacred space" dictates that once territory belongs to Islam, it can never again be surrendered, as explained by Clare M. Lopez, a former CIA operations officer who is now a senior fellow at the Center for Security Policy:

> The concept of "sacred space" is well-developed in Islamic law (shariah) and holds that all land on earth has been given by Allah to Muslims in perpetuity. According to this belief, inasmuch as the world already belongs in its entirety to Muslims, they are both destined and obligated to dominate it. In practice, however, pursuit of this global objective proceeds incrementally and includes both advances and retreats. Land already once conquered or occupied by Muslims, whenever in history that may have occurred, is considered *waqf*, or a holy endowment from Allah to the *ummah* (the Muslim people) forever. If such space has been lost in battle or for any other reason, it is the duty of all Muslims to regain it, by jihad if necessary.[18]

This concept of sacred space is a key reason that the Middle East conflict will never end. Back in AD 637, Muslim armies besieged and conquered Jerusalem, and in 692, the Dome of the Rock was completed on the Temple Mount, directly above the site where the Jewish temple once stood. But today the Holy Land is occupied by Israel, which means there can be no peace until the Muslims win back what they perceive to be their land.

The doctrine of sacred space is what leads Muslim conquerors to build their mosques and other structures right on top of destroyed churches and other religious structures. Even private homes are affected by this idea of sacred space. The thinking is that once land is in Muslim hands, it should remain in Muslim ownership so that more territory is set aside for the growth of Muslim communities and the larger Muslim advance. Patrick Sookhdeo, in his book *Faith, Power and Territory: A Handbook of British Islam,* says that migrant Muslim communities in the West "sacralize" new areas for Islam through the occupation of their mosques and private homes.[19] As explained in *Shariah: The Threat to America,* "This tactic (in the U.S.) often involves Muslim real estate agents who ensure that homes occupied by Muslims will always be occupied by Muslim families."[20]

In addition, Muslims attempt to demonstrate the superiority of Islam by making their mosques the highest and biggest building in the immediate area. According to the Center for Security Policy, much of the money for these extravagant building programs comes from Saudi Arabia.[21] Worth noting is that many mosques are built larger than would seem necessary. That's because their planners are anticipating future growth. They are looking ahead to an Islamic future.

At the time of this writing, the debate still continues over the proposed building of a mosque near Ground Zero. In this case, the plan is for a warehouse damaged by the 9/11 attacks to be torn down so the new structure can be built. The plan was to call the project Cordoba House, which generated great controversy because Cordoba is the name of a Christian city in Spain that was conquered by Muslims in the eighth century. In keeping with Islamic practice, the invaders converted a cathedral into what is the third-largest mosque complex in the world. So for Muslims, the name Cordoba House has definite significance—to the point of strongly suggesting the idea of conquest with regard to the site of Ground Zero.[22] The public outcry was so great that more recently the project was renamed Park51 (a reference to the address, 51 Park Place).

There are some who say the fact the United States grants freedom of religion is an argument for allowing Muslims to build a mosque where they want, in accordance with zoning regulations and other laws. Yet there are many who question whether it's appropriate to permit a victory mosque to be built a mere two blocks from the site where thousands of families lost loved ones on 9/11, the site where radical Islam triumphed. Paul Sipos, a member of NYC Community Board 1, made this observation:

> If the Japanese decided to open a cultural center across from Pearl Harbor, that would be insensitive. If the Germans opened a Bach choral society across from Auschwitz, even after all these years, that would be an insensitive setting. I have absolutely nothing against Islam. I just think: Why there?[23]

The Whole World a Mosque

There is additional significance to the whole matter of building mosques wherever possible and observing the concept of sacred space, as explained in *The Mosque Exposed*:

> Muhammad said that the earth had been declared to him a mosque...In practical terms, this means Muhammad and his followers are to conquer the whole world and cleanse it, purge it from all kinds of *kufr*, meaning apostasy. Therefore, the mosque's mission or function is not to be limited to prayer and religious services only, but extends to physically and practically how to bring the earth under Islamic dominion.[24]

So in a very real sense, we can say Islam is committed to purging the whole earth by transforming existing houses of worship, such as churches, into mosques.

Abu Ala Maududi, a leading Islamic scholar, put it this way: "In reality Islam is a revolutionary ideology, a revolutionary program (agenda) to alter the social order of the whole world, and rebuild it in conformity with its own tenets and the ideals."[25] And, if you think that is not clear enough, he continues, "Islam is not merely a religious creed or compound name for a few forms of worship, but a comprehensive system which envisages to annihilate all tyrannical and evil systems in the world and enforce its own program of reform which it deems best for the well being of mankind."[26]

So when a church is turned into a mosque, Islam has conquered another piece of property and transferred it from the "house of war" to the "house of peace." Muhammad's vision of the whole world becoming a mosque is another step closer to fulfillment. This makes it appear as though Muhammad is triumphing over Jesus.

Could It Happen Here?

In the early centuries AD, Christianity was widespread in Syria, Iraq, and other Middle Eastern countries. No one would have imagined it would ever die out to the extent that it did. As for Asia Minor, where the seven churches of Revelation were located, Jenkins writes, "A thousand years ago, the Christians of Asia Minor held the same assurance [that their region was fundamentally Christian], yet that region today bears the name of Turkey, a country that nationally claims 99% Muslim loyalty."[27] Jenkins warns, "At least as far as particular regions of continents are concerned, Christianity does not come with a warranty."[28]

The point, of course, is that much of what we call the Islamic world today was at one time Christian—whether Iraq, Iran, Syria, and of course, Turkey. These countries had a strong Christian presence and many churches. Today, the few Christians who live in these places risk their lives if they attempt to share their faith with others.

Could their story be our story? If you have visited Europe, you know that many cathedrals are, for the most part, empty. The last country Rebecca and I visited before returning home from our tour of the seven churches was Greece. As we caught a cab to the airport in Athens, we saw a magazine in the backseat with an article that listed examples of cathedrals that had been purchased and turned into hotels, bookstores, restaurants, and mosques.

What Islam historically has done by force is now being accomplished in Europe through the purchase of churches and other properties, the building of mosques, and the growing insistence that Europeans respect the rights of Muslims in the name of cultural or religious sensitivity. The non-Muslims of Europe, paralyzed by political correctness and having self-consciously despised their Christian past, are powerless to withstand Islam's growing presence. If they will not attend church, why should these structures not be sold and used by a religion that takes its faith seriously? We can confidently predict that these countries—with their empty cathedrals and pride in secular values—will experience the exponential expansion of Islam, and the Europe we once knew will come to an end.[29]

HOW THE TRANSFORMATION OCCURS

What is happening peacefully in Europe these days is happening by force in Muslim countries. The few Christian churches that have been allowed to exist are either being closed down or destroyed. For example, in December 2010, Muslims converted a house in Egypt into a mosque so that two nearby Coptic churches could no longer hold services. There is a rule in Egypt that states that no church is permitted within 100 meters (about 110 yards) of a mosque. On a Thursday evening, some Muslims hung a cloth sign outside of a four-story house, proclaiming the building was now a mosque. And on Friday, some 3000 Muslims showed up to pray at the site. This, of course, meant the churches had to shut down, for they were now in violation of the law.

"We are devastated," said a local Copt. "This church cost the poor people 7 million Egyptian pounds, which we collected by having to go without a lot in our homes, and there comes the governor and state security, angry because we built a dome and destroy it, kill our children, leave others maimed and the rest in prison for a very long time."[30]

This Coptic Christian was referring to an incident that had taken place a few weeks earlier, when Egyptian authorities attempted to shut down the construction of one of the churches, located in Talbiya. Some 5000 security forces came to storm the church and use tear gas on those inside the building, including women and children. Two Coptic Christians were killed, many more were injured, and 200 were arrested—including women and children—with 170 of them held on allegedly false charges.[31]

And churches are being destroyed as well. A Coptic church in Alexandria was bombed on January 1, 2011, with 23 people killed, and a church in the Helwan province was burned down in March 2011.[32]

Whether peacefully or by force, Islam is spreading. In the case of Europe and the United Kingdom, secularism has weakened the churches to the point they are not able to withstand the growing Muslim influence, and political correctness is silencing both governments and individuals from saying anything critical of Islam, even if it's legitimate.

But this should not cause us as Christians to despair. We have a reason to remain hopeful.

JESUS' EVENTUAL TRIUMPH

Lest we become dispirited by Islam's victories in many countries of the world, let us keep in mind what the future holds. The eventual triumph of Jesus over all the nations of the earth is taught in dozens of passages of Scripture. Let us never forget there is coming a day when *the cross will eclipse the crescent throughout the whole world*.

Consider Egypt, for example. The ancient prophet Isaiah made this amazing prediction:

> In that day there will be an altar to the LORD in the heart of Egypt, and a monument to the LORD at its border. It will be a sign and witness to the LORD Almighty in the land of Egypt. When they cry out to the LORD because of their oppressors, he will send them a savior and defender, and he will rescue them. So the LORD will make himself known to the Egyptians, and in that day they will acknowledge the LORD…The LORD Almighty will bless them, saying, "Blessed be Egypt my people, Assyria my handiwork, and Israel my inheritance" (Isaiah 19:19-21,25).

Many Bible teachers believe this passage will be fulfilled literally during the millennium, after the glorious return of Jesus Christ to the earth. So, although its fulfillment is yet future, we should embrace our challenges of the present day with optimism and joy. Yes, Islam is replacing churches with mosques, but there is coming a day when the church—that is, God's people—will triumph for all eternity. We can serve the Lord in this world with the ringing assurance that Jesus *will* triumph over Muhammad.

Meanwhile, however, a weak and sickly church is not a credit to our triumphant Christ. My friend David Bryant (of the ministry Proclaim Hope!) wept when we were told about a young mother who was injured in a car crash and placed on life support. Our conversation then turned to the church, and David said, "That is the way I see the church of Jesus Christ today—it's on life support. We have lost the vision as to who Jesus is and why His exaltation in our lives would rid us of fear of the future, and give us a buoyant hope for the future."

"When a Muslim views a Christian" says Larry Poston, "he sees a person who wears his Christianity like a casual garment, useful for show on certain occasions but tossed aside when not needed. He sees Christians as captives of a materialistic culture that has co-opted Christianity by marketing Christian music, books, clothing and other paraphernalia."[33] Tragically true.

THE NEED TO STAY STRONG

I conclude this chapter with a question: Why are we so weak when our Lord and Savior is so strong? Why are churches in Europe and the United Kingdom dying out while mosques are growing in number? Jesus warned the church in Ephesus that if the people didn't repent He would come and "remove [their] lampstand from its place" (Revelation 2:5). That warning was not just for Ephesus, but for all the churches of Revelation and today's churches as well.

The churches of Revelation eventually lost the simplicity and purity of the gospel, and hundreds of years later, when Islam came into Asia Minor, whatever was left of these churches was uprooted. A church on life support cannot rise up and walk.

So what is the first lesson we can learn from the seven churches?

Don't assume any given church's continued existence is assured. We as Christians need to remain faithful to God and take a stand for the faith. All across Europe and the United Kingdom we are seeing what happens to a church that is in a weakened state. We cannot assume that if we are strong now, we will remain so.

Will the levees hold?

— The Triumph of the Cross —

A Personal Testimony

I was born in Lebanon in 1960 in a conservative Muslim family. I came from a family that claimed descent from the tribe of Muhammad, the prophet of Islam. I grew up in an environment of much strife between Muslims and Christians in Lebanon. The tension was evident everywhere—even encounters between young Muslim and Christian boys would turn bloody. When I was seven, a Christian boy hit me on the head with a stick that had a nail in it, and blood splattered over my face and I was dragged home crying. So we viewed Christians as our enemies, although I now realize many of those who called themselves Christians were Christian in name only, and were not believers whose lives had been changed by Christ.

I went to a conservative Muslim school, and there was a mosque next door. The imam at the mosque started giving me books and said the world was divided into two parts: Islam and the world of infidels. He said it is the duty of the Muslims to convert the other part of the world or subjugate it by force. He said, "We are part of a global Islam movement that extends from India to Morocco, and one day we will rise together and join hands and establish a global Muslim state."

At the age of 12, I joined the Muslim Brotherhood. I started my military training at a camp at the age of 13. There we were taught how to shoot rifles, rocket-propelled grenades, and mortars. The man who taught us how to use the rifle said, "If you want to shoot straight, imagine there is a Christian in your sights. Then you will shoot straight." That is an example of the hatred Muslims have toward Christians and Jews.

In 1975, when civil war broke out in Lebanon, my brother and I helped shell the main Christian neighborhood in Beirut. I felt uneasy about it, but a Brotherhood leader convinced me what we were doing was justified. In 1980, my brother was gunned down by Christian militia, and I was devastated. I couldn't focus on my studies anymore. I dropped all my courses except one on cultural studies, comparative literature, and religions. In that class, the professor was comparing

Greek mythology, the Bible, the Quran, and Western philosophy. As a Muslim, I considered the Bible unclean, but because it was part of the curriculum, I listened to the professor. When she got to the New Testament, she read from the Sermon on the Mount, "Love your enemies." That stunned me. Who could love his enemies? It was like hearing the voice of God in stereo. The figure of Jesus leaped out at me. After all, my enemy wasn't just someone who cut me off in traffic or refused to have lunch with me. My enemy had killed my only brother, my only sibling, my only friend, and I was bitterly determined to take vengeance.

When Jesus was asked about the greatest commandment, He said, "'Love the Lord your God with all your heart and with all your soul and with all your mind.' This is the first and greatest commandment. And the second is like it: 'Love your neighbor as yourself.'" As a Muslim I spent three hours a day memorizing the Quran, and I thought this was the way to love God. But Jesus' words struck me. I thought, *Maybe I am missing the truth. Maybe I should read the Bible.*

So I did. But to be fair, I continued memorizing the Quran. That's when I noticed the hate language, the hate culture in the Quran. So I explored other religions as well. But they all taught reaching God through human effort—and it became clear that cannot be done.

Only Jesus Christ can help us reach God. He descended to us, and "the Word became flesh and made his dwelling among us." When I received Christ as Savior, I was set free from the burdens of Islam, of trying to please God through my own efforts. I experienced a peace beyond any peace I could have imagined. God gave me a new heart. And instead of seeking vengeance against those who had helped kill my brother, I began going to church to hear more about Jesus.

—Hicham

The Shadow of the Crescent

"If anyone desires a religion other than
Islam (submission to Allah),
never will it be accepted of him
and in the Hereafter he will be in the ranks
of those who have lost (all spiritual good)."

Sura 3:85[1]

Chapter Three

Lesson #2:
Faithfulness to Christ Requires an
Acceptance of Persecution

*These are the words of him who has the sharp, double-
edged sword. I know where you live—where Satan has
his throne. Yet you remain true to my name. You did
not renounce your faith in me, not even in the days of
Antipas, my faithful witness, who was put to death in
your city—where Satan lives (Revelation 2:12-13).*

—Jesus, to the church in Pergamum

Put yourself in the shoes of the Christians who were trying to survive when the Turks conquered the various cities of Asia Minor
in the latter half of the Middle Ages. Imagine that you are a member
of one of the churches in Ephesus, Pergamum, or Sardis. You want to
remain true to your Christian convictions, but at the same time you
have children to feed and clothe. You need a job in order to live, and
you need the fellowship of other believers, even when the church is
being oppressed. You are given the option of converting to Islam to
escape persecution, or you could choose to remain true to your Christian faith and live a life of servitude under Muslim rule. Or you could
be put to death.

Given those grim choices, Christianity didn't have much of a chance for survival. Indeed, in time, the demise of the church in this part of the world was virtually complete. Historian Philip Jenkins states that in 1050, the region "had 373 bishoprics, and the citizens were virtually all Christian, members of the Orthodox Church. Four hundred years later...we can find just three bishops."[2] He adds, "From the eleventh century onward, the Christian landscape of Asia Minor was destroyed piecemeal,"[3] and "the Turks shredded Christian ecclesiastical institutions beyond repair."[4]

With the coming of Islam in the Middle Ages, we're told that "church hierarchies were destroyed, priests and monks were killed, enslaved, or expelled, monasteries and cathedrals fell silent."[5] In his excellent book *Islamic Imperialism: A History*, Efraim Karsh documents the evidence that Islam is an imperialist movement that forced itself on neighboring lands: "As a universal religion, Islam envisages a global political order in which all of humankind will lie under Muslim rule as either believers or subject communities."[6] The desire to subjugate the people of the world to Islam, is of course, one of its most enduring goals.

CONVERSION, SERVITUDE, OR DEATH

When Muslim invaders captured a city or territory, in the instances when the conquered populations weren't killed outright, they were given three choices: convert to Islam, be killed, or be forced into a life of servitude or slavery. Many people, when given these options, converted to Islam so that they could escape either persecution or the sword. Some converted willingly because they knew little about this religion. They didn't know what they were consenting to, but they were willing to give it a try because it seemed a better alternative than death. In some cases, the captives saw their Muslim captors in a better light than their former Byzantine rulers, many of whom were corrupt and oppressive.

A Pact of Surrender

Those who refused to convert to Islam were either forced into servitude or slavery. Christians and Jews, because they were "Peoples of the Book" (the Bible), were sometimes offered protective status provided they were willing to enter into a "pact of surrender [that] came to be known as a *dhimma* or 'covenant of liability.'...The *dhimma* pact fixed the legal, social and economic place of non-Muslims in the Islamic state."[7] Those who agreed to this arrangement were known as *dhimmis*. They were servants for perpetuity, and in exchange for the "privilege" of being allowed to live within the Muslim community, they were required to pay oppressive taxes and follow strict codes of conduct that assured continuous public humiliation under their Muslim overlords. In effect, these non-Muslims were often little more than slaves. They were granted a small measure of religious freedom, but they had to abide by very restrictive conditions, which, if violated, could mean severe punishment or death.

This practice of allowing conquered peoples to live in servitude—particularly in the earlier centuries of Islamic conquest—served a very pragmatic purpose. Karsh explains:

> At the time of the conquests the Arabs were a marginal group, lacking substantial material resources, with a dearth of bureaucratic and administrative experience and a limited literary and cultural tradition. It was only natural for them to take whatever they could from the great cultural and intellectual centers that had come under their rule in order to strengthen their own imperial prowess.[8]

In fact, Muslim victors sometimes discouraged the conversion of non-Muslims because those who subjected themselves to *dhimmi* status were an economic asset to the Muslim community. These captives comprised a ready-made labor force and a source of income from the various taxes that were imposed on them.

As might be expected, Muhammad himself taught that Jews and Christians could be allowed to live under certain conditions. The Quran states, "Fight against those who do not believe in Allah... of those who have been given the Book, until they pay the *jizya* out of hand and are humbled" (Sura 9:29). The phrase "those who have been given the Book" refers to Jews and Christians, and the *jizya* was a tax required of every adult male *dhimmi*. This tax was paid annually and served as a constant reminder of the payee's status as a defeated person.

The Pact's Terms of Subjection

The *dhimma* pact granted a rather superficial protection to the Jews and Christians who lived under Muslim rule. They were secure from future attack as long as they abided by the oppressive conditions and laws placed upon them. While the terms of this pact varied from place to place, in general, here are the basic rules *dhimmi* had to follow in exchange for permission to remain alive:

- They could not build new places of worship, and those that had been ruined in conquest could not be repaired or rebuilt.
- They had to house and feed Muslim soldiers.
- They had to offer hospitality to all Muslim travelers for three days.
- They could not put their religion on public display.
- They could not proselytize anyone to their religion.
- If any of their kin wanted to convert to Islam, they could not prevent them from doing so.
- They could not raise a hand against or strike a Muslim.
- They could not wear garments that in any way resembled those worn by Muslims.
- They could not bear arms or swords.
- They could not display crosses or print or sell books pertaining to their religion.
- They could not bury their dead near dead Muslims.
- They could not build their homes on higher ground than Muslim homes.
- They had to give up their seats to Muslims who wanted them.

Those *dhimmis* who failed to comply with these and other restrictions forfeited their lives and possessions: "A protected person who violates his protection agreement, whether by refusing to pay the head tax [*jizya*] or to submit to the laws of the community...makes his person and his goods 'licit' [*halal*—freely available to be killed or captured by Muslims]."9

Obviously, this wasn't so much a pact of protection as it was a terms of surrender. And the severe restrictions in this pact made it difficult, if not impossible, for Jews and Christians to exercise their faith.

If you watched the many television commentaries that aired after 9/11, you probably heard Muslim authorities defend their religion by saying that historically, Muslims have expressed tolerance toward Christians. As proof, they would point to the *dhimmi* pacts that offered "security" to Christians who lived among their Muslim conquerors. But they omit the fact such pacts were granted only to those who gave their lives over to permanent servitude, and any failure to observe the pact usually meant death.

With regard to Jews, there were some instances historically of Muslim rulers and governing authorities granting protection that was somewhat favorable. For example, during the Spanish Inquisition, when Catholics were persecuting Jews, many Jews fled from Spain and Portugal to go to North Africa. They were welcomed in the Ottoman Empire, especially Morocco and Algeria. Although they had to comply with the restrictions placed on *dhimmis*, at least life under Muslim rule offered them some opportunities.

In fact, Sultan Bayezid II, who began his rule in 1481, welcomed the Jews and "sarcastically thanked Ferdinand for sending him some of his best subjects, thus 'impoverishing his own lands while enriching his (Bayezid's)."10 Bayezid II decreed to his governors that no Jew should be harmed, for he realized they could contribute to the cultural and economic development of the Ottoman Empire.

THE TREATMENT OF DHIMMI

In the Middle Ages, under the pact of *dhimmi*, the treatment of Christians was not uniform. In some locales, Christians were treated quite kindly, though the legal, economic, and social restrictions imposed upon them made it clear they were a people of inferior status. Even then, "Christians were treated rather better than other groups,"[11] and in fact there were some areas in which "long periods of good interfaith relations...prevailed."[12] That is why in some Muslim regions, Christian communities continued to exist for decades or even centuries after Islamic rule had been established.

Middle East historian Bernard Lewis explains the reason for the limited tolerance Muslims sometimes showed to Christians. Muslims viewed Christianity as a "predecessor" religion. It was "a religion which had been true and had possessed an authentic revelation, but was incomplete and now superseded by Islam."[13] He gives this further explanation:

> For the Muslim, Christianity was an abrogated religion, which its followers absurdly insisted on retaining, instead of accepting God's final word. They could be tolerated if they submitted. If they did not they were to be fought until they were overcome and either accepted the truth of the Muslim faith or submitted to the authority of the Muslim state.[14]

Bat Ye'or, in her book *The Decline of Eastern Christianity Under Islam*, describes the conditions that existed under the Umayyad Caliphate, which was the second of the four major Arab caliphates that ruled after the death of Muhammad. She explains that under the Umayyads, Christians "represented the large majority of the Islamic state's subjects and...its principal taxpayers...Moreover, these conquered populations had mastered the techniques of civilization: state administration, agriculture, trade, architecture, and various crafts."[15] For this reason, "a conciliatory attitude was adopted toward the active and hard-working vanquished people; they were left in charge of the administration and collection of taxes but under the control of the Islamic state, whose power and resources they increased."[16]

But under the Umar Caliphate, Efraim Karsh notes that conditions grew more hostile:

[*Dhimmi*] suffered from social indignities and at times open persecution. Their religious activities outside the churches and synagogues were curtailed…the construction of new church buildings prohibited, and the proselytizing of Muslims was made a capital offense punishable by death. Jews and Christians had to wear distinctive clothes to distinguish them from their Muslim lords, could ride only on donkeys, not horses, could not marry Muslim women, had to vacate their seats wherever Muslims wanted to sit, [and] were excluded from positions of power.[17]

THE PRESSURE TO CONVERT

In the instances when Christians were pressured to convert to Islam, they were told that all true Christians were really already Muslims. Islam regards itself as the most complete and final religion, with Christianity and Judaism in its early roots. After all, Abraham is regarded as the father of all three major world religions: Judaism, Christianity, and Islam. Muslims believe that Judaism and Christianity had been abrogated and had become corrupted, and that if these religions were purified, all Jews and Christians would become Muslims.

Muhammad himself taught that Abraham was actually a Muslim rather than a Jew (Sura 3:67). In the Quran, it is said the disciples identified themselves as Muslims (Sura 3:52; 5:111). Because Islam would ultimately triumph over all other religions (Sura 48:28), and it had superseded Judaism and Christianity, "it would no longer be acceptable for Jews—or Christians—to follow their old religion; they had to acknowledge Muhammad, and become Muslims too, like everyone else."[18]

THE VICTORY OF ISLAM

A question I have often pondered is this: Why has Islam been able to obliterate the church in a way that Communism has not? Think, for example, of the remarkable growth of the church in China despite severe persecution. Today, according to the Chinese Academy of Social Sciences, we are told that there are some 23 million Christians in China, and when unregistered churches are taken into account, the estimates range from 40 to 130 million.[19] That's astonishing when we consider the many hardships and restrictions that have been imposed upon Chinese believers under Communism. Compare this with the fact that, for all practical purposes, the church has been extinguished in Muslim regions such as North Africa, Asia Minor, and the Middle East. All that remains are tiny, scattered pockets of believers who are but a miniscule fraction of the whole population.

Financial Ruin

One of the reasons the church was wiped out is that, from an economic standpoint, conversion to Islam was attractive. Those who remained Christians and became *dhimmi* had to pay the *jizya*, a prohibitive tax that fell on the shoulders of those who refused to convert. What is more, the Christians were greatly humiliated by the many conditions imposed on them as a reminder of their inferior status.

The method of collecting taxes from Christians is described as follows:

> Although the ritual varied in its specific features, its essential character was an enactment of a beheading, in which one of the recurrent features was a blow to the neck of the dhimmi, at the very point when he makes his payment.
>
> To understand the significance of neck striking, let us turn to the Quran:
>
> > When thy Lord inspired the angels, (saying): I am with you. So make those who believe stand firm. I will throw fear into the hearts of those who disbelieve. Then smite the necks and smite of them each finger. That is because they opposed Allah and His messenger (Q8:12-13; see also Q47:4).
>
> ...The jizya payment was thus a ritualized decapitation, symbolizing the very penalty which the payment was designed to avoid.[20]

This ritual, then, made it clear that the *dhimmi* deserved to be beheaded, but he was being exempted because he was paying a tax instead. The Egyptian jurist al-Adawi (who died in 1787) described the procedure this way:

> Following this [the handing over of the *jizya* payment] the emir will strike the *dhimmi* on the neck with his fist; a man will stand near the emir to chase away the *dhimmi* in haste; then a second and a third will come forward to suffer the same treatment as well as all those to follow. All [Muslims] will be admitted to enjoy this spectacle. None will be allowed to delegate a third party to pay the *jizya* in his stead, for they must suffer this degradation personally.[21]

This is just one of the many ways Muslims oppressed the *dhimmi*. While Christian parents may have been willing to endure such treatment, they could not bear to see their children so grievously humiliated. Therefore they would convert to Islam—out of concern for their loved ones.

In recent decades, historical revisionists, particularly from within the Muslim community, have downplayed the severity of the *jizya* tax, claiming it was rarely enforced, that it was like any other tax, that *dhimmis* enjoyed equal rights, and so on. But accounts dating as far back as the eighth century report that many *dhimmis* were taxed into extreme poverty, finding it necessary to sell everything they had and let their families starve. When they were unable to pay, they would go into hiding or be forced into slavery. "Money was extorted by blows, torture, and death—particularly by crucifixion."[22]

Marital Prohibitions

Another reason Islam succeeded in wiping out Christianity—and Communism didn't—is because Muslim men were encouraged to marry Christian women, who then would be forced to convert to Islam. But Christian men were strictly forbidden to marry Muslim women. This made it difficult for a Christian heritage to continue.

Even today, in Africa, a Muslim man will sometimes marry a Christian woman with the express intention of either using the marriage to force her to convert to Islam or having children with her who will be raised as Muslims. And if the woman is unwilling to convert, the Muslim husband has the right to divorce her and take away the children to ensure they will be raised as Muslims. Then he is free to remarry to a Muslim woman if he wants.

These restrictions explain why it was very difficult for Christians under Muslim rule to propagate their faith to the next generation. With Muslim men marrying their Christian daughters and their Christian sons forbidden to marry Muslim women, Christians found it difficult to survive through the centuries.

THE CRY OF THE CHURCHES

Let's return to the Christian churches that were in Asia Minor at the time of the first Muslim conquests long ago. As we have already noted, when these Christians were conquered, they didn't have much choice. They could go into servitude, slavery, or be killed.

We also have to keep in mind that these Christians did not have the information that we possess today about the history and the teachings of the Muslim faith. Many could not read; they only knew what they had heard from others. On the surface, Islam may have seemed compatible with Christianity because it taught there was only one God, and of course the Quran makes occasional references to Jesus. And the fact that Muslims taught that Islam had abrogated Christianity and the Quran was God's final revelation made the transfer of one's loyalties attractive.

What is more, conversion to Islam was easy. A person simply had to recite out loud, with total sincerity, the *shahadah*, a creed that declared, "I confess that there is no god but Allah, and I confess that Muhammad is Allah's Messenger." That was enough to make a person a Muslim. This conversion required no repentance from sin, no change of heart. That seemed simple enough. But what many people didn't realize is that Islam offered a door that was easy to enter, but that door was bolted from the inside. Woe to the person who wanted to convert back to Christianity! He was either ostracized from the Muslim community or killed.

First and Last Words

The creed "There is no god but Allah, and Muhammad is the Prophet of Allah" is the first statement uttered into a Muslim baby's ears when it is born. And Muslims are urged, if possible, to say these words just prior to their death. If a dying person is unable to make this declaration, another person can do it on their behalf.

Dietrich Bonhoeffer, who was hung because of his opposition to Hitler, made a poignant observation about Philippians 1:29, which says, "To you it has been granted for Christ's sake, not only to believe in Him, but also to suffer for His sake" (NASB). Bonhoeffer is quoted as saying that we gladly accept the first gift mentioned in the verse— "to you it has been granted...to believe in Him"—but we balk at the second gift: "to suffer for His sake." But *both* faith and suffering are gifts from God.

FREEDOM AND FAITHFULNESS

In 1521, when Martin Luther declared at the Diet of Worms, "My conscience is taken captive by God's Word... [and] to act against our conscience is neither safe for us, nor open to us," he introduced the revolutionary idea that in matters of religion, people should be free to follow their own conscience. And although it took many years before this principle was fully realized in Europe, it came to fruition because brave people, such as Luther, insisted that following God was more important than obeying the laws of men. This vision of freedom informed the Founding Fathers of the United States, who knew that such freedom had to rest on an affirmation of faith in a God who gave to mankind "certain unalienable rights."

Islam, of course, does not respect freedom of conscience. Rather, it keeps its adherents bound by fear—fear that if they were to leave their faith they would be killed, most likely by members of their own families.

In Chicago, whenever I get into a cab driven by a Muslim, I always initiate a friendly dialogue with him. After talking with him about the role of Jesus in the Quran, I ask this question: "If you were to convert to Christianity, do you think you should be put to death?" Some drivers say no, and others say yes. When I ask who should kill them, they are usually unsure, but volunteer that "someone who is in charge" should do the deed. So even here in America, some Muslims hold to the view that to convert from Islam to Christianity could very well mean the loss of their life.

Muslims who convert to Christianity do so for many reasons. Some meet a Christian who shares the gospel with them. Others observe the love and kindness of Christians in action over a period of time, and as a result, are attracted to the Christian faith.

One convert explained to one of our pastors at The Moody Church that he accepted Christ after reading John chapter 6 in the Bible, where Jesus respected His disciples' freedom of choice and gave them the option of leaving Him. After many of them left, "Jesus said to the Twelve, 'Do you also want to go away?'" (verse 67 NKJV). The implication is that they could have left Him if they had wanted to. How contrary to Muhammad, who commanded that those who left his teachings be put to death. In the mind of this convert, Jesus was to be admired for respecting freedom of conscience.

Why does Islam not allow such freedom? There are two reasons: one is the strict prohibition against Muslims converting to Christianity. To do so is to be an apostate. In some Muslim countries, a person who leaves Islam will face severe punishment, imprisonment, or execution. Even in the West, Muslims who convert are almost always rejected by their families, ostracized and persecuted by the Muslim community, and are the recipients of death threats.

The other reason Islam prohibits freedom of conscience is more practical: If Islam were to no longer observe conversion as apostasy, there is little doubt that tens of thousands—if not millions—of Muslims would reject Islam for another religion, or for no religion at all. It is fear that keeps Muslims bound to Islam, not their own search for truth.

When Lina Joy, a Malay woman, wanted to have her conversion to Christianity recognized by the Malaysian courts, the Arabic media network Al-Jazeera suggested that "if Malaysia allows conversions to Christianity this could trigger off 'mass conversions' from Islam."[23] No doubt it would! After several years of legal battles, Lina Joy was denied her request that she be identified as a Christian on her ID card.

SILENCING FREE SPEECH

Today in the West, Islam uses the stifling of free speech in an attempt to assert its superiority and get non-Muslims, in a sense, to acknowledge their *dhimmi* status. An example of this is what happened in June 1997 to Canadian pastor Mark Harding. When the local high school in his town decided to set aside a special room for Muslim students so they could pray during school hours, Harding protested, saying that students of other religions received no similar special privileges. He went to the school and handed out pamphlets that pointed out the violence Muslims have committed against non-Muslims in foreign lands. "The point I was trying to make is you shouldn't have a violent religion like Islam allowed in a school when Christianity or Hinduism or Buddhism is not allowed."[24]

Harding was accused of "willfully promoting hatred" in violation of Canada's hate speech law simply for being critical of Islam. He was then forced to undergo two years of probation and 340 hours of community service at the Islamic Society of North America (ISNA). Part of the community service included indoctrination sessions about Islam, which were conducted by Mohammad Ashraf, the general secretary of the Islam center. It was either this, or go to jail.

Ashraf warned Harding that during the indoctrination sessions, nothing negative could be said about Islam or Muhammad. What's more, Harding was placed under a gag order so he could not speak publicly about his case.

Harding, an evangelical Christian pastor, says he loves Muslims and that his protests were not motivated by hate. After Harding was indicted in 1997, he received more than 3000 hate-filled phone calls, and many included death threats. On his first day of trial, he needed police protection from a large crowd of Muslims chanting, "Infidel, you will burn in hell."[25] And throughout the duration of the trial, some of the Muslim onlookers in the courtroom would silently run a finger across their neck from ear to ear.

All this took place because some Muslims perceived Harding as being guilty of hate speech. They were offended that he would voice any criticism of Islam, no matter whether it was legitimate or accurate.

Paul Marshall, a senior fellow at the Hudson Institute's Center for Religious Freedom, observes that "a growing threat to our freedom of speech is the attempt to stifle religious discussion in the name of preventing 'defamation of' or 'insults to' religion, especially Islam."[26] He explains how groups like the Organization of Islamic Cooperation (OIC) have worked aggressively with the United Nations to get Western governments to implement what are known as blasphemy laws, or controls on speech about Islam. The OIC's charter states one of its objectives is "to combat defamation of Islam," but it "does not define what speech should be outlawed."[27] The definition of "hate speech" is deliberately left vague, of course, for that makes it easier to silence debate about Islam altogether.

When Telling the Truth Becomes Hate Speech

While on the surface hate-speech laws might seem a reasonable step toward prohibiting discrimination and harassment in society, the problem is this: Once restrictions are placed on what people are allowed to say, there is no longer true freedom of speech. It is virtually impossible to uphold the freedom of expression and, at the same time, impose limits on that expression.

What's more, who gets to determine whether someone's statement is truly hate speech or not? When it comes to hate-speech laws, all that's needed to trigger an accusation of wrongdoing is for a Muslim to claim that he was offended or hurt. So even if you make an absolutely truthful statement about Islam, if a Muslim decides he doesn't like it, then solely on the basis of his own subjective perception, he can take you to court for having committed a hate-speech crime.

Consider the following scenario: The oppression and mistreatment of women in Islamic countries is well documented. Paul Marshall and Nina Shea point out that "efforts to defend the human rights of Muslim women are frequently denounced as a form of 'insulting Islam.'"[28] So if you were in a country with hate-speech laws and you expressed heartfelt concern over the plight of Muslim women and their lack of equal rights, you could be arrested and indicted for religious discrimination.

It's Already Happening

In their book *Silenced*, Marshall and Shea discuss blasphemy laws and their impact on freedom worldwide, and cite numerous legal cases that have already been brought against Westerners who "have been prosecuted and even convicted under Western blasphemy and hate-speech laws."[29] They say such laws "have created a complicated legal patchwork that threatens the right to speak freely about and within Islam,"[30] and that "the result is a direct denial of individual freedoms, an indirect chilling of speech, legal confusion, rising sectarian expectations of further restrictions, the exacerbation of tensions among religious groups, and secular courts being put in the untenable position of pronouncing judgment on the doctrines of a multitude of religions."[31]

There are many well-meaning individuals who support the establishment of hate-speech laws for the sake of religious and cultural sensitivity. But as one source points out, "We have comforted and deluded ourselves by calling our self-censorship the silence of respect. In reality, it is the silence of fear. We have called it the silence of tolerance; actually, it is the silence of cultural acquiescence."[32]

....

A VICIOUS CATCH-22

In an article titled "Moderate Muslims Turning Radical?" William Federer "highlights the unintended consequences" of the extraordinary level of tolerance the West has shown toward Islam. What many don't realize is that such tolerance binds the West into a no-win dilemma:

If the West naively promotes tolerance of a belief system that does not promote tolerance, it is effectively promoting intolerance.

If the West refuses to promote an intolerant belief system, it is accused of being intolerant.[33]

Either way, Islam wins and the West loses. While religious and cultural tolerance are commendable goals, it's an impossible pursuit when the West, on the one hand, seeks a tolerance that applies to all equally, and Islam, on the other hand, is intolerant toward other belief systems. It's vital that Westerners recognize that "whereas 'world peace' in the West means peaceful coexistence, 'world peace' in Islam means the world submitting to the will of Allah."[34]

HOW SHOULD WE RESPOND?

What if we today were to find ourselves in a situation that demanded we compromise our Christian faith? And we had a full understanding of what was at stake? For the vast majority of us in the West, this may take the shape of not voicing criticism against Islam. It might mean acquiescing to the pressures of political correctness and staying silent rather than speaking the truth. Or maybe it could mean the threat of jail time, as in Mark Harding's case. Or perhaps there may come a day when the consequences are more severe.

How should we respond?

Three men in the Old Testament serve as a tremendous example of how to be faithful, even under a government that doesn't recognize freedom of religion. The scene took place in Babylon, where Daniel and his friends were held captive. Nebuchadnezzar had made an image of gold and set it up on a plain. He decreed that at a given time, when music was heard, all the people were to fall down and worship the golden image. Those who didn't would "immediately be thrown into a blazing furnace" (Daniel 3:6). But Daniel's three friends, Shadrach, Meshach, and Abednego, replied, "If we are thrown into the blazing furnace, the God we serve is able to deliver us from it, and he will deliver us from Your Majesty's hand. *But even if he does not, we want you to know, Your Majesty, that we will not serve your gods or worship the image of gold you have set up*" (verses 17-18).

How should we respond when we are stripped of our freedoms? How should we react when we are commanded to do something that goes against our conscience, or more pointedly, requires us to disobey God?

The New Testament apostles echoed the same refrain voiced by Daniel's friends in the Old Testament. When told by Jewish religious leaders that they could not proclaim the gospel message, the apostles answered, "Which is right in God's eyes: to listen to you, or to him? You be the judges! As for us, we cannot help speaking about what we have seen and heard" (Acts 4:19-20). On another occasion, when they were told again not to speak about Jesus, they said, "We must obey God rather than human beings" (Acts 5:29). Very simply, they were saying, "We will remain steadfast in our commitment to Christ, even to the point of persecution and death."

Jesus never promised we would live in countries with freedom of conscience. What He did promise us is that He would walk with us through whatever fire we are expected to endure. He gave His disciples candid instructions about the soon-to-come companionship of the Holy Spirit, and then He followed with this warning:

All this I have told you so that you will not fall away. They will put you out of the synagogue; in fact, the time is coming when anyone who kills you will think they are offering a service to God. They will do such things because they have not known the Father or me. I have told you this, so that when their time comes you will remember that I warned you about them (John 16:1-4).

Jesus warned His followers of persecution, even to the point of death. Even so, we are called to remain faithful.

Consider the words of Bishop Ding, who headed the Three-Self Patriotic Movement of Protestant churches in China, which is the government-approved church in mainland China. He was speaking to a group of us who had the privilege of visiting with him in China back in 1984. We had no idea where he stood theologically because he was the government's approved representative to the churches. But he told us, "I know you are evangelicals; I know what you believe. If you were to travel the length and breadth of China you would find Christians who believe what you do…persecution wiped out theological liberalism in China."

Of course! I thought to myself. Those who are theologically liberal—who hold to a low view of God and His Word—do not believe that Jesus was divine. They teach that the Bible is a purely human book. Consequently, they are not willing to die for their faith. Quite literally, they have nothing worth dying for! But true believers know that Christ is more valuable than life itself. And so it is that the Christianity that has survived in Communist China is largely of the biblical variety.

Read the history of Christianity, and you will have to agree that true Christians have had to learn that it is not necessary to have religious freedom to stay faithful to God. I subscribe to *Voice of the Martyrs*, a publication that reports about our brothers and sisters in Christ who live in predominantly Muslim countries and experience threats, imprisonment, and violent deaths. Christians are sometimes asked to dig their own graves; they are being stoned, tortured, and shot. We need to remind ourselves of what Jesus said: "Do not be afraid of those who kill the body but cannot kill the soul. Rather, be afraid of the One who can destroy both soul and body in hell" (Matthew 10:28). If we refuse to speak out because we are afraid, it shows that we have built our life around things that are temporal, not eternal.

Christ was beaten and then nailed to a cross. If we are His followers, then should we expect better treatment? Faithfulness in persecution proves that Christ is more valuable to us than life itself.

The apostle Paul, who was martyred, left us a legacy: "I eagerly expect and hope that I will in no way be ashamed, but will have sufficient courage so that now as always Christ will be exalted in my body, whether by life or by death. For to me, to live is Christ and to die is gain" (Philippians 1:20-21).

Time is short; eternity is long. Faithfulness in this life will be rewarded in the next.

The churches in Asia Minor had their light extinguished many centuries ago. What would they tell us today if they could? They would say that persecution for Christ is to be expected, and that we must remain faithful no matter how high the cost.

— The Triumph of the Cross —

A Personal Testimony

I was born in Pakistan during the 1960s, and my family has lived in the US for some 30 years now. My dad used to be a major in the Pakistani army.

I went to college in California and met a woman who would invite students to go to church. For a while, I refused. Later, I became a math tutor, and among the students I helped was Rudy, who was from Mexico. He invited me to go to church with him, and for the first time I heard the gospel. Afterward, I got angry at Rudy and told him I wanted to remain a Muslim.

In 1987, I moved to Boston and took evening classes at Harvard University and worked at a hotel at the same time. One day I came down with a flu that wouldn't go away. None of the doctors I visited could figure out what was wrong. Because of extreme fatigue and exhaustion, I could barely walk or talk and slept 14 to 15 hours a day. So I moved back to Chicago to live with my parents and recover. I thought about what Rudy had said about praying for me, and I started reading the Bible in secret, away from my parents' home. Matthew 7:7 stood out to me: "Ask and it will be given to you; seek and you will find; knock and the door will be opened to you."

In September of 1988, I accepted Jesus as my personal Savior and repented of my sins. Rest and peace came into my life, and I continued to read about Christ, who I realized was more than a mere prophet, as Islam taught.

One day my mom found my Bible in my backpack. "This is a

Muslim home," she said, and she demanded that I leave. I walked the streets of Chicago looking for a place to stay, and God brought along a Filipino Christian man with whom I stayed with for a few days. Then a friend offered me a place to stay until I could find a job. I still struggled with my illness, but kept on praying and reading the Bible and joined a church.

Then I met the woman who is now my wife, and I shared Christ with her. She became a Christian, and we got married. I have since fully recovered from my illness, and I have continued to keep my promise to Jesus that I would serve Him for the rest of my life.

—Name withheld

The Shadow of the Crescent

"Our belief is that Islam is the final divine religion,
supersedes all other divine religions,
and that all other religions are abrogated
by the prophet hood of Mohammad...
no one has the right to stay on his/her Christianity or Judaism..."

Dr. Main Khalid Al-Qudah[1]

Chapter Four

Lesson #3:
Even When a Church Is in the Devil's Hands, It Is Still in God's Hands

I know your afflictions and your poverty—yet you are rich!...Do not be afraid of what you are about to suffer. I tell you, the devil will put some of you in prison to test you, and you will suffer persecution for ten days. Be faithful, even to the point of death, and I will give you life as your victor's crown (Revelation 2:9-10).

—JESUS, TO THE CHURCH IN SMYRNA

The history of Smyrna reminds us that Satan has great power to intimidate and destroy. Yet he does not have ultimate power, for he cannot change the eternal destiny of anyone who belongs to Christ. Yes, throughout history there are many instances in which a church has been thrown into the hands of the devil, and it has not survived—at least in its visible form. However, through it all, God's people are kept secure. Jesus gave Himself up for the church, and He has promised never to abandon her.

When our tour group arrived in Smyrna by bus, most of us knew little of the city's fascinating past. Of course, we were aware of Jesus' first-century prophecy that the church in Smyrna would face persecution, but the details of what happened in the centuries afterward was only casually addressed by our tour guides. Many people are unaware that in Smyrna took place one of the most heart-wrenching episodes of persecution that can be found in the annals of Christian history.

FIRST-CENTURY PERSECUTION

Let's begin by looking at the more immediate context of Jesus' prediction. He started His letter to the church by saying, "I know your afflictions and your poverty—yet you are rich!" (Revelation 2:9). Like the other cities mentioned in Revelation chapters 2–3, Smyrna had temples erected to Roman gods and goddesses to which the citizens were expected to bow. So when the Christians refused to participate in emperor worship, they were vilified. Because of their faithfulness, they endured poverty—probably because they could not participate in some of the trades and businesses that may have had immoral or unethical dealings involved. It may be some couldn't get jobs because they wouldn't worship the emperor.

The Christians in Smyrna were also slandered by those who said they were Jews but were not (verse 9). That likely refers to people who claimed to be Jews in order to escape persecution. As a rule, Rome did not persecute the Jews. This slander may have taken the form of attacks on their character or mockery for their faith.

Smyrna's best-known martyr was Polycarp, the bishop of the church in Lyon. At the time Jesus' letter in Revelation 2 was read to the congregation, Polycarp was very likely a part of that church. According to the early church father Irenaeus, Polycarp was taught directly by the apostle John himself. In the year AD 156, as the Roman persecution worsened, Polycarp's friends urged the bishop to flee the city to spare his life, but he was tracked down and captured. So gracious was he that he offered food and drink to his captors. He was repeatedly asked to recant his Christian faith, but he refused to do so. Then he was brought into an arena and threatened with death. When he was given one last opportunity to deny Christ, he replied, "Eighty and six years I have served Him, and He has done me no wrong. How can I blaspheme my King and my Savior?"

When Polycarp was warned that wild beasts were waiting for him should he refuse to recant, he replied, "Call them. It is unthinkable for me to repent from what is good to turn to what is evil." With that answer, the proconsul changed his mind and said that because Polycarp had despised the beasts, he would be burned by fire.

And so it was that when Polycarp was bound and the fire was prepared, he prayed, "O Lord God Almighty, the Father of your beloved and blessed Son Jesus Christ, by whom we have received the knowledge of you...I give you thanks that you count me worthy to be numbered among your martyrs, sharing the cup of Christ." Then the fire was lit. And thus it was that Polycarp, though seemingly in the hands of the devil, was of course ultimately in the hands of God.

Such suffering was but a small preview of the horrors that still awaited Smyrna.

LATER PERSECUTIONS

Brutality was routinely practiced by many different invading armies in Asia Minor and the surrounding lands during the early centuries after Christ and all through the Middle Ages. For example, in the 1360s, the Muslim warlord Aksak Timur captured cities of the Middle East, and as a tribute to his victories, he would pile up a giant pyramid consisting of the skulls of all his victims, including children. Smyrna suffered this fate in 1402, and in Timur's crusade of ethnic cleansing against the Christians, he boasted of "washing the sword of Islam in the blood of the infidels."[2]

Smyrna's suffering, however, was far from over. The barbarism faced in 1402 pales in comparison to what happened in 1922. Hundreds of thousands of men, women, and children were caught in a human bloodbath on a scale that the world until that time had never seen before. When it was over, the *New York Times* would carry the headline "Smyrna Wiped Out."[3]

Here is the story.

THE BACKGROUND TO SMYRNA'S DESTRUCTION

Keep in mind that in World War I, Turkey sided with Germany, and therefore found itself at war against the Allied Forces, including Britain, France, Russia, Greece, and the United States. Part of Turkey's border is up against Russia, and the Turks, fearing the advance of the Russian armies, orchestrated a propaganda campaign saying that the Armenians in their midst were in league with the enemy and therefore were a threat to the security of the Ottoman Empire. Because the Armenians were non-Muslims living under Islamic rule, they held *dhimmi* status, and thus were viewed with contempt by the Turks.

Armenians within the city of Constantinople were the first to be arrested and massacred by the Turks, and from there, the hostilities spread to Armenians in other parts of the region. The atrocities committed against the Armenians defy description—for example, men had horseshoes nailed to their feet, and women were gang-raped.

When trains filled with Armenians being deported to death camps crossed a bridge, mothers would throw their infants out the windows into the water below, preferring to spare their little ones from the more horrible fate that surely awaited them at the death camps. A Greek Christian, Stylianos T. Ayanoglou, an eyewitness to some of the tragedies, reported, "I remember the screams and the smell of burning flesh as hundreds of Armenians were crowded into a building, which was then set on fire. I had witnessed cartloads of bodies, charred or half-burned, being dumped into the river near my home in Adana."[4]

The massacres carried out by the Turks during and immediately after World War I were so extensive that it is estimated that more than a million Christian Armenians were exterminated. One historian wrote, "The bloodstained annals of the East contain no record of massacres more unprovoked, more widespread or more terrible than those perpetrated by the Turkish Government upon the Christians of Anatolia and Armenia in 1915."[5] The magnitude of these atrocities led Polish Jewish lawyer Raphael Lemkin to coin the word *genocide,* meaning "acts of extermination directed against the ethnic, religious, or social collectivities whatever the motive (political, religious, etc.)."[6]

In the end, the Allied Forces won World War I. And Turkey, because it had sided with Germany, had little option except to sign an armistice, conceding defeat. But that didn't help quiet the tensions in the region.

THE GREAT IDEA

What followed is both troubling and fascinating. The story is told in detail in the book *Paradise Lost—Smyrna 1922: The Destruction of Islam's City of Tolerance* by Giles Milton, who collected eyewitness accounts of Smyrna's utter destruction and shared them in the book.[7] Milton also explains the "The Great Idea"—a foolish plan concocted by England and Greece with the goal of recapturing Turkey for the Greeks. Because Turkey had been weakened by World War I and the country was in the hands of the Allies, the British and Greeks believed they now had the opportunity to punish Turkey for its cruel treatment and massacre of the Armenians.

Initially, the Greeks and Britons won many victories, and it appeared as if they might recapture Turkey. But they could never have predicted the horrific change of events about to take place.

TURNAROUND AND REVENGE

Meet the Turkish hero who changed everything.

If you have ever visited Turkey, you know that statues and pictures of Mustafa Kemal Ataturk dot the country. He is highly regarded as the hero who made Turkey the country it is today. His positive influence is seen everywhere, and he is rightly called the father of modern Turkey.

When England and Greece invaded Turkey, it was Ataturk who pulled the Turks together and plotted the uprising that would fight back. Ataturk was a shrewd tactician and a feared commander. At first he won small battles against the British. Then he took on the Greeks, who, though they fought valiantly, were no match for Ataturk and his efficient army.

PUNISHING SMYRNA

Soon the war provoked by England and Greece was seen to be a foolish mistake. They had underestimated the determination of the Turkish nationalists. Under the capable leadership of Ataturk, the Turks recaptured territories that had been occupied by the Allies. When they retook Smyrna, the Armenians breathed a sigh of relief. They figured that because the Turks had won and taken Smyrna back, life would return to normal for them.

Unfortunately, the Turks were bent on revenge. They wanted to punish Smyrna, which had long been a Greek city. As Sir Valentine Chirol put it, "After the Turks had smashed the Greek armies they turned the essentially Greek city (Smyrna) into an ash heap as proof of their victory."[8] The Turkish soldiers sealed off the Armenian portion of Smyrna and began to ransack homes and businesses and brutally massacre the inhabitants. They placed barrels of petroleum inside buildings, then took bundles of rags dipped in petroleum and threw them through the windows, using these to set fire to the city. Those Christians who had managed to evade the killing up till now by hiding in basements could not escape the flames.

One eyewitness wrote, "Nothing—no words—can describe the awful effect of the city…One appalling mass of flames, the water front covered with dark masses of despairing humanity."[9] Fernand de Cramer wrote, "Picture to yourself a crowd so dense that you could scarcely touch the ground with your feet and you turned upon yourself like grains of sand in a whirlwind. Amid piercing shrieks and blows, people falling into the sea, a smoke so hot that upon my word I thought my entrails were on fire."[10]

Countless thousands of people were trapped. As the fire blazed, they fled toward the sea, hoping to escape the approaching flames. But there was no place to go. It was either die in the flames, or jump into the waters of the Aegean Sea.

Understandably, most of the terrified people preferred to drown rather than be burned alive. Smyrna's bay became filled with floating corpses. One eyewitness said the sea was so full of bodies that if you fell into the water, you would not drown but land on floating human beings in various stages of drowning and death.

The missionary Anna Birge reported, "Among the many dead bodies, we saw men, women and children shot to death, bodies drawn up in horribly strained postures, with expressions portraying the endurance of excruciating pain."[11] By the time the ordeal was over, many thousands were dead and the city was leveled to the ground. Churches and hospitals were no more. And the official name of the city was changed to Izmir.

Now, nearly 100 years later, I'm told there are Christian churches in Smyrna, but their numbers are very small. Christians are not allowed to openly spread their faith, and anything they do cannot be done in view of the prying eyes of the Muslim authorities. The numbers are small, the converts are few.

DID THE GATES OF HELL PREVAIL?

I bring up Smyrna's past not to focus so much on the atrocities committed by the Turkish army, but to raise an important question: Where was God when all this took place? After all, didn't Jesus promise that He would build His church and "the gates of Hades will not overcome it" (Matthew 16:18)? Does the utter devastation that occurred in Smyrna mean that Jesus failed to protect His church?

Some would say that seems to be the case.

There are some who interpret Matthew 16:18 as saying the church can withstand the gates of Hades such that it cannot be harmed. But I would contend Matthew 16:18 isn't a promise to shelter Christians from persecution. In fact, nowhere in Scripture do we find any kind of assurance that we will *not* encounter suffering—whether it be trials of a minor nature or horrors of the magnitude encountered by the Christians in Smyrna.

More to the point, I included this account about Smyrna's devastation so we could have a proper understanding of the relationship between God, the devil, and the church.

Let's take a closer look at Matthew 16:18. Speaking to Peter,

Jesus said, "You are Peter, and on this rock I will build my church, and the gates of Hades will not overcome it." Regardless of how we understand Peter's relationship to the church, 1 Corinthians 3:11 makes it clear that Christ is the foundation upon which the church is built. And the Jews of Jesus' day would have understood "the gates of Hades" to refer to the physical death of Jesus.[12] In other words, the Lord was telling His disciples that His death would not prevent His church from being built.

The RSV rendering of Matthew 16:18 captures this meaning when it reads, "The powers of death shall not prevail against it." In short, the death of Jesus would not prevent the church from being built. Indeed, His martyrdom was necessary for the church to be established. Nor does the death of God's people thwart Christ's plans to raise up a people who belong to Him.

So Matthew 16:18 is not a promise that churches will always survive, but rather that the death of Christ and His people will never prevent Him from doing what He has set out to do. As we know, thousands of churches close every year—sometimes for good reasons, sometimes for carnal reasons, such as a lack of vision, lack of funds, or a congregational split. And when the church as a whole declines in one place, it grows in others. Even as the church is declining in America, we are told that it is growing rapidly in Central and South America and parts of Africa.

That said, it is necessary for us as believers to think carefully about how we understand suffering from a biblical standpoint. How do we understand the relationship between God, the devil, and the church? Surely Smyrna is a case study well worth examining if we want to better understand what the church can expect when it comes to persecution.

ONLY WITH GOD'S PERMISSION

Let us begin by considering Jesus' warning to the believers in Smyrna. He said, "Do not be afraid of what you are about to suffer. I tell you, the devil will put some of you in prison to test you, and you will suffer persecution for ten days" (Revelation 2:10).

First, we can take comfort in the fact that Jesus knew, in advance, what the church would have to endure. He knew what was going to happen. And He not only foresaw the sufferings of believers in the first century, but the sufferings of believers for all time, including today. We can take consolation in the fact that nothing escapes the eyes of the Almighty. And nothing that happens to us will ever take Him by surprise.

Second, note that Jesus possesses sovereign control over the extent of the suffering that the believers in Smyrna would face. He said, "You will suffer persecution for ten days." We don't know what is meant by "ten days"—was Jesus talking about ten literal days, or ten periods of persecution? Are the ten days symbolic of a longer period? Regardless of how we're to understand the phrase "ten days," the point He was making is this: All the powers of hell combined could not extend the persecution to *eleven* days! Jesus has His hand on the thermostat. No matter how much affliction the devil desires to unleash, he is still subject to God. He cannot usurp God's ultimate control over all things.

Jesus knew what He was talking about based on personal experience. When He was arrested, note that the Roman soldiers "bound Him" (John 18:12). Does this mean the men who mistreated Jesus were stronger than Him? When Satan was allowed this victory over the Son of God, did this show that the devil and his purposes were superior—at least at that time?

Of course not. When the soldiers came to arrest Jesus, He handed Himself over to them. He said, "Am I leading a rebellion, that you have come with swords and clubs? Every day I was with you in the temple courts, and you did not lay a hand on me. But this is your hour—when darkness reigns" (Luke 22:52-53). Jesus voluntarily gave Himself up to His enemies because this was the hour when darkness was allowed to rule. His crucifixion could not have happened without His personal permission. "The reason my Father loves me is that I lay down my life—only to take it up again. No one takes it from me, but I lay it down of my own accord. I have authority to lay it down and authority to take it up again" (John 10:17-18).

So Jesus submitted Himself into the hands of evil men. But there comes a point when the hands of men can only do so much, and then the hands of God take over. When Jesus died, His final words were, "Father, into your hands I commit my spirit" (Luke 23:46). He was crucified by human hands, but He died under the Father's watchful care.

GOD RULES THE AFFAIRS OF MEN

My point is that the church, just like Jesus, has suffered under the hands of the devil, but each victory Satan experiences is but a temporary blip on the divine calendar of God's complete sovereignty over all the ages. Although Jesus was crucified in weakness, He was in Satan's hands only by divine appointment—only because God allowed it. Peter explained, "This man was handed over to you by God's deliberate plan and foreknowledge; and you, with the help of wicked men, put him to death by nailing him to the cross" (Acts 2:23).

So where was God during those fateful days in Smyrna in 1922? The Turkish army could not have massacred the Christian Armenians unless they had authority "from above," just as Pilate did when he gave the word for Jesus to be crucified (John 19:11).

We should never minimize the power of the devil, nor deny that his trademark is violence, hatred, and the destruction of God's people. And yet we must always see that God is bigger, stronger, and mightier—not just in strength but in wisdom. God is in charge; He rules the affairs of men. The devil wants to be in control, but he's not. The phrase "the LORD of hosts" appears repeatedly all through the Old Testament to affirm that behind the visible rulers of the world is the invisible God of the universe.

How strong is Satan? As strong as God allows him to be, and not one whit more. He is so weak that a single angel, acting under God's authority, will someday come down from heaven with a key to open the pit and throw the devil into it for 1000 years (Revelation 20:1-3). All evil is ultimately under God's authority. As Martin Luther is quoted as saying, "Even the devil is God's devil!"

The fact of God's sovereignty and His perfect plan to bring glory to Himself even through the evil schemes of men must be the cornerstone of any plausible explanation of the kind of persecution and slaughter that took place in Smyrna. God has a much larger purpose that we will not understand on this side of heaven. And we, as His children, do not live by human explanations, but place our full trust in His promises.

We can also take great assurance in the truth that a violent death cannot separate a believer from God's love and grace. When Paul asked, "Who shall separate us from the love of Christ?" he answered that neither "trouble or hardship or persecution or famine or nakedness or danger or sword" can hold back God's care (Romans 8:35). In Acts 12, on the night before his scheduled trial, Peter was sound asleep between prison guards. James had been killed, and Peter had every reason to believe he was next. Yet that night, with the confidence of God filling his soul, he *slept*. He knew that for him, death would be gain.

Those Christians who conclude that evil triumphs because God is too weak to hold Satan back will find no hope in their distress. But those who trust that God is still firmly in control even when they suffer great persecution know that they will one day be compensated for the sacrifices they endure. They share the apostle Paul's conviction "that our present sufferings are not worth comparing with the glory that will be revealed in us" (Romans 8:18). And they are sustained by the fact that the greater their present suffering, the greater their future glory.

TRUSTING GOD NO MATTER WHAT HAPPENS

We who live in the West can be heartened by two facts. First, no matter what suffering might lie in our future, countless thousands of our brothers and sisters in Christ have endured much worse. Of these, untold numbers suffered faithfully, fulfilling God's will for their lives. And second, we must remember that when we are persecuted, we are still held firmly in the hands of God, not the hands of men. As Jesus said, no one can pluck us out of His hands (John 10:28-29). Therefore, we have no reason to fear the future.

To ancient Israel, a nation well acquainted with bloody massacres, massive deportations, and lost wars, God gave this promise:

I, the LORD, have called you in righteousness; I will take hold of your hand. I will keep you and will make you to be a covenant for the people and a light for the Gentiles, to open eyes that are blind, to free captives from prison and to release from the dungeon those who sit in darkness (Isaiah 42:6-7).

Even as we are held in God's hands and we suffer, we are to be a witness to those who are in spiritual darkness. We are not to retreat in resignation or fear, but to step forward as bold witnesses who proclaim God's saving grace. Let us prove once and for all that we value Christ more than our own comforts or even life itself.

No matter how bad things get, no matter whether it seems Satan has the upper hand, God is in control. And that was true for the believers in the church at Smyrna. "Be faithful, even to the point of death," Jesus said to this church, "and I will give you life as your victor's crown" (Revelation 2:10). That promise applied to the Christians in ancient Smyrna, and it still applies to us today.

Even when we are seemingly thrown into the hands of the devil, we are still in the hands of God.

— The Triumph of the Cross —

A Personal Testimony

Abdul grew up in northern Nigeria in a pious Muslim family. When he was still a young boy, his parents decided to hand him over to an imam, who taught Abdul what Muslims believe and required him to learn the Quran by heart.

In time, some Muslim leaders recognized that Abdul was a talented boy. So they gave him a special task: He was to visit Christian churches, then report everything back to his Muslim friends. He went so far as to tell one pastor he wanted to receive Christ, and he went to baptism classes and got baptized. The church even asked him to preach. All this time, he was still a Muslim spy.

One day Abdul was invited to a special event by the youth group of his church. More than 1000 people attended the service. When an old man got up to preach, Abdul laughed quietly, figuring the sermon wouldn't be very good. The man began to teach about Elijah, then read, "How long will you hesitate between two opinions? If the LORD is God, follow Him; but if Baal, follow him" (1 Kings 18:21 NASB). Abdul was stunned. He felt as if this preacher was speaking to him alone. He wondered, *Who told this man about me?* At the end of the sermon the preacher said, "Make the right decision today—stand up to show us that you have decided to follow Christ." Abdul found himself standing—and he was the only one in the crowd doing so.

That was the day the Lord found Abdul. And it was also the day he began to experience persecution. His Muslim friends wanted to kill him. To save him, his church hid him in a small village. An elderly pastor cared for him and discipled him. Abdul later married the pastor's daughter, Mary, and together they dedicated their lives to winning Muslims for Christ.

Their decision came with a high price. One day more than 1000 Muslims surrounded the house in which Abdul and his family lived, wanting to kill them. Miraculously, the Lord spared the family. A few years later, Muslim fanatics brutally murdered Abdul and Mary's oldest son—all because the couple dared to testify about Christ to Muslims.

Today Abdul works in northern Nigeria as a missionary. He heads a group of about 35 "farmer evangelists" who work in rural Islamic villages. The Islamist terrorist group Boko Haram threatens him regularly, and is committed to wiping out Christianity in Nigeria. And yet Abdul continues to follow the Lord's call to minister to Muslims and reach them for Christ.

—shared by a friend of Abdul's

The Shadow of the Crescent

"Destroying the cross is an Islamic obligation."

Slogan on a poster in Eastern Afghanistan[1]

Chapter Five

Lesson #4:
The Crescent Cannot
Destroy the Cross

Now I say to the rest of you in Thyatira...hold on to what
you have until I come. To the one who is victorious and
does my will to the end, I will give authority over the
nations—that one "will rule them with an iron scepter
and will dash them to pieces like pottery"
(Revelation 2:24-27).

—JESUS, TO THE CHURCH AT THYATIRA

No Muslim can pray in the presence of a cross."
I learned that the first time I visited the Church of Holy Wisdom in Istanbul several years ago. Our Muslim guide took us on an in-depth tour and pointed out that all crosses (including those that were a part of the original structure) had been chiseled out. This was especially apparent as we toured the balcony—we could see that all of the crosses that had been in the building had either been removed or defaced. That's when our guide explained, "No Muslim can pray in the presence of a cross."

Throughout history, Muslims have not only demolished thousands of churches, but have also burned Bibles and destroyed crosses.

For example, the city of Antioch was captured in 1268 by the Mamluk general Baybars, who afterward wrote to Count Bohemund VI (the ruler of Antioch, who had been away in Tripoli at the time), explaining to him what he would have seen if he had been in the city:

> You would have seen crosses in your churches smashed, pages of the false Testaments scattered, the Patriarchs' tombs overturned. You would have seen your Muslim enemy trampling on the place where you celebrate the Mass, cutting the throats of monks, priests and deacons upon the altars, bringing sudden death to the Patriarchs and slavery to the royal princes. You would have seen fire running through your palaces, your dead burned in this world before going down to the fires of the next, your place unrecognizable, the Church of St. Paul and that of the Cathedral of St. Peter pulled down and destroyed...[2]

Whether in Asia Minor, North Africa, or the Middle East, crosses have been destroyed as Muslims have replaced this symbol with the crescent. Given that the cross represents the heart of the Christian faith, it should come as no surprise that Muslims are so strongly opposed to it. In fact, if we want to understand just how great the divide is between Islam and Christianity, we need only to look to Jesus and the cross.

WAS JESUS CRUCIFIED?

One reason Muslims despise the cross is because they believe Jesus was never crucified. The primary text in the Quran that denies the crucifixion is Sura 4:157-159, where the biblical declaration that Jesus had been nailed to a cross is given an alternate explanation:

> They claim we killed the Messiah Jesus, son of Mary, the apostle of God. But they killed him not, nor did they crucify him. They were under the illusion that they had. Those who differ on this matter are full of doubts. They have no real knowledge but follow only conjecture. Assuredly they did not kill him. On the contrary, God raised him to himself, and God is all powerful, all-wise...

So, according to the Quran, the Jews did not succeed in killing Jesus, who, in the Quran, is called "the apostle of God."

Some Muslim interpreters say that the Jews killed someone whom God made to *look like* Jesus.[3] This, however, makes God seem guilty of deception and illusion. Why would God be party to a deceitful and unjust act by having someone else who looked like Jesus die on the cross instead of Jesus Himself? God would have been guilty of falsehood, leading people to believe that it was Jesus who had been crucified, when in fact it was someone else.[4]

Yet we must keep in mind that the Quran did not come into existence until more than 500 years after the cross, when it was written by Muhammad. By contrast, the accounts recorded in the Bible were documented by a number of independent eyewitnesses whose testimonies have been preserved in manuscripts that date very close to the time of Jesus. Muslims respond to this by saying that Allah spoke through Muhammad, and Allah would not have made a mistake; therefore, what was spoken through Muhammad has no mistakes.

It's interesting to note that only 74 out of 6236 verses in the Quran have any connection with Jesus, and more than 40 of those are indirect references.[5] Of the few passages in the Quran that mention Jesus, most are about His birth, and only one says anything about the crucifixion, saying, "They killed him not" (Sura 4:157). The New Testament Gospels, however, devote a significant amount of space to Jesus' death on the cross. In fact, Mark and John say nothing about Jesus' birth, yet they describe His crucifixion and resurrection in great detail.

Even the fact that the apostle Peter vehemently opposed Jesus' own prediction that He would be crucified and buried adds to the credibility of the New Testament account. When Jesus "began to explain to his disciples that he must go to Jerusalem and suffer…and that he must be killed…Peter took him aside and began to rebuke him. 'Never, Lord!' he said. 'This shall never happen to you!'" (Matthew 16:21-22). Jesus then said to Peter, "Get behind me, Satan! You are a stumbling block to me; you do not have in mind the concerns of God, but merely human concerns" (verse 23).

Peter's problem was that he could not accept a crucified Messiah. To hear that Jesus would be put to death was unthinkable. Peter's urging that Jesus avoid the crucifixion struck at the heart of God's everlasting covenant. The cross was predetermined to be the hinge on which God's purpose for mankind would turn. Without it, there would be no removal of sin, no redemption, no hope of humanity being reconciled to God. This would have suited Satan's purposes all too nicely.

The fact is, what Satan wanted is confirmed in Matthew 4:9, where Satan advised Jesus to skip the crucifixion. There, high on a mountain, the tempter said to the Son of God, "All this I will give you…if you will bow down and worship me." Satan wanted to make a bargain with Jesus. He invited our Lord to bow in worship to him and grasp the kingdoms of the world without dying. Satan's words of hate and Peter's words of misguided love were in unison. Peter's supposed wisdom and the devil's plan were identical. Clearly, *the devil would want us to believe that Jesus was not crucified.*

For Jesus, however, no other option was under consideration. Despite the horror that awaited Him, the cross *had* to be. If Jesus had been a false messiah bent on staging a messianic coup, He certainly would not have chosen to go to Jerusalem to get Himself crucified. He would have taken pains to fulfill the popular messianic expectations of the day—namely, to stage a revolt against the Romans who occupied Israel, and set up a human kingdom. The fact that Jesus countered public opinion and expectations and instead died on the cross confirms the authenticity of His claims about Himself.

If Jesus had taken Peter's suggestion, Peter's own redemption would never have been possible. Without the cross, there would have been no forgiveness, no reconciliation, and no final triumph of Jesus over death and hell. The cross is the hub that holds all the spokes of God's eternal purposes together.

The bottom line here is that Muslims deny Jesus' death on the cross. According to them, "the cross did not happen…and there is an Islamic consensus to say, 'It need not happen, and moreover, it should not happen. It did not happen historically, it did not happen redemptively and it should not morally happen to Jesus.'"[6] Therefore, Christianity should have no cross, and the very symbol itself is offensive to devout Muslims.

DARK CHAPTERS OF CHRISTIAN HISTORY

Muslims despise the cross for another reason—one that is more immediate in their consciousness. The Crusaders often fought against the Muslims under the banner of the cross. The European Crusades that were launched to free the Holy Land from the Turks more than 800 years ago are often cited as a pretext for Muslims who insist that they are still trying to "even the score" today.

Setting the Record Straight

Let's back up for a moment and get some historical context: In the seventh century, Muslim invaders entered the Holy Land unprovoked to capture Christian lands. First they conquered Syria. Then, because the Holy Land was largely unprotected, the Muslim forces were able to capture it without much resistance.

Robert Spencer, a scholar of Islamic history, theology, and law, explains what followed:

> In the Holy Land, the conquest of Jerusalem in 638 stood at the beginning of centuries of Muslim aggression; Christians in the Holy Land faced an escalating spiral of persecution...
>
> Brutal subordination and violence became the rule of the day for Christians in the Holy Land...Early in the ninth century the persecutions grew so severe that large numbers of Christians fled for Constantinople and other Christian cities.
>
> ...[I]n 1004, the sixth Fatimid Caliph, Abu 'Ali al-Mansur al-Hakim...ordered the destruction of churches, the burning of crosses, and the seizure of church property. He moved against the Jews with similar ferocity. Over the next ten years thirty thousand churches were destroyed, and untold numbers of Christians converted to Islam simply to save their lives.[7]

From the seventh to the tenth centuries, Muslims conquered "fully two-thirds of the Christian world."[8] Not until the eleventh century did Europe finally respond. So it was hundreds of years of unrelenting violence and persecution by Islamic armies that sparked the Crusades. Thomas F. Madden, among the world's foremost authorities on the Crusades, explains, "The crusades were in every way a *defensive war*."9

Today, there are many—even in the Western media—who perpetrate the notion that the Crusades were an unprovoked, imperialistic attack upon peaceful Muslims. In reality, the Crusades were preceded by centuries of horrific Islamic invasions and widespread cruelty and killings against Christians. The Crusades, therefore, had a legitimate goal—the defense of Christians and their lands, and a desire to free Jerusalem so that Christian pilgrims could once again visit the sacred sites associated with the death, resurrection, and ministry of Jesus.

When Pope Urban II recruited his armies for the First Crusade, he had the emblem of the cross placed on the soldiers' uniforms. He also promised the remission of sins to those who took "a pilgrim vow to persist in the way of God to the end, or until death."10 Some soldiers went so far as to burn the sign of the cross into their flesh, like a tattoo. Pope Urban II also warned that any soldier who deserted from the army would be considered an outlaw. I'm sorry to say that Pope Urban's actions and challenge to his army could be described as an abysmal form of Christian jihad.

What's more, Pope Urban's armies included untrained volunteers bent on mayhem and revenge. There are also reports that some of the Crusader armies were undisciplined and would attack their Muslim enemies, including women and children, in a ruthless manner. While this conduct did not represent the Crusaders as a whole, the fact is, some of the armies were badly managed and unruly. For this reason, in the minds of Muslims, the cross—which was highly visible on the Crusaders' uniforms—remains a negative symbol.

A Proper Christian Response

While historically far more people have been massacred under the banner of the crescent than ever under the banner of the cross, this is not a numbers game. The Bible is clear that Christians should "not repay anyone evil for evil" (Romans 12:17). We humbly confess that those soldiers who, under the banner of the cross, violated the principles that were to be upheld by the Crusaders ended up besmirching the name of Christ. Today, rightly or wrongly, Muslims still point to their wanton behavior as the reason for modern-day terrorist acts against "Christian" Westerners.

When the Roman soldiers approached the Lord Jesus Christ in the Garden of Gethsemane to arrest Him, the apostle Peter drew his sword. Jesus rebuked him, saying, "Put your sword back in its place... for all who draw the sword will die by the sword" (Matthew 26:52). This confusion of swords—relying upon a sword of steel rather than the sword of the Spirit—has bedeviled the Christian church over the course of its history. To join the army of one's country was legitimate for matters of state, but to fight in a so-called "holy war" is a discredit to Christ.

The reformer Martin Luther, for all of his blustering comments about the Jews and Turks of his day, repeatedly emphasized that no person should go to war under the banner of the cross.[11] Samuel Zwemer, a lifetime missionary to Muslims who went on to become a professor of missions at Princeton Theological Seminary, said, "The Crusades were a colossal error on the part of Christendom. They showed zeal but without knowledge, passion without the love of Christ."[12]

Obviously, many of the Crusaders were not true Christians who understood the New Testament doctrine of salvation. We can be certain most were probably Christian in name only, and not true followers of Christ. What's more, the fact Pope Urban II would even promise the remission of sins to the pilgrims who "took up the cross" to liberate formerly Christian lands is proof enough that he himself had buried the gospel amid political and religious agendas.

All that to say, we must be sensitive to the feelings of Muslims when it comes to the cross—even if we are convinced they have greatly misunderstood both its meaning and message. We must help them separate the truth about the cross from the misuses of the cross that have occurred in history. That doesn't mean, however, that we should obscure the cross—either as a symbol, nor especially the message which lies at the heart of it. We have no reason to be ashamed of the cross. We need to speak about the cross with both clarity and sensitivity.

THE CONFLICT OVER THE CROSS

We should note that Muslims were destroying crosses long before the Crusades, long before they were ever sewn onto the garments of soldiers. When Muslim invaders entered Jerusalem in 637, they did away with all crosses and would not allow them to be displayed. The symbol that lies at the heart of the Christian faith was utterly abolished. And that's the way it has been ever since. Where Islam has prevailed, there is no room for both the cross and the crescent.

Now, we can perhaps understand the rejection and destruction of Christian crosses in Muslim-dominated lands. But what about in places such as the United Kingdom and the United States? Remarkably, in the name of cultural sensitivity, more and more Western institutions and individuals are being told they should remove crosses from wherever Muslims might see them, such as hospital rooms, or even from the exterior of churches. This is done under the guise of not needlessly provoking Muslims in our midst.

However, the reverse has never been true. You will never find evidence that the crescent has ever been removed or hidden in Muslim countries so as not to offend the sensibilities of Christians who remember the large multitudes of believers who were killed under its banner.

As Christians, it is important that we endeavor to proclaim the truth with love and sensitivity, and not in a way that brings reproach upon Christ. But that doesn't mean we who live in Western nations should feel it is necessary to accommodate Muslims by taking down crosses. Tragically, rather than being willing to stand up for Christ, we are stepping aside and suppressing our Christian influence in the name of cultural and religious sensitivity. And even when we are in disagreement with such acquiescence, we are reluctant to voice our objection to this censorship of the Christian faith.

GOOD-BYE TO THE CROSS

In a provocative article titled "Away with Crucifixes, Crosses, and Christmas," Daniel Pipes, the founder and director of Middle East Forum, documents specific examples of how Muslims have demanded the removal of crosses on display in public places, particularly in Europe.[13] For example, in England, the chief inspector of prisons, Anne Owers, prohibited prison officials from wearing St. George's Cross tiepins, even though this cross appears on the national flag of England. Muslims complained about the cross's supposed connection to the Crusades—never mind the fact St. George was executed by the Roman emperor Diocletian in 303, a few centuries *before* the time of Muhammad, and even more centuries before the Crusades took place.

Pipes also reported about a Turkish lawyer who, in 2007, was watching a Champions League soccer match and became offended when he noted that the Inter Milan team's uniform had a large red cross on it. He filed a complaint, seeking damages for himself and a large fine against Inter Milan because the uniforms displayed a "Crusader-style" cross that allegedly represented "Western racist superiority over Islam." He also wanted the results of the game annulled.[14]

A respondent to Pipes's article observed it's interesting that Muslims should take offense to the cross, but Christians cannot take offense to public displays of the Islamic faith. He mentioned the Saudi flag, which carries the statement, "There is no deity but God and Muhammad is his Messenger," beneath which appears a sword. What if Christians were to say they were offended by that statement and the image of the sword? Unfortunately, the so-called cultural sensitivity today works in only one direction. Hospitals and prisons in Western countries are asked to remove the cross, but that could never be requested of the crescent in Muslim-majority lands.

In April 2009, senior staff at the Royal North Shore Hospital in Sydney, Australia ordered that crucifixes, Bibles, and other Christian symbols be removed from the hospital chapel so that Muslims, Hindus, and other non-Christians would not be offended.[15] And in 2010, Muslim patients objected to crosses in the surgical department of Bad Soden hospital in Frankfurt, Germany, so employees removed them.[16] Such actions are becoming increasingly common in hospitals in Western nations.

With the rise of Muslim influence in the Western world, we can expect many more requests that Christian symbols be removed or prohibited. Politically correct government and administrative officials, unable to make appropriate religious judgments, bend over backward to accommodate Muslims who are allegedly offended by symbols or expressions of the Christian faith. They are typically all too eager to appease Muslims, figuring that the removal of so-called offensive symbols will ensure peaceful relations. But what they are really doing is *censoring* expressions of the Christian faith while freely *permitting* expressions of the Islamic faith. In a good-faith effort to exhibit tolerance *toward* Islam, Western governments are actually encouraging the intolerance exhibited *by* Islam.

As Western leaders increasingly cave to Muslim demands that infringe on freedom of religion, it would be easy for us to get discouraged about the erosion of our religious liberties. But these attacks on the cross should inspire us to be all the more eager to carry our cross for Christ. Jesus urged us to take up the cross and follow Him. That is a high honor indeed. May we never let cultural pressures diminish the cross in our churches or our lives. Instead, may we echo the words of the apostle Paul in Galatians 6:14: "May I never boast except in the cross of our Lord Jesus Christ, through which the world has been crucified to me, and I to the world."

TWO SYMBOLS, TWO SALVATIONS

The cross and the crescent represent two radically different understandings of salvation. Muslims claim they honor Christ more than Christians do because they believe that God let Jesus escape the crucifixion and took Him directly to heaven. But Christianity teaches that the death of Jesus on the cross was God's finest hour so far as we as sinners are concerned. There, both the love and justice of God were mutually satisfied, making it possible for the lost to be reconciled to the Almighty. Love wanted to redeem us, but justice demanded that we pay for our sin, which for us sinners is impossible. Thus God chose to take the initiative and satisfy His own demands, and Christ died for us on the cross.

We must help our Muslim friends understand that at the cross, God's love and holiness came together. Both attributes were upheld in their fullest expression. The holiness of God was upheld because God's just demands for sin were satisfied by the death of Christ. John Piper put it this way:

> There is a holy curse hanging over all sin. Not to punish would be unjust. The demeaning of God would be endorsed…Therefore God sends his own Son to absorb his wrath and bear the curse for all who trust him, "Christ redeemed us from the curse of the law by becoming a curse for us" (Gal. 3:13).[17]

And then the love of God was upheld because Christ's payment for our sins made it possible for God to extend forgiveness and the gift of His own righteousness.

Follow the reasoning: Because the wages of sin is death, and because we are all sinners, either we had to experience an eternal death or else someone had to stand in our place so that we could be exempt from sin's ultimate penalty. Our substitute had to meet all of God's requirements—He had to be perfectly holy and perfectly obedient. As sinners both by nature and by choice, we have no ability to meet God's demands. Only Jesus, who was sinless, had these credentials. Piper emphasizes God's attributes further: "If God were not *just*, there would be no *demand* for his Son to suffer and die. And if God were not *loving*, there would be no *willingness* for his Son to suffer and die. But God is both just and loving. Therefore his love is willing to meet the demands of his justice."[18] Jesus' suffering was terrible for the simple reason that our sin is terrible.

Contrast this with Islam. The Quran teaches that people commit sin, but they are not sinful. Sin is an act of disobedience to God rather than evidence of a broken relationship with God. As Bible scholar Ron Rhodes notes, "They do believe that sin exists, but they believe people commit sins not because they have a sinful nature, but because of human weakness and forgetfulness (Sura 4:28)."[19] In Islam, there is no need for God to redeem humanity because sin is paid for by you personally. Muslim Muhammad Asad wrote, "Every Muslim is his own redeemer; he bears all possibilities of spiritual success and failure within his heart."[20]

What's more, Muslims can make up for their bad deeds by doing good ones. For example, Sura 2:271 teaches that doing acts of charity can help take away sin. In fact, even the manner in which you do your charity makes a difference. Sura 2:271 says that to "declare" your charities is "good," but to remain "anonymous" about them "remits *more* of your sins."

So for Muslims, the idea that one's good deeds must outweigh one's bad deeds is very real. According to the Quran, "The balance that day will be true; those whose scale of good will be heavy, will prosper; those whose scale will be light, will find their souls in perdition" (Sura 7:8).

By contrast, Christianity teaches that sin is so serious and God's holiness so demanding that sin cannot be overlooked by the Almighty. Christianity agrees with Islam that every sin will be paid for. But Islam teaches that we can pay for our own sin and hope that eventually we will go to paradise. In stark contrast, Christianity says there is no one righteous—no, not one (Romans 3:10). Sinners cannot pay for their sins; only a holy substitute can do that. We have a debt that only God Himself can pay. That is why it was necessary for Christ to die in our place.

That's what made the crucifixion necessary. Christ *had* to die on the cross—contrary to what Muslims claim. The cross wasn't a show of weakness on Jesus' part. Rather, it demonstrated His great power, for His subsequent resurrection proved that He had triumphed over sin and death. Those who attempt to reach God other ways—as Muslims do, by attempting to pay for their own sins and by doing enough good deeds—diminish the wonder of what Christ did on the cross. Without the cross, there can be no crown.

Muslims cannot know the assurance of salvation, for in the end, Allah does with each person as he desires. According to the Hadith, Muhammad himself said he was unsure of his eternal salvation. He wrote, "Though I am an Apostle of Allah, yet I do not know what Allah will do to me!" (Bukhari 5.58.266). And the Quran states that only death by jihad assures a person of instant access into paradise.

Christians, however, can know the assurance of their salvation.

That's because salvation is a free gift made available through the sacrifice and triumph of Jesus. No matter how great our sin, Jesus' sacrifice on our behalf was greater. Because it is Christ who obtained our salvation and gives it to us, we cannot and will not lose it. As the apostle John said, "Whoever has the Son has life; whoever does not have the Son of God does not have life. I write these things to you who believe in the name of the Son of God so that you may know that you have eternal life" (1 John 5:12-13).

This free gift is available to anyone who receives Christ as Savior: "To all who did receive him, to those who believed in his name, he gave the right to become children of God" (John 1:12).

CROSSES VERSUS THE WORK OF THE CROSS

Can the crescent obliterate the cross? Muslims have proven that they can indeed destroy crosses. They did so when they invaded Christians' lands long ago, and today they intimidate Westerners into removing crosses from public view. But can they destroy *the* cross—that is, the great work Jesus accomplished when He was crucified? Destroying a symbol is one thing; destroying the reality of Jesus' victory over sin and the devil is quite another. Jesus' great triumph will forever remain undiminished in light of the temporary victories of those bent on replacing crosses with crescents. Crosses are temporal, but the work of the cross is beyond the reach of its enemies. That is why a day is coming when the cross will forever replace the crescent.

Satan knows that no matter how many crosses are destroyed, his doom was sealed when Jesus died as a sacrifice for sinners. "And having disarmed the powers and authorities, he made a public spectacle of them, triumphing over them by the cross" (Colossians 2:15). For a person to burn a flag is not the same thing as destroying a country. And for a Muslim to destroy a cross is not the same thing as diminishing the triumph of Jesus.

Muslims do not honor Jesus more than Christians do. They deny the cross, whereas Christians see the crucifixion as the most breathtaking expression of God's love ever. On the cross, He intervened on our behalf and accomplished, at a great sacrifice, what we could not.

"God so loved the world that he gave his one and only Son, that whoever believes in him shall not perish but have eternal life" (John 3:16).

This victory not only secured our salvation, it also demonstrated the triumph of Jesus over all His foes. In the end, the confessions of the various world religions will be rewritten to acknowledge that Jesus is the King of kings and Lord of lords.

THE VANISHING MESSAGE OF THE CROSS

Some time ago I read a book that told the story of how England went from being a largely Christian country that sent missionaries around the world to becoming the largely post-Christian, atheistic country it is today.[21] I remember the author made the remark that during the transition period, the gospel was still preached, but it was so bedecked with flowers that no one could see it.

The cross bedecked with flowers!

Tragically, much of the evangelical church today has lost its confidence that the preaching of the cross is "the power of God that brings salvation" (Romans 1:16). I fear that what many people assume is the gospel is not really the gospel at all, but rather a message diluted by popular culture.

Listen to much of the "gospel" preached in America, and you will find these themes running through it: Man is essentially good, God wants you happy and personally fulfilled, the key to real change is positive thinking, and it is virtuous to be open to other belief systems.

What you will not find is an emphasis on the depravity of man, the holiness of God, and the urgent need to humble ourselves and approach God through Christ's sacrifice alone. Nor is much said about the sacrifices and persecution we can expect to face as followers of Christ, and Scripture's commands for us to live a holy life.

I know of a Muslim family that recently converted to Christianity at great personal cost. They visited a large, well-known church with the hope that they would hear instruction from God's Word. Instead, the pastor preached a sermon on the benefits of good nutrition. Needless to say, the family was stunned and disappointed.

Today's church has, to a large extent, abandoned the very message that is most desperately needed at this critical hour of history. At a time when we need to engage our culture with the one message that has any hope of transforming it, many Christians have set aside the power of the gospel and replaced it with man-made programs, strategies, and gimmicks intended to attract the lost. Those won't work, because there is nothing outside the gospel that has the power to bring real change to lives.

The apostles found themselves up against social, political, and religious barriers that they could not move. They had no political clout, no connections with people in high places who could help them out. From a human perspective, they were doomed to fail, and they had absolutely nothing to offer.

And yet they turned the world upside down.

The apostles were motivated by the conviction that God had entered their world and, through Christ's death and resurrection, made it possible for even the most notorious sinner to be transformed. This confidence gave them an impact that was much greater than their numbers might suggest. Faced with ridicule, ostracism, and persecution, they kept the main thing the main thing. Even if no one had believed, they would have continued to do God's work, leaving the results in His hands.

The cross is the hinge on which the door of history swings; it is the hub that holds the spokes of God's purposes together. The Old Testament prophets pointed toward it, and the New Testament prophets proclaimed it. When we cling to that old rugged cross, as the old but familiar song encourages us to do, and we proclaim it, we will see results. This is the heart of our message; this alone will enable us to combat the encroaching darkness.

Some years ago I read this remarkable account:

> During China's Boxer Rebellion of 1900, insurgents captured a mission station, blocked all the gates but one, and in front of that one gate placed a cross flat on the ground. Then the word was passed to those inside that any who trampled the cross underfoot would be permitted their freedom and life, but that any refusing would be shot. Terribly frightened, the first seven students trampled the cross under their feet and were allowed to go free. But the eighth student, a young girl, refused to commit

the sacrilegious act. Kneeling beside the cross in prayer for strength, she arose and moved carefully around the cross, and went out to face the firing squad. Strengthened by her example, every one of the remaining ninety-two students followed her to the firing squad.[22]

Were those who refused to trample on the cross winners or losers? In this life they appeared losers, but they are winners in the life to come. Indeed, eternity will reverse many of the verdicts of time.

— The Triumph of the Cross —

A Personal Testimony

I was born in Kuwait to a Muslim family and attended a Muslim school in Jordan. As a little girl, I did not experience love; rather I was reared in an atmosphere of anger and fear and violence. I don't blame my parents for this—they were victims of similar upbringings by their parents.

I became a devoted Muslim at the age of 10 when I began wearing the hijab (a cover for my hair) and at the age of 13, the abaya (a long dress to my ankles). I did special fasting and prayed five times a day to grow closer to Allah. I read the Quran and studied at the mosque, but still felt dirty and shameful even though I remained a virgin till my wedding day.

When I got married, I was excited because I thought that at last I would be loved. The man who became my husband had previously married an American woman, but after he became an American citizen, he divorced her and married me, a Muslim girl. I was also thrilled about living in America. But I soon learned that I had to obey my husband's rules without questioning, or I would be yelled at or beaten up. Soon we had a child together. I tried hard to please my husband, but he continued to beat me frequently. One night I was so badly beaten I thought I would die. I called the police to report his abuse, which a Muslim wife is told she should never do.

I was befriended by a Christian and began attending church with her. I had been taught to believe that Christians were infidels because they made Jesus the only Son of God. Despite this, I kept going to church and learned more about Jesus. Meanwhile, I was in the process of divorcing my husband. A few months before the divorce was finalized, he sexually assaulted me; I felt broken and ashamed and wanted to die. A month later, I discovered I was pregnant with our second child.

In church, I felt uncomfortable saying the name of Jesus and prayed to Allah instead. At the same time, I asked Christians to pray for me. For months I struggled over what I should do. When I heard a song that proclaimed freedom is found in Jesus, I then prayed to Him and asked Him to be my Savior and Lord. Immediately, I felt my heart changed; I now had a connection with Jesus and I was at peace.

For a while I still went to the mosque, and the imams angrily told me I should go back to my husband. They tried to make me stop going to church. I finally reached a point when I said to myself, "No more!" Then I determined that I would leave the mosque. When I called my parents in Jordan and told them that I had decided to become a Christian because of the love shown to me at church, they were angry, and they have since disowned me.

My life story began with anger and abuse, but God's healing love found me and has been poured over me ever since! Jesus, the Son of God, died for me, and that is the greatest love gift I could ever receive. Growing up, I was taught to hate the cross, but now I love the message of the cross because of all that Jesus did for me on Calvary. "I trust in your unfailing love; my heart rejoices in your salvation. I will sing the LORD's praise, for he has been good to me" (Psalm 13:5-6).

—Majida

The Shadow of the Crescent

"Islam is the solution."

Slogan of the Muslim Brotherhood

Chapter Six

Lesson #5:
Compromise Weakens
the Church

I know your deeds; you have a reputation for being alive,
but you are dead (Revelation 3:1).

—JESUS, TO THE CHURCH AT SARDIS

It is time for us to reflect on what we have learned about Islam
and the church, and to ask ourselves: What responsibility did the
churches in Asia Minor have in contributing to their own demise?
What made them vulnerable in the face of Islamic aggression? Could
it be that they had compromised in ways that weakened their ability to withstand the Muslim assault? To put it differently, might they
have been able to survive longer if they had been more committed to
a New Testament form of Christianity that was not intimidated by
the threat of oppression and martyrdom?

In this fifth lesson, we will focus on the condition of the churches
themselves and draw some important conclusions that relate directly
to our Western Christian culture. We must ask ourselves if we will
do better than they in maintaining our witness if serious persecution
were to come our way.

But first we need to recognize that churches have sometimes been obliterated by persecution through no fault of their own. As we have already learned, Tertullian, the famous early church theologian of North Africa, said that the blood of the martyrs is the seed of the church. That is, persecution spurs growth. However, there have been times when it heralded the death of the church. Sometimes churches have faced persecution so intense that entire congregations have been wiped out. As Philip Jenkins observed in *The Lost History of Christianity*, during the fourteenth century, "wholesale massacres" by Islamic conquerors thoroughly destroyed churches in the Middle East. And "whole Christian communities were annihilated across central Asia... Christianity now disappears in Persia, and across southern and central Iraq."[1]

During the horrific Armenian Genocide in 1915, Turkish authorities in the Ottoman Empire were determined to "complete the eradication of the empire's Christians," and "entire congregations were burned alive inside churches during Sunday services."[2]

Even today we hear in the news about militant Islamist groups or violent mobs who attack an entire church. For example, on October 31, 2010, "Islamic extremists attacked worshipers at the Syrian Catholic Church of Baghdad, killing 59 Christians and severely injuring more than 80 others...Several gunmen armed with automatic weapons and explosives entered the church during a worship service and opened fire on the worshipers."[3]

In the same way that a person might be killed even though he or she stays true to the faith (that is what martyrdom is all about), it is entirely possible for death to come to faithful churches. Even the Lord Jesus Christ was faithful to the Father, and yet He did not avoid death at the hands of wicked men who nailed Him to the cross. Some churches are destroyed *because* they are faithful to the gospel, and not because they were unfaithful. In other words, faithfulness does not guarantee a church will survive.

But there are also times when a church is weakened and eventually dies because of various compromises made with the world. Although we cannot know all the reasons God allowed Islam to triumph over

Christianity in Asia Minor, we do know that a weakened church that has bought into the values of the prevailing culture is much more likely to succumb to deception or wilt under persecution in contrast to a church that is deeply committed to living out the gospel regardless of the cost.

By the time Islam came to Asia Minor, the churches in the region most likely had already been weakened by various compromises. To suggest this is not unreasonable, for it's clear that compromise was already a problem a few hundred years earlier when Jesus wrote His letters to the seven churches.

Perhaps the most destructive compromise was the corrosive relationship between the churches and the local political environment. As the churches intermingled politics with doctrine and church polity, they lost their focus and became prey for the deception of Islam. More on this in a moment—first, let's look at the compromises Jesus addressed in connection with the churches in Revelation 2–3.

MORAL COMPROMISE

When we read Jesus' letters to the seven churches, we note that He rebuked them most often for moral compromise. For example, to those in Pergamum who tolerated the Nicolaitans (who condoned immorality), He warned, "Repent therefore! Otherwise, I will soon come to you and will fight against them with the sword of my mouth" (Revelation 2:16). Imagine Jesus coming with a sword to fight against His own disobedient people in His church!

To those in Thyatira who tolerated Jezebel, He said, "So I will cast her on a bed of suffering, and I will make those who commit adultery with her suffer intensely, unless they repent of their ways. I will strike her children dead. Then all the churches will know that I am he who searches hearts and minds, and I will repay each of you according to your deeds" (Revelation 2:22-23). This tells us the lengths to which Jesus is willing to go to discipline an impure church.

As far as Jesus is concerned, when a church tolerates immorality, it is ready for severe judgment. Why? Moral compromise weakens a church's ability to withstand the pressures of society and false doctrine. Such a church accommodates itself to the spirit of the age. The rot within cannot withstand the storm without.

Perhaps the church in Sardis is most instructive on the matter of morality. Jesus said to these people, "I know your deeds; you have a reputation of being alive but you are dead" (Revelation 3:1). Imagine: On the surface, this church gave the appearance of being healthy. But Jesus applied His stethoscope to the body at Sardis and concluded that despite all the outward signs, the church was a corpse. "You are dead" was His solemn verdict.

If you had been with us at Sardis on our tour of the seven churches, you would have noticed the ruins of an ancient fourth-century church building right up against a pagan temple. Of course, these buildings would not have been in existence when Jesus sent His letter to this church three or four centuries earlier. Still, these ruins might give a clue as to the sin that prevailed in ancient Sardis.

We have to ask: Why was this church built right next to a pagan temple? We can interpret this in one of two ways. Perhaps the Christians said, "We want to build a church right where Satan dwells; we want to shine a light into the moral and spiritual darkness around us. We want to evangelize pagans." This would have been a positive sign; it is good if a church desires to be a light in the middle of the immoral culture around it.

Or there is another way to look at this: Perhaps the church felt at home next to the pagan temple. Its members might have attended both the church services and the pagan rituals next door. If so, the church was sold out to the culture and adopted the ways and means of the sensual society in which it lived. If that were the case, the church's location adjacent to the pagan temple was an indication that moral and spiritual decay had set in.

Sadly, the second interpretation is most likely correct. As far back as the first century AD, Jesus already found it necessary to warn the Sardis congregation about the immorality that had become embedded within it. After telling the people they had a reputation for being alive but in fact were dead, Jesus added, "Yet you have a few people in Sardis who have not soiled their clothes. They will walk with me, dressed in white, for they are worthy" (Revelation 3:4).

Evidently the majority of the church members had "soiled their clothes" by the immorality around them. Yet thankfully, even as in our day, there were a few church members who maintained their purity in the midst of the decadent culture around them. These were the overcomers who kept themselves pure from the pressure of compromise. They had kept themselves unspotted from the world.

COMPROMISE IN AMERICAN CHURCHES

What is the spiritual state of the American church? We cannot doubt that we have been weakened by compromise—especially by the inroads that sexual immorality has made into our churches. The saints at Sardis might have had to deal with the presence of a pagan brothel next door, but they did not have to fight the tsunami of pornography that is so readily available at our newsstands and on the Internet. Their children were not brought up in homes exposed to the seductive power of television with its enticing images of sensuality, violence, and occultism. Whatever their temptations, the people in the church in Sardis did not have to live in a world where all of these enticements were available to them on a desktop computer or mobile device that can be accessed in private.

I fear that we in the West are so seriously morally compromised that we will find it increasingly difficult to withstand the attacks that are coming against the church—whether from secularism in general or the spread of Islam. We are yielding ourselves and compromising with regard to the values that nibble away at our single-minded commitment to Jesus Christ. We say we want to be faithful to Christ but cannot find the strength to do so.

The deadening effects of worldly sensuality stifles our witness. What Christian is going to joyfully share his or her faith while, at the same time, struggling with the residual guilt of a porn addiction? What parents are going to help their children learn biblical values about money, time, and pleasure if they themselves have succumbed to the world's gratifications? Our moral compromises make us weak and vulnerable to whatever wind of adversity comes against us. Only a church that is living in full submission and obedience to Christ and is practicing proper church discipline can maintain standards of purity that will withstand the enemies of Christ, whoever or whatever they may be.

Consider the churches of Western Europe. For the most part, the people there have rejected their Christian heritage and opted for the hedonistic values of personal affluence and radical self-absorption. Today their empty cathedrals are wistfully called "The Tombs of God." I have in my possession a European magazine that illustrates how European church buildings are being turned into mosques, restaurants, and hotels. And if the trend continues, God may very well permit Islam to obliterate Europe's Christian heritage and the blessings of freedom of conscience, freedom of worship, and religious tolerance, all of which grew out of that heritage.

What warning did Jesus give to the church in Sardis? "Remember, therefore, what you have received and heard; hold it fast, and repent. But if you do not wake up, I will come like a thief, and you will not know at what time I will come to you" (Revelation 3:3).

Likewise today, we do not know when Jesus will come. He may come for His bride, the church, and snatch us away to heaven very soon. Or He may delay His coming, withdraw His protection, and let us be fodder for our enemies. Meanwhile, the words of Jesus shout to us across the centuries: "Wake up! Strengthen what remains and is about to die, for I have not found your deeds complete in the sight of my God" (Revelation 3:2). If Jesus warned the church in Pergamum, "I will soon come to you and will fight against them [those who teach immoral things in your midst] with the sword of my mouth" (2:16), we can know with certainty He won't hesitate to discipline an impure church today.

Jesus hates moral and spiritual compromise.

THE KINDS OF COMPROMISE TO WATCH FOR

Let's review some of the other kinds of compromise that can weaken us as believers.

The Compromise of Consumerism

As we toured the ruins of the ancient city of Laodicea, the letter that Jesus wrote to this church repeatedly went through my mind. We surveyed ruins that marked the foundations of houses and buildings dating back to the first century. (No one lives in ancient Laodicea today; there is a newer city by that same name in the vicinity.) As we walked among the ruins, I thought that perhaps they were symbolic of what happens to a church that does not repent of wrongdoing. In this area there was at one time a body of believers who smugly thought that they did not need anything, but today they are only a distant memory. Their prosperous culture that gave them the false assurance that they were quite fine, thank you, now lies in a heap of scattered rocks—a monument to a city whose church had long since been obliterated.

Specifically, Jesus highlighted three shortcomings of the church: "You say, 'I am rich; I have acquired wealth and do not need a thing.' But you do not realize that you are wretched, pitiful, poor, blind and naked" (Revelation 3:17). Because Laodicea was located near a number of important trade routes, it was a prosperous city. The citizens became wealthy trading cloth, garments, and carpets. So even the people in the Laodicean church were saying, "I am rich...and do not need a thing." But Jesus saw them differently. From His point of view, they were "wretched" and "pitiful" (verse 17).

Furthermore, Laodicea was close to a temple of Aesculapius, the Greek god of medicine and healing. The residents of Laodicea took pride in their manufacture of treatments for healing various diseases, including a powdery salve known to help sore or weak eyes. Despite the fact they boasted of having good eyesight, Jesus said they were spiritually blind.

So, Jesus said the people in this church were *poor* despite their wealth; they were *blind* despite their healing powder for eye problems; and they were *naked* despite their clothing guilds. We should be especially alert to the fact that Jesus' view of the church was radically different than the view the church had of itself.

Don't miss this: The problem with the Laodiceans was not that they were spiritually poor, blind, and naked. There is a cure for these vices, and it's called *repentance*. The deeper problem was that they were in this wretched condition and thought they were doing very well! It was their inability to assess themselves as Jesus saw them that made them think they had no need for repentance. Though they could see just fine physically, they were blind spiritually.

Little wonder the letter ends with Jesus outside of the church, knocking on the door, seeking entrance. "Here I am! I stand at the door and knock," He said. Imagine Jesus on the outside of His own church! He was squeezed out not because of false doctrine or even explicit immorality; He left because the church members had no room for Him amid the prosperity they enjoyed. Apparently He was never invited back in, or at least not for long. Eventually the church was no more, and today it lies as a memory amid the ruins of a city that itself no longer exists.

This letter of Jesus, perhaps more than any other, pictures the American church: affluent and enjoying the perks that come with the American way of life. In a word, we are very susceptible to the compromise of consumerism, a compromise so easily justified we don't even see it when it is before us. Who needs God to satisfy the deepest longings of the soul when we have so many ways to fulfill ourselves through all kinds of pursuits, activities, and entertainment? Our schedules are packed with distractions that distance us from God, and our abundance makes it easy for fulfillment to be found in material goods.

In short, our world is crammed full of things and activities that in and of themselves aren't inherently sinful, but we allow them to fill the void which only God can fill. In this way we become practical polytheists: We worship God Himself on Sunday, then indulge ourselves with the gods of materialism and self-fulfillment the rest of the week, and then we serve the god of entertainment all weekend (with a few hours carved out for church on Sunday morning). And, like the Laodiceans, we have difficulty seeing that from which we should repent.

Perhaps our greatest failure is that we have equated the American way of life with the Christian way of life. Our inability (or unwillingness) to distinguish between the two has weakened us and made us vulnerable to the cultural currents that are intended to throw us off course and obliterate our witness. The letter to Laodicea comes from the heart of Jesus to us in America today.

The Compromise of a Weakened Gospel

There are at least a couple different ways in which a weakened gospel is affecting the church today.

First, there is a more general kind of gospel compromise in the sense that believers are watering down the gospel message in an attempt to make Christianity look more appealing to unbelievers. They proclaim God as a genie eager to make people happy, speak of Jesus' love without mentioning sin and the need to repent of it, and present a Christianity free from suffering and hardship. Instead of helping the lost to see their desperate need for Christ and relying upon the Holy Spirit's ministry of convicting people's hearts through the gospel message itself, they rely on human ingenuity and persuasion to entice people and make Christ as attractive as possible. That, however, will not work, for the apostle Paul said the gospel of Christ *alone* is "the power of God that brings salvation" (Romans 1:16).

Second (and more relevant to the topic of this book), some people today have become advocates of what is called *Chrislam*—that is, the bringing together of Christianity and Islam. These people say that because the Quran mentions Jesus and shares some elements in common with the Bible, Islam has common ground with Christianity. They teach that Christians and Muslims worship the same God, so in the interest of unity, we must give deference to both religions.

The Insider Movement, different in emphasis but still problematic, teaches it is possible to be a Christian and remain a Muslim at the same time. The proponents of this movement claim "that Muhammad was a prophet from God, the Quran is at least partially-inspired Scripture, and it is possible for Muslims to retain their Muslim identity as 'Muslim followers of Christ.'"[4] Certain religious practices must be "reinterpreted," to be sure, but because the Quran holds Jesus to be a prophet, it is believed that the common ground between the Jesus of the Quran and the Jesus of the New Testament is sufficient enough to lead people to faith in the real Jesus. Thus, Muslims are told they can follow Christ without abandoning their religion. This approach has sparked a far-ranging controversy within Christian ministries involved in outreach efforts in Muslim countries.

This is not the place to present a critique of this new form of syncretism, except to say that it is difficult—in fact, impossible—for a person to receive Christ as Savior and remain a Muslim. Islam explicitly denies the deity of Christ, His crucifixion, and that He alone is the way to salvation. Christianity teaches that salvation is possible only because of Christ's deity and His crucifixion. At the core, the two belief systems are at complete odds with each other. The two faiths cannot be reconciled, for the differences between the two religions are vast and the supposed similarities really aren't.

So a person simply cannot become a Christian without leaving Islam. For those who are interested in the current state of this growing controversy, let me recommend the book *Chrislam: How Missionaries Are Promoting an Islamized Gospel.*[5]

So a second kind of compromise we need to watch for is unfaithfulness to the gospel. Here we are reminded of what Jesus wrote to the church in Ephesus: "If you do not repent, I will come to you and remove your lampstand from its place" (Revelation 2:5). You can visit Ephesus today and see that the candlelight of the gospel has been long snuffed out—for more than 1000 years, in fact.

The point Jesus made to Ephesus still applies to churches today: He will judge those who dilute the essence of the gospel and embrace other agendas. Let us never think, *It won't happen to us.* May we never assume we won't succumb to the temptation to soften the gospel, to diminish in our love for Christ to the point of making the gospel something it is not. We need to remain watchful, lest the flame on our candle begin flickering without us noticing it.

The Compromise of Institutionalized Christianity

Yet another kind of compromise that weakens the church is institutionalized Christianity. The churches in Asia Minor were wedded to the political powers of the day in such a way that when the governing leaders were replaced by Muslim rulers, the church no longer survived. In other words, when the political structures of a region collapsed, the churches in that area collapsed as well.

In an earlier chapter I pointed out that the Church of Holy Wisdom was dedicated by the Emperor Justinian in AD 537, and it still stands today as a tribute to his reign and political power. But we must pause and ask: Why was this emperor building a church? Emperors aren't usually noted for their theological or biblical acumen and values. Unfortunately, Justinian, as did some of the emperors before him, saw himself as the head of the church. And in the Byzantine Empire, Constantinople (present-day Istanbul) was seen as the capital of the world, and the church was viewed as the spiritual arm of political power. Thus the emperors used the church to further their designs for the Byzantine Empire.

Ever since Constantine the Great's victory over Rome in AD 312, the emperors over the Roman world saw themselves as the head of the church. In the words of one writer, this new alignment ushered in "an epoch of fantastic building projects—basilicas whose rich ornamentation drew its inspiration not from the Bible but from the eastern opulence of an Empire which perceived its glory in the genius of man rather than the grace of God."[6] The emperors used the church for their own political purposes and fought wars over points of biblical doctrine, with error often winning the day.

The church as found in the New Testament book of Acts was gone, and in its place was a church that had fossilized into religious forms and rituals. As the buildings grew more splendid, so did the rites and the ceremonies of the church. The appointed clergy led their congregations in formal Greek or Latin liturgies, and many of the people did not understand the languages spoken by those who officiated. Thus many churchgoers eventually came to depend on the clergy for their faith rather than seek a personal relationship with God through the Scriptures. As the priests became more powerful and functioned as intermediaries between people and God, the common person's relationship with God became substituted by his or her relationship with the church, and churchgoers became content with merely being present for the rituals and doing only what was required of them.

So when the Ottoman invaders fought against the political rulers of the Byzantine Empire, they were, in effect, also fighting against the church. No doubt a church that had been schooled to depend upon the clergy, the necessity of buildings, and poorly understood rituals fared badly when the Muslim conquerors came. Of course we can sympathize with the people because many of them were unable to read, and some accepted Islam knowing little or nothing about the religion. For them, it was probably enough that this new religion shared with Christianity a belief in one God. Others of course, chose the route of martyrdom, for they understood the incompatibility of the two faiths.

So it's largely understandable that when Muslim armies came and captured the church buildings and destroyed the power of the clergy, the Christians did not know how to survive the onslaught. With the loss of the buildings came the destruction of the church—with the abdication of the clergy, grace was no longer available for the people. To put it clearly, the fortunes of the church were so closely tied with the fortunes of the state that without the support of the "Christian" state and the rituals it prescribed, the church essentially collapsed. Once the political structure was destroyed, there was no independent church left to survive.

Contrast this with the early Christians in the book of Acts, who were able to withstand persecution because the church was independent of the political structures around it. The same can be said about the church in China during the cultural revolution. Even though the government turned church buildings into warehouses and confiscated Bibles and Christian literature, the people who make up the church have not only survived, but have grown in number. Alan Hirsch comments,

> We know that persecuted Jesus movements that are forced underground usually adopt a more cell-like structure, and are forced to rely largely on relational networks in order to sustain themselves as self-conscious Christian communities. But in order to survive in the context of persecution, they have to jettison all unnecessary impediments, including that of a predominantly institutional conception of *ecclesia*.[7]

Missiologists tell us that today there are an estimated 30 to 50 million believers in China who do not belong to an institutional church. This is not Christianity from the top down, but from the bottom up!

I am not saying that we should do away with church buildings or pastors (after all, I am also the pastor of a congregation that happens to meets in a beautiful structure!). But we want to make sure we don't lose sight of what a church really is—the people, and not the building or an organization. That's why it's so beneficial for churches to meet in smaller communities for study, prayer, and accountability. Centralized churches must ask how they can decentralize their ministries so that no matter what might happen to the building or ecclesiastical structure or leadership, the people themselves can continue to function as a church body.

We can only speculate about what might have happened if the early churches in Asia Minor or North Africa had separated themselves from the political powers around them and sought God and His blessing alone. What if those who were educated had taught believers to read the Scriptures and helped copy the Scriptures for themselves? If each had diligently passed on what he had learned to his children and his grandchildren, perhaps the history of the church in these now-Muslim regions would have been different.

Augustine wisely observed, "Men build cities and men destroy cities, but the City of God they didn't build and cannot destroy." Let's remember that the church is not buildings; it is not institutions or clergy. The church is the people of God wherever they are found worshipping the Lord, serving Him, and proclaiming the gospel of salvation in Christ alone. And as believers pass their faith on to their children, the church will be better equipped to survive hostility and persecution.

A LESSON FOR AMERICA

How dependent is the American church on buildings, pastors, and denominations? If we who are pastors and teachers were jailed, could our churches survive? If we were less concerned about our traditions and structures and followed more closely the model of the early church, the answer might be yes.

In America, our churches have, for the most part, followed an attraction model: Come to our church because we have great music, superb teaching, and wonderful family ministries. But the people in the early church saw themselves as called to live out their faith in the midst of a lost world, representing Christ to the unbelievers around them. They came together and met in homes or outdoors, strengthened one another in their small groups or communities, then went back out into the world. They had what we call a missional model—a commitment to representing the life of Christ wherever they found themselves.

The US government has been at least tolerant of Christianity, and many of our presidents have professed to be Christian, at least in name. But as our government and courts have become more secularized, and as society has displayed increased hostility toward expressions of the Christian faith and its uniqueness, how can we survive? There may come a day when we are forced to become a Jesus movement that exists in small, relational groups rather than in structured denominations and ecclesiastical buildings.

If churches were to lose their tax-exempt status, and speech laws were changed to the point that voicing even legitimate concerns about Islam was treated as a punishable offense, would the church survive? The answer to that question depends on what we understand the church to be. If we emphasize the church as an institution with buildings and assets, the answer, regrettably, might be no. But if we believe that the church is the people of God meeting together in groups to worship and serve, the answer is probably yes. Going back to Augustine's observation, earthly kingdoms may crumble, but the heavenly city—the church—is eternal.

In saying all this, I am not trying to romanticize persecution and make it appear as though it is always the cure for a worldly church. Nor am I saying we should welcome persecution so we will be driven back to a more primitive and unencumbered form of Christianity. I believe the church in America has been spared of major persecution so far because many Christians here have been mightily used by God to spread the gospel to the world. Almost certainly that would end if and when persecution became more intrusive and hampered our ministries. My point is simply that we must prepare ourselves for the possibility that there may come a day when our present religious freedoms diminish significantly or end, and that could happen if the Islamist agenda for America were to shift into high gear.

DOES CHRISTIANITY HAVE A FUTURE IN AMERICA?

During Holy Week in 2011, the BBC hosted a program in the United Kingdom titled "Does Christianity Have a Future?"[8] Participants included atheists who saw no reason to think that Christianity would survive. They said that atheists lived by the same standards of decency, forgiveness, and compassion as churchgoers—thus there was no need for people to adhere to a "Christian faith," and the church was irrelevant. Those on the program who argued in favor of Christianity's survival were left unable to provide an adequate response. Why indeed should the church survive if atheists also possessed a credible form of morality?

What was largely missing in the discussion was the radical nature of the message of the gospel, which says that Jesus came down to earth to rescue us from our sins and give us eternal life. Apart from people's need for a Savior, Christianity has no meaning. The good news of salvation through Christ and becoming a new person is something that atheists do not have, needless to say. But liberal churches, which are void of the gospel and instead simply promote good moral teaching, are by and large irrelevant in a culture that claims even an atheist can be moral.

A blogger, evidently a Catholic, contributed some astute observations to the discussion, and I'm sure he spoke for many Britons—both Catholic and Protestant—when he said this:

> I think the main issue is that in so many cases the gospel is not proclaimed. I was at Mass just now, and there was a young fellow in the row behind me. He had his head in his hands much of the time, like one either in despair, or else very bored. I was also bored. The Mass, as offered and experienced, is so childish,

casual, banal, lame. Of course there are some places where this is not the case, and I thank God for those places.

I think what people, especially young people, are rejecting, is not Christianity per se, but the banal, lame, pseudo-Christianity, the humanistic "gospel," what I would call in my own church "Catholic Lite." This is what they reject because it is not life-giving, it is not the gospel—it is a lame, emasculated, humanistic counterfeit, which does not challenge, does not call sinners to repentance, does not offer life. Until the fullness of the gospel is proclaimed, and a fitting worship of God offered in the Mass, the young people will stay away, whilst the older people eventually die off.

. I think a major issue now in the church in Ireland is the old wine skins, new wine problem—our bishops and priests, for the most part, are seemingly incapable of standing up to the mark—to present the real gospel to the people and to get with the programme. Where the growth is you will find fidelity and orthodoxy, while lameness produces no good fruit, only more lameness.[9]

Lameness produces no good fruit, only more lameness! That is true not only in Ireland, but also in America. Does Christianity have a future here? Of course our situation is not as dire as that in the United Kingdom and Europe. After all, church attendance is much higher, and we have far more healthier churches. But make no mistake: If we compromise the gospel—and many so-called evangelical churches already do so—we will have no reason to stand when the difficulties come. Let the seven churches of Revelation be a warning to us: If we compromise morally or spiritually—if we lose the gospel and the transformed lives that accompany it—the church will be vulnerable when hostility and persecution come, and in time, it will diminish or die out.

A LESSON FOR US FROM ISLAM

Brother Andrew, whom I had the opportunity to meet many years ago, is known mainly for his work of smuggling Bibles into Russia during the dark days of Communism. Today he spreads the gospel in Muslim countries, eschewing political issues and focusing exclusively on the gospel. He has even shared the good news within the leadership of Hamas and similar terrorist organizations.

Brother Andrew tells the story of sloshing through a muddy path in Lebanon with a man whom he believed to be second in command in Hamas and the imam (spiritual leader) of a nearby camp. Andrew asked the imam, "Do you have your prayers every day, five times a day?" The imam replied, "Yes, of course."

"So where do you pray? I do not see a mosque."

The imam stroked his scraggly beard for a moment and then answered, "Every tent is a mosque."

What a lesson! We already know the mosque is important to Islam, but evidently it is not essential. When there is no mosque available, every tent becomes a mosque. Imagine the strength we would have as Christians if we viewed every home as a house of prayer, or every home as a church!

THE SEED THAT WOULD NOT DIE

In some ways the church can be likened to a tree. When a tree is cut down to the stump, new life can grow from it. Isaiah, an Old Testament prophet, used this very illustration in a message he received from God—a message of judgment and rebirth.

First, he was to warn God's people of impending judgment, which came in the form of the Babylonian invasion, in which the people of Judah were taken into captivity. But he was also to proclaim hope for the future. "Though a tenth remains in the land, it will again be laid waste. But as the terebinth and oak leave stumps when they are cut down, so the holy seed will be the stump in the land" (Isaiah 6:13). The holy seed and the stump that grows in the land, is of course Christ, who will come out of Israel as a Redeemer and King.

The stump of a terebinth tree may appear to be dead, but in time it can give off new shoots and give life and hope to a parched land. From its stump new seed can be scattered.

Recently I read an article about the bristlecone pine,[10] which grows primarily in the high-elevation mountain areas of eastern California, Utah, and Nevada. Some of these trees have been alive for many centuries. Incredibly, there is even one that is said to be more than 46 centuries old and predates the Egyptian pyramids—it's called the Methuselah Tree (named after Methuselah in the book of Genesis, who lived for 969 years).

Robert Mohlenbrock, a botanist, studied this ancient pine in the Inyo National Forest. These trees live in very harsh conditions at 10,000-foot elevations. It turns out that the bristlecone pine has special traits that enable it to cope in one of the most austere and unfriendly environments on the planet.

First, these pines *grow slowly*. They are watered by less than 12 inches of precipitation a year, and their growing season is a mere six weeks. They are also rooted in a limestone substrate with few nutrients. Under these conditions, their girth grows very slowly—perhaps only an inch per century.

Second, these trees put down an *extensive root system*. Their root systems are impressive compared to what you see of the tree above the ground. This enables the tree to have greater access to whatever little resources are available in the soil.

The great redwood trees, which also grow in California, teach us about the need for trees to have good root systems. If you could peer into the soil beneath the trees, you would see a giant conglomeration of roots by which the trees are intertwined with one another. This interconnectedness means a tree that stands far from water can survive because it is able to draw moisture from the roots of trees that are closer to water. It is this system of interconnected roots that enable the redwoods to survive in harsh climates. And they survive or suffer together because their roots are intertwined.

Perhaps there is a lesson here for us: We need churches with deep roots—roots in the soil of Scripture, and roots that connect lives together. When this happens, churches are able to grow people who know what they believe and are willing to suffer for the faith. We need sustaining connections with God's Word and each other.

Third, the bristlecone pine has a built-in *resistance to disease*. The tree has a dense wood that shields it from invasion by insects, bacteria, and fungi. Likewise, the church should consider barriers that would protect it from rot and decay—this is, spiritual rot from within and persecution from without. When Jesus spoke to the seven churches of Revelation 2–3, He mostly addressed rot from within—immorality and spiritual compromise. When Paul spoke about the need for the Christians in Corinth to discipline a church member, he said, "A little yeast leavens the whole batch of dough" (1 Corinthians 5:6). In other words, without biblical discipline that confronts sin in the life of a believer, the entire church will become diseased. A church must also develop a resistance to enemies from without, such as false doctrine and worldly values.

Fourth, the bristlecone pine *remains small in size.* "When the green part of the tree dies from a lightning strike, for instance, the tree copes by letting an equally significant part of its tissue and bark die as well. This way, the remaining greenery has a smaller total organism to support."[11] Likewise, we should encourage small groups to develop within the church to ensure ongoing life on the basis of people, and not the institution itself.

And there are times when a bristlecone pine will allow most of itself to die so that a small part of it can live. A parallel of this in the church would be letting go of old ways of doing things that are hindering growth. It is this kind of efficiency that enables the bristlecone pine to live for a long time.

Finally, the only times the bristlecone pine sheds its seeds are when it is struck by lightning or it is surrounded by the intense heat of a forest fire. The capsule that holds the seeds does not break open unless it is exposed to great heat. Likewise, sometimes the church does not multiply until it faces intense persecution. Although Islam has frequently destroyed churches in whole regions, there have also been times when remnants have survived, and their seed has given birth to new growth.

Some botanists once made an incredible find of 28 bristlecone pine seeds. They eagerly planted the seeds, but none survived because the conditions in which they were planted were too favorable. Wouldn't it make sense that churches might not fare well in overly friendly settings either? A church that is too comfortable with the world around it can easily become complacent or even apathetic.

GROWING DEEP AND INTERCONNECTED

Ponder this question: What can your church do—or what can *you* do—to grow deeper and more interconnected roots to prepare for the storm that is sure to come? One small but important step is to cut down on worldly distractions and spend more time reading the Scriptures. We must have our roots deeply planted in the soil of God's Word. And we must connect with other believers in fellowship and accountability. Our repentance must be deep and lasting, and our courage must be consistent and contagious.

When that happens, we will have equipped ourselves to endure.

— The Triumph of the Cross —

A Personal Testimony

Stylianos T. Ayanoglou was born into a Christian family in Adana, Turkey, in 1878. Through a series of providences he came to know Bhari Pasha, the ruthless governor of Adana, who had been trained in the sultan's palace in Istanbul on how to administer cruel forms of punishment. The sultan regarded Pasha as a son, and Pasha, as governor, had the power to kill, extract money, and inflict any form of punishment he deemed necessary.

Pasha heard that Stylianos was distributing Bibles in cooperation with The American Bible Society, and so called him in for a hearing. Stylianos went to see the feared Pasha, praying that God would give him wisdom. When it came time to explain his work, Stylianos did not hedge. He said, "I represent and sell the Bible, the Word of God, which no man can hinder or destroy." Pasha erupted in anger and insisted that Stylianos sign a decree that he would not distribute any more Bibles. But Stylianos refused, even though he was threatened with jail time.

Days later, Stylianos climbed the steps of a mosque not too far from the Pasha's palace. He began to fearlessly recite a poem he had written, and when a crowd gathered and the authorities asked him to leave, he opened his Bible and began to read from 1 Corinthians

13, the great chapter on love. The crowd listened intently, many not aware that the Bible had such a message of universal love and compassion for all people.

Armed with Bibles and Christian booklets, Stylianos then traveled to Seleucia with a companion, and both shared their faith in Christ with others. One morning a man woke them up at an early hour, saying, "I know this is early, but I couldn't wait any longer. I am weighed down with the guilt of my sin. I long to be forgiven and free." Stylianos then told him the gospel and led him to faith in Christ. Others who heard Stylianos and his companion also put their faith in Christ.

One night while sleeping in a hotel room, Stylianos was awakened by a man who was to interrogate him about his activities. When Stylianos told him he was there to give out Bibles, the man became angry. "Don't talk to me about the Bible. How can you praise and love such a book after all the crimes that have been committed in the name of Christianity?"

Stylianos then read slowly the entire love chapter of 1 Corinthians 13, and the man listened intently. Then the man took the Bible and read the entire chapter for himself. "I have never in all my life read such a beautiful passage as this," he said. He continued, "Although I should not allow you to distribute Bibles, I can't stand in the way of a man who holds to such an amazing book."

No wonder Stylianos believed that love was the bridge to any human heart!

—Excerpted from Stylianos's self-published *Far Above Rubies*

The Shadow of the Crescent

"Mahdi [the Twelfth Imam] and Messiah are two
different personalities
but they come at the same time,
Mahdi as Imam and Jesus as his follower."

Muslim website article "The Twelfth Imam"[1]

Chapter Seven

Lesson #6:
Things Are Not What
They Appear to Be

*Be faithful, even to the point of death, and I will give you
life as your victor's crown (Revelation 2:10).*

—Jesus, to the church at Smyrna

There are Muslims who say that the success of their past military conquests proves the superiority of their religion. No less than Muhammad himself pointed to his own military victories as evidence of his superiority among the prophets.[2] Even a tour guide in Istanbul, Turkey, told me personally that in the same way Christianity proved its superiority over paganism by conquering it, Islam has proved its superiority by conquering Christian lands.

When I talked to a Muslim friend about how some Muslims teach that their religion is superior on account of their past military successes, he objected. However, this teaching is found in the Quran. The best example is Muhammad's interpretation of the famous battle of Badr, which took place on March 13, 624.

First, a bit of background: Muhammad was born and raised in Mecca. When he began claiming to others that he had received revelations from God, most people rejected him and his message. Eventually

Muhammad and his small band of followers went to Medina. There, he began to prepare to do battle against those in Mecca.

When word reached Muhammad that a caravan bearing money and goods was en route from Syria to Mecca, Muhammad decided to attack. The Meccans heard about Muhammad's plans, and sent nearly a thousand reinforcements to guard the caravan. This show of force initially terrified Muhammad and his 300 or so men, and they wondered if they should retreat. But Muhammad and his forces marched forward, and although they were outnumbered three to one, they won the battle. This victory, which is still celebrated by Muslims today, has gone down as one of the most important in their history.

In the Quran, Muhammad's victory is ascribed to divine intervention. Allah is said to have sent 3000 angels to help, and 5000 were available, if needed (Sura 3:123-125). And we are told regarding the killing of the Meccans, "You did not kill them, but God killed them" (Sura 8:17). This surprising outcome, in spite of overwhelming odds, was regarded as a warning to those who failed to honor Muhammad as a messenger of Allah.

Muhammad was said to have declared that he was superior to all the prophets who preceded him: "I have been helped by terror (in the hearts of enemies); spoils have been made lawful to me...I have been sent to all mankind and the line of prophets is closed with me."[3] 'Ali Tabari, an Islamic scholar in the ninth century, wrote this in his defense of Islam: "His [Muhammad's] victory over the nations is also by necessity and by undeniable arguments a manifest sign of his prophetic office."[4]

So what evidence can Muslims point to as proof that Muhammad is superior to Jesus, and Islam is superior to Christianity? Take a look through history and consider all the lands that have been conquered for Islam, and remember as well to count the many thousands of churches that have been destroyed or turned into mosques. Then ask yourself this question: In all that time, how many mosques have been turned into *churches*? And how many Muslim countries have gone on to become *Christian* nations?

Beginning with Muhammad's conquests, Islam has continued to spread across the earth, and today it is rising in influence and power all across the West. In fact, in terms of numerical growth, Islam today is outpacing Christianity. That's not only because of mere population growth; it's also because there are large numbers of Christians being killed in Muslim lands today. The problem is so serious that in February 2012, *Newsweek* magazine's cover bore the title, "The War on Christians." The article explains that in recent years, "the violent oppression of Christian minorities has become the norm in Muslim-majority nations stretching from West Africa and the Middle East to South Asia and Oceania."[5] This persecution is ongoing, persistent, and widespread—we're not talking about mere isolated incidents.

For example, in Nigeria, churches are being burned and worshippers massacred as the Islamic presence moves from north to south. In 2011 alone, one Islamist radical group known as Boko Haram "killed at least 510 people and burned down or destroyed more than 350 churches...They use guns, gasoline bombs, and even machetes, shouting 'Allahu akbar' ('God is great') while launching attacks on unsuspecting citizens."[6] This group's goal is to completely eradicate Christianity in Nigeria.

In July 2012, a Muslim convert to Christianity was beheaded in Tunisia, and the grisly murder was shown on Eygptian TV.

> The footage shows a young man being held down by masked men with a knife to his throat. One man chants a number of Muslim prayers in Arabic, mostly condemning Christianity. The man holding the knife to the Christian convert's throat begins to cut, slowly severing the head amid cries of "Allahu Akbar" ("god is great")...
>
> "The footage of this brutal beheading is the latest alarming indication of the violent threat to religious freedom in the post-Arab Spring order," said a Barnabas Fund spokesperson. [The Barnabas Fund is a ministry that aids Christians who are persecuted and suffer for their faith.][7]

Especially tragic in this escalating wave of violence against Christians is the Western media's silence. Why are we not hearing more about this? One possible reason for the reluctance to report such incidents "may be fear of provoking additional violence. Another is most likely the influence of lobbying groups such as the Organization of Islamic Cooperation [OIC]...and the Council on American-Islamic Relations [CAIR]"[8]—both of which have shamed the media from coverage that is in any way perceived as anti-Muslim. And it should come as no surprise to us that the writer of the *Newsweek* article, Ayaan Hirsi Ali, who grew up Muslim and renounced Islam in 2002, has had to live in hiding due to constant threats against her life for her outspoken stance on shariah, free speech, and women's rights.[9]

So how should we as Christians respond to all this? Does Islam's rapid spread prove the superiority and eventual triumph of Islam? Does this indicate that Islam is the one true religion revealed from Allah that has abrogated Judaism and Christianity and has the right to dominate all others?

The answer is a resounding no. As the Bible confirms, God sometimes allows His enemies to win, and to win big. But it won't always be that way. Islam's successes are not proof of its ultimate superiority. *Things are not what they appear to be.*

An Astute Observation

When asked about the atrocities that Muslims carry out against Christians in countries like Nigeria, some Muslim representatives will give the excuse that what we're seeing in such regions of the world is actually a political battle, and not a religious one. When I talked about this recently with a prominent Christian minister who speaks frequently in Muslim countries, he recounted for me a conversation he had with a pastor in Malaysia. The pastor's church had been vandalized and looted by local Muslims. As the pastor shared about what happened, the Christian minister observed, "Islam is really a political ideology that uses religion to protect and support it. Without the protection of religion it might not even survive." The Malaysian pastor agreed wholeheartedly.

WHEN GOD GIVES VICTORY TO HIS ENEMIES

We've already learned that there have been times when God has allowed churches to be destroyed—not because they were unfaithful to the gospel, but precisely because they were faithful to their calling. There is no reason for us to assume that God permitted some churches in Nigeria, the Sudan, or Indonesia to be obliterated because they were unfaithful to the gospel. Faithfulness does not grant a church immunity from persecution any more than it grants us immunity from martyrdom.

In fact, Scripture confirms that God has used evil nations to judge His own people. When God told the prophet Habakkuk that He was raising up the wicked Babylonians to come against Judah to destroy her, the prophet struggled with this revelation. Habakkuk, in effect, told God that this was contrary to His attributes of holiness and justice. Furthermore, Judah, despite her many evils, was still more righteous than the Babylonians. So the prophet asked, "Why are you silent while the wicked swallow up those more righteous than themselves?" (Habakkuk 1:13).

To be sure, the Babylonians were more evil than the people of Judah, but God still used Babylon to bring judgment against Judah. And of course, the Babylonian conquest happened just as God predicted. The Babylonians came against Judah, destroyed the temple that Solomon had built, and took many of the Jewish people to Babylon. Among the captives were Daniel and his friends, who had to learn how to survive in the midst of an idolatrous, pagan nation.

Roughly 100 years earlier, God used the wicked Assyrians to punish the northern tribes of Israel. Though both Babylon and Assyria were pagan nations, God permitted them to decimate His people. That doesn't mean, however, that the Assyrians and Babylonians had gained favor in His eyes. Eventually, God brought judgment against them. With God, righteousness ultimately prevails.

In the same way, whatever victories Islam has known to this day have been permitted by the hand of God. But it's all temporary. In the end, the Lord Jesus Christ will stand victorious. He will set up His kingdom on earth, and all will kneel to His authority.

So when we see how Islam is spreading through the West today, we might complain as Habakkuk did and say, "Lord, how can this be? In Muslim countries, those who convert from Islam to Christianity are imprisoned or killed. And Islam denies Jesus' deity and His crucifixion. Then there are the terrorists who strap bombs to themselves and blow up marketplaces, wedding receptions, and hotels. How can you allow Islam to prevail?"

And yet we need to remember that, as happened with Israel, God could be trying to get the attention of Western Europe and America. We have thousands of churches; we have Bibles available for everyone to read; we have an abundance of Christian television and radio; we have Christian books that address every imaginable need; we have conferences and seminars and retreats galore. And above all, we have the freedom to preach the gospel, to witness to our friends, and to live for Christ.

And yet the church isn't all it could be. Many Christians today don't take sin seriously. They aren't concerned about living holy lives. They are walking in the flesh rather than in the Spirit. They're consumed with worldly pursuits, and God and His Word are not the priorities they should be. People come to church to feel good about themselves rather than to seek and worship the Lord. They cling to their temporal comforts and their lives, valuing them more than the glory of God and the rewards of eternity. And when it comes to showing Christ's light to others, they're ashamed. They long for acceptance by the world around them. So they soften the hard edges of the Christian faith and talk about Christ's love but say nothing about sin because they don't want to offend anyone.

As a result, the church has become weak. And this has made it all the easier for Islam to encroach upon Western society. Rather than show love to our Muslim friends and at the same time warn the world of Islam's deceptions, we succumb to appeasement so we don't offend.

So in the same way that God used the Babylonians to turn the people of Judah from their wicked ways, God could very well be using the spread of Islam to stir Western Christians from their slumber.

SPECTACULAR REVERSALS

We can take heart knowing that in the end, God will judge all things fairly. Some of those who win in this life will end up becoming losers in the next, and some who appear to be losers in this life will win in the next. In fact, Jesus promised that if we lose our life for His sake, we will find it (Matthew 10:39).

In the New Testament, Paul contrasted this world with the next: "Therefore we do not lose heart. Though outwardly we are wasting away, yet inwardly we are being renewed day by day. For our light and momentary troubles are achieving for us an eternal glory that far outweighs them all. So we fix our eyes not on what is seen, but on what is unseen, since what is seen is temporary, but what is unseen is eternal" (2 Corinthians 4:16-18).

What is seen is temporary, and what is not seen is eternal! The things of this present world will not last. Jesus will prevail, and of His kingdom "there will be no end" (Isaiah 9:7).

THE REVERSAL OF WEALTH AND COMFORT

Jesus taught that we cannot judge who is blessed and who is cursed simply by looking at their worldly successes or failures. On a number of occasions, I've asked young people this question: Would you rather be a rich person with fashionable clothes and an expensive home, or a poor beggar who searches through garbage to eke out his daily existence? Obviously we would all rather be self-sufficient from a financial standpoint. No one is waiting to trade places with a poor, sickly person.

Yet Jesus told a story that illustrated how, in eternity, the fortunes that people experienced on earth might very well be reversed. In Luke 16, we read about a rich man who lived in abundance and comfort, and a poor man covered with sores that were licked by scavenger dogs. When the beggar died, the angels carried him to a place of comfort at Abraham's side. And when the rich man died, he went to Hades, where he suffered torment (Luke 16:19-31). What you see of people here on earth is deceptive; only in eternity will we see where people really stand. Only then will we know who the real winners and losers are.

Christianity makes no claim that faith in God will produce victory over one's enemies in this world. As an example, we need look no further than to Christ, who submitted Himself to those who sought to kill Him. He knew that when they succeeded, they would celebrate their victory. But that was not the end of the story. When Jesus' enemies came to get Him, He calmly told them, "This is your hour—when darkness reigns" (Luke 22:53). In effect, Jesus said, "Today you win."

Three days after Jesus' crucifixion, of course, the story was quite different. He rose from the dead, and later ascended to heaven. From there, He will someday return with His angels:

> This will happen when the Lord Jesus is revealed from heaven in blazing fire with his powerful angels. He will punish those who do not know God and do not obey the gospel of our Lord Jesus. They will be punished with everlasting destruction and shut out from the presence of the Lord and from the glory of his might on the day he comes to be glorified in his holy people and to be marveled at among all those who have believed (2 Thessalonians 1:7-10).

Justice will be done, even though we think it is centuries overdue. Eternity will bring to light all that was craftily hidden on earth. Victory in this world is no proof of victory in the next.

A LESSON FROM ANTICHRIST

If political and military victories are an indicator of the truthfulness of a religion, then the religion of the future Antichrist will be the most "truthful" of all time. I say this not because I believe that the Antichrist will be a Muslim, but to call attention to the fact that even the greatest political and religious power in all human history will be headed up by one who is entirely opposed to truth. Read this stunning account of what will happen under the Antichrist:

> [He] was given power to wage war against God's holy people and to conquer them. And [he] was given authority over every tribe, people, language and nation. All inhabitants of the earth

will worship the beast—all whose names have not been written in the Lamb's book of life, the Lamb who was slain from the creation of the world (Revelation 13:7-8).

What will all the people of the earth do? They will worship the beast (the Antichrist). Why? First, many will conclude that his incredible power proves that he has the "right religion" and is therefore worthy of worship. Second, people will worship him no doubt because of fear—fear of what might happen to them if they dare challenge him. Either way, in betting terms, people will put their money on the beast, so to speak, because they are convinced he is on the winning side. They will bow down because, from their perspective, power is proof of religious superiority.

Scripture tells us the Antichrist will make war against the followers of Jesus and conquer them. He will put them to death for refusing to take his mark. Christians will clearly be in the minority, and will not be able to fight back. The overwhelming superiority of the beast's political and religious power will be worldwide and uncontestable. This will be evil's most glorious day; this will be Satan's headiest triumph.

But just two short chapters later, we see a spectacular reversal. At this point, God's wrath has been poured out upon the earth, and John writes the following:

I saw what looked like a sea of glass glowing with fire and, standing beside the sea, those who had been victorious over the beast and its image and over the number of its name. They held harps given them by God and sang the song of God's servant Moses and of the Lamb (Revelation 15:2-3).

What follows is an exuberant song of praise to God for His power and deliverance.

Here we see the saints in heaven "victorious over the beast and its image and over the number of its name." The saints are now in the presence of God, in a place of indescribable beauty and joy. Their experiences on earth in no way foreshadowed their final destiny. Things were not what they appeared to be!

And, in sharp contrast, we see how the career of the Antichrist will end: "The beast was captured, and with it the false prophet who had performed the signs on its behalf…The two of them were thrown alive into the fiery lake of burning sulfur" (Revelation 19:20). And later Satan will join them in the lake of fire, where "they will be tormented day and night for ever and ever" (Revelation 20:10).

What a difference two chapters make!

In Revelation 13, the Antichrist is ruling over the whole earth and conquering the saints. But in chapter 15, the saints are celebrating their victory over the Antichrist. Evil can engulf the whole earth, and yet the eternal purposes and plan of God are not affected. Or, to put it more accurately, the purposes and plan of God actually include the evil that engulfs the earth. No matter how bad things get, God will prevail. Nothing can thwart Him from carrying out what He wills to do.

The fact that the Antichrist will one day rule the world and be worshipped by everyone will not be an indication that he is right or that his religion is superior. And that's true for all religions—truth and error do not change on account of the numbers who line up on one side or the other. Truth is truth, and error is error, no matter what the majority vote would indicate. The ability of one religion or nation to dominate another does not prove its superiority.

FAITH BRIDGES THE GAP BETWEEN TIME AND ETERNITY

Why does God allow Christians to endure so much suffering? In the case of Antichrist and the Tribulation, God will allow evil to triumph to test the faithfulness and endurance of His people (Revelation 13:10). He wants to see who will remain steadfast despite the pressure, despite the lure of political and religious power and prestige. Will His people trust His promises even though there is no visible evidence that they will win in the end?

During the lifetime of Martin Luther, the Turks were aggressive in their expansion of the Ottoman Empire. Under Suleiman the Magnificent (1494–1566), Turkish armies swept their way across Eastern and Central Europe, taking Belgrade in 1521, the island of Rhodes in 1522, then most of Hungary in 1526. In 1529 Suleiman besieged Vienna and appeared to be on the verge of victory. If the city had fallen, "all of Germany would have been at the mercy of the Turkish armies."[10] But the Austrians turned Suleiman back, giving him his first defeat.

What did Luther have to say about the Muslims' successes as a guarantee of their eventual triumph? This is what he wrote:

> The Turk maintains with such assurance that he is the people of God that he does not hesitate to give his life and head as a pledge...God adorns him with the finest and highest gifts, and deals with the opposite manner with Christians. As for the Christians [God] subjects them to the cross and hands them over to their adversaries to be killed like sheep to the slaughter (Rom. 8:28). On this account the Turk taunts us in the most insolent manner...When the Turks saw corpses lying here and there with their noses cut off, they laughed at the misery of those who had been slain and with virulent sarcasm they repeated these words, "Jesus Mary!" It is as if they were saying, "Where is their God now?"[11]

By way of historical note, the victorious Turks were not only feared, but some Christians in Luther's era converted to Islam because they wanted to back a winner. For the sake of their families, their friends, and their own lives, they sided with the Ottoman Empire. Clearly, it seemed as if God had abandoned the Christians and taken up the cause of the Turks.

So we return to Luther's question: Where is the God of the Christians now?

Luther helps us here. He went on to say that the Turks believed that the Christians had been rejected and cast aside by God. But even when it appears all is lost, we must take God at His word. We must trust His assurances that someday, wrongs will be made right, and justice will prevail.

So what are we to do when the enemy prevails? Luther gives us this answer:

> We have nothing from God except the pure Word, namely that the Lord Jesus sits at the right hand of God the Father and is the Judge of the living and the dead, and that through Him we are kings and priests (Rev. 1:6). And even though God hides Himself now, in the end, all enemies will be put under his feet (I Cor. 15:25).[12]

In other words, we must continue to believe God's promises, knowing that things are not what they appear to be. Military victories today are no proof of ultimate triumph tomorrow. *We do not have to win in this life in order to win in the next.*

We who are Christians may appear to be losing in this life, but rest assured we will not lose in the life to come. Eternity, not time, determines superiority, justice, and truth. In heaven we will sing, "Salvation and glory and power belong to our God, for true and just are his judgments" (Revelation 19:1-2).

Events on earth are viewed very differently from the vantage point of heaven.

WRAPPING UP HISTORY

We as Christians can take comfort in the fact the Bible does not teach that we can judge the superiority of one religion over any other by virtue of its military victories or the number of followers it has. Make no mistake: In the end, He who is just and true will win a decisive victory over all His enemies. At the return of Christ, all those who opposed Him will be shown to have worshipped a false god or followed a false prophet. Though "might does not make right," as the saying goes, *He who is right will come with might.* The basis of Christ's power is righteousness, holiness, and goodness.

In the end, the power of Christ—along with His mercy, faithfulness, and justice—will be displayed. He will come with power to justly judge those who rejected Him, and show unbending mercy to those who are His followers. He is at once truth and love, power and justice.

Muslim theology says Jesus will return to earth at the second coming and convert all people, including Christians, to Islam. He will establish a reign of peace and establish Islamic law in all the nations of the earth. Jews and Christians will come to believe in the Jesus of the Quran; Jews will see Jesus as a prophet and Christians will realize He is not the Son of God. Jesus will destroy the cross, and this will make Christians realize that Jesus was not crucified. He will live on the earth for 40 years, and once His mission is accomplished, He will die a natural death and will be buried in Medina next to Muhammad. His death will serve as the signal for what Muslims believe will be the general resurrection.[13]

According to Shia theology (a branch of Islam), the Twelfth Imam, who lived during the ninth century, will return as messiah. Until now he has been in hiding, but when Allah reveals him and he returns, he will bring Jesus with him. Jesus will serve this Imam and force all people to choose between this Imam and death. One Islamic website makes this statement about the relationship between the Twelfth Imam (Mahdi) and Jesus: "As we see Imam Mahdi is from the Ahlul Bayt of Prophet Muhammad, so he can not be Jesus (the Messiah; al-Maseeh). Mahdi and Messiah are two different personalities but they come at the same time, Mahdi as Imam and Jesus as his follower."[14]

This stands in sharp contrast to the New Testament account of Jesus' final triumph, in which He will be exalted by God the Father and will reign supreme over all the earth. He will not be anyone's follower. The apostle Paul wrote this regarding Jesus' future return:

> He will pay back trouble to those who trouble you and give relief to you who are troubled, and to us as well. This will happen when the Lord Jesus is revealed from heaven in blazing fire with his powerful angels. He will punish those who do not know God and do not obey the gospel of our Lord Jesus. They will be punished with everlasting destruction and shut out from the presence of the Lord and from the glory of his might on the day he comes to be glorified in his holy people and to be marveled at among all those who have believed (2 Thessalonians 1:6-10).

In that day, all rivals will acknowledge that Jesus is ruler over all. When He returns, not only will every eye see Him (Matthew 24:30), but every knee will bow. The One who was crucified will be declared the King of kings and Lord of lords. The cross will be replaced by a crown:

Being found in appearance as a man,
he humbled himself
by becoming obedient to death—
even death on a cross!
Therefore God exalted him to the highest place
and gave him the name that is above every name,
that at the name of Jesus every knee should bow,
in heaven and on earth and under the earth,
and every tongue acknowledge that Jesus Christ is Lord,
to the glory of God the Father (Philippians 2:8-11).

So in the end, Gandhi will confess that Jesus is Lord, to the glory of God the Father. Buddha and Krishna will confess Jesus is Lord, to the glory of God the Father. And there among them will be Muhammad, also confessing that Jesus Christ is Lord, to the glory of God the Father. Our Savior will return as Judge and King, and before Him all will be required to bow.

It is not necessary to win in this world in order to win in the next. Things are not what they appear to be.

— The Triumph of the Cross —

A Personal Testimony

I was born and grew up in an upper-middle-class Egyptian Muslim family in Kuwait. From the time I was 5 until I was 17 years old, I had a recurring nightmare in which I dreamed I was swimming in the ocean and all of a sudden I would start drowning in a whirlpool. I would gasp for air and try to swim out of it as I was suffocating. Then I would wake up from the nightmare with a wet bed.

I always felt there was some kind of separation between me and God. I tried praying five times a day and following the Muslim rituals as a child and teenager, but because of my sins, I believed God would punish me. I sought God's mercy and wanted to be close to Him, but I still felt a void in me.

My one brother died in a terrible car accident when I was 17. During that year, I had been teaching Arabic to some Americans in

Kuwait. We became friends, and at first I didn't know they were missionaries. One day, as I was trying to influence one person for Islam, he gave me a Bible to read. I asked him to read the Quran, and he said he would read it as I read the Bible. When I asked him why he wasn't Muslim, he said he would become a Muslim if the Quran gave him the peace that he had experienced when he read the Bible.

One day during that same year, I knelt in prayer and asked God whether he was the God of Islam, Christianity, or Judaism, and asked Him to please show Himself to me. One night after that, Jesus came to me in a dream and said, "I am the way, the truth, and the life, and I will show you the way." I hadn't read the Bible yet, so I didn't know that was a verse in the Bible. My body tingled all over, and I sensed the dream really was from God. Around this same time, my nightmares stopped.

I started going to an evangelical church in Kuwait with a Pakistani friend who was also searching for answers in his life. We had both had a lot of difficulties in our childhoods and we came to Christ at the same time. The church was international and had an American pastor who was very nice to me. I committed myself to Christ there in Kuwait and was baptized. My family was angry, and I clung to Romans 8:28 when my family turned against me and my father threatened to disinherit me. Later I went to a university in Egypt and met some missionaries and other Christians there, who have helped me grow in my faith. I thank God for the Christians in Egypt and Kuwait who have encouraged me.

—Name withheld

The Shadow of the Crescent

"I have no doubt in my mind, Muslims sooner or later
will be the moral leadership of America.
It depends on me and you, either we do it now
or we do it after a hundred years,
but this country will become a Muslim country."

Abdurahman Alamoudi [1]

Chapter Eight

Lesson #7:
The Remnant Will Triumph

Whoever has ears, let them hear what the
Spirit says to the churches!

—JESUS, TO EACH OF THE SEVEN CHURCHES OF REVELATION

In every one of the seven letters to the churches of Revelation, Jesus called out to those within the congregation who were really *listening*. He knew that every church has some believers who get it and others who don't. Spiritual deafness is everywhere, but among the deaf He can always find at least a few who can hear and are willing to obey the message. Jesus ended each letter with this: "Whoever has ears, let them hear." He knew that only those who had an ear to hear would actually *hear*. He also knew that a listening church could be a powerful witness to the world.

God's means of victory is usually to work through a remnant. When tribulation comes, He chooses to uphold His name using a few people rather than the whole crowd. When Jesus said, "Whoever has ears, let them hear," He might well have been separating the true believers from those who were Christians in name only and showed no evidence that they understood the gospel and its implications.

So what do we do when life gets difficult for the church? Hunker down and wait out the storm and hope we will have at least bits and pieces of Christianity left after the hurricane makes landfall? No, we prepare for the storm, and we move forward with confidence knowing that we can count on Christ to bring His church safely through it all.

As we see the growing influence of Islam all around us—in every level of government, education, business, finance, the legal system, and more—and we see Islamists exploiting the freedoms of speech and religion to further their agenda, there is temptation for the church to give in, to remain silent, to appease in the hopes of preserving peace. But that approach permits Islam to prevail, and it betrays a lack of trust in God's power and protection. I do not doubt that God has allowed Islam to spread to the extent that it has for a reason. Far from weakening the church, Islam could be used by God to strengthen it.

If the church rises to the challenge, this could be a time when we see countless Muslims all around us come to faith in Christ. There is unrest in the Muslim community; many Muslims are weary of the emptiness of Islam, the cruelty directed toward women, and the inability of Islam to bring peace to the human heart. And Muslims who live in the West have some freedom to investigate and pursue Christianity without the fear of persecution or even death, which is what they would face in their home countries.

According to those who work in outreach ministries to Muslims, "today worldwide there are more Muslims becoming Christians than at any time in history."[2] Thabiti Anyabwile—a former Muslim who is now a Christian pastor—has this to say:

Increasingly, God seems pleased to bring the Muslim world right to our doorsteps. The work of cross-cultural evangelism and missions has never been more accessible. With some confidence and reliance on God and His gospel, we may yet be the generation that sees history's greatest revival among Muslim peoples.[3]

J.D. Greear, a pastor and missionary to Muslims, makes this observation:

For the first time in history, Muslims in just about every part of the world have been exposed to life outside of their communities. Many Muslim college students, through international study, television, or the Internet, have started to question their faith and the assumptions they have grown up with.[4]

There are even Muslims who have said they were drawn to Jesus through dreams. We should not be skeptical of that. Some have said that after they had such a dream, they met a Christian who shared the gospel with them, or they began reading a Bible, which led them to the good news of the gospel. The dream might not lead them directly to Christ, but it prepared the way and opened their heart to the gospel message.

Consider this: When God led the wise men using the star in the East, note that the star did not take them to Bethlehem, but to Jerusalem, where they met Jewish scribes who knew about Micah's prophecy that Jesus was to be born in Bethlehem (Micah 5:2). God did not bypass His Word; a star or a dream can only take someone so far. Eventually a person needs to hear or read God's Word and learn the way to salvation. But we can be encouraged by the fact that Muslims are coming to Christ and converting to Christianity—not only in America and in Europe, but in Muslim countries as well. One pastor who sponsors ministries in Iraq told me there are thousands of Muslims coming to Christ in that country.

That said, the road going forward will not be easy. The church in the West can expect hardship, setbacks, and discouragement. We can expect opposition.

WHAT WE CAN EXPECT IN THE DAYS AHEAD

Remember that the real threat to the United States is not so much terrorism, but Islamism, which intends to challenge our constitutional liberties and take advantage of political correctness to silence discussion and debate about Islam and to undermine our national security, as national security expert Andrew McCarthy observes:

[*Both* terrorists and Islamists] want the same thing, the Islamicization of society...Non-terrorist Islamists want to overthrow the

United States government every bit as much as the terrorists do. They are not moderates. Their differences with the terrorists are over means and methods, not goals.[5]

One of the key means Islamists will use to make progress toward this goal is to silence any form of opposition, even legitimate ones. This is being accomplished in many different ways.

For example, one key weapon used against Christians is false accusations. False evidence—such as portraying Muslims as victims of imagined discrimination or misunderstandings—is presented so that the media and society at large can resort either to ridicule or a dismissive attitude that puts those who love the gospel in the worst possible light. There are even some who say that the church is the enemy—that Christians are the jihadists.[6] They state that Americans have nothing to fear from Muslims; rather, it is the narrow-minded, bigoted Christians who are stirring trouble. Americans need not fear shariah law, they say. Rather, they should fear Christians who wish to impose their agenda on the United States.

One way Christians are portrayed negatively is through projection. For example, some people will point to a lone "professedly Christian" killer of an abortion doctor and claim that the killer's behavior represents how dangerous all Christians are. They conclude that Christians pose the same threat to America as terrorist bombers who target innocent civilians. Never mind that Christians have vehemently denounced violence as a means of ending abortion; never mind that it was one lone person who killed the abortion doctor. But in the twisted logic followed by much of secular society, Christians are said to be just as much a threat to our nation as Muslim extremists.

A frequent type of false evidence we hear about is accusations against Christians who are said to have done something horribly disrespectful and offensive to Islam. For example, when Muslims in a country like Pakistan want to incite violence against Christians, they will often accuse a missionary or pastor of dishonoring Muhammad by desecrating a Quran. That happened in 2011 in Gujrunwala, Pakistan—"two Christian men...[were] accused of desecrating the Qur'an by writing on it and burning pages." However, "it soon became clear the accusations were fabricated after the police employed a handwriting expert to test whether the men wrote the offending words."[7] Still, Muslim mobs attacked a Christian church and school as well as some homes, wounding 50 and causing many Christians to flee.

It's fairly common to hear of trumped-up charges and allegations made against Christians for dishonoring the Quran; and the accused are often killed, jailed, or brutally persecuted. Many such reports can be found on the website ReligiousWatch.com, which reports on numerous cases of religious persecution worldwide.

During the Danish cartoons crisis in 2006, in which 12 cartoons printed in a Danish paper were condemned by Muslim leaders and governments, it is alleged that some additional cartoons were created showing Muhammad in an even worse light—presumably in order to whip Muslim crowds into a frenzy and incite violence against Europeans. Interestingly, the original set of cartoons was published in September 2005, and the "supposedly...spontaneous outrage in the 'Muslim Street' did not occur until *several months later.*"[8] Disappointed at the initial lack of indignation, three Danish imams got together in an attempt to generate outrage over the cartoons. As they did so, they not only spread copies of the original 12 cartoons, but added "three significantly more offensive, entirely unrelated drawings, whose origin is murky."[9]

These same imams also "made wildly exaggerated claims about repression against Muslims in Denmark; for example, asserting that they are not legally permitted to build mosques."[10] This explosive combination of the original cartoons and false or exaggerated evidence, of course, provoked the tempest the imams wanted, and violent riots broke out worldwide, causing more than 200 deaths. The result? Newspapers and publishers have become extremely wary about carrying content that might be perceived as insulting Islam in some way, even if that content is accurate. For fear of stirring a hornet's nest, the media has imposed censorship upon itself.

This is a prime example of how voices are being silenced.

Next, there is what's called "legal jihad" or "Islamic lawfare," in which Muslim individuals and advocacy groups take advantage of the

US legal system to sue for alleged infractions that can be cast as some form of discrimination against Muslims or Islam. In 2010, a Muslim woman who had already worked for two years at a Disney hotel knowingly violated Disney's 50-year dress code one day by wearing a hijab on the job. Disney offered to transfer her to a position that would permit her to dress however she wished, but she refused. Other US businesses have been sued by Muslim women who have insisted on their right to wear hijabs or head scarves. In 2007, Target stores in Minneapolis were forced to accommodate Muslim cashiers who refused to handle pork products in the checkout line. And there are other large businesses—including Wal-Mart—that have been pressured or sued into providing a variety of special exemptions or privileges for Muslim employees during their work hours. Of course, the companies are expected to honor these demands regardless of the inconveniences imposed upon non-Muslim coworkers and customers.[11]

We can expect such abuses of the law to increase in the years to come, and we can expect that anyone who voices legitimate concerns about granting special exemptions to Muslims will be called names: Islamophobic, prejudiced, racist, demagogues, fearmongers, purveyors of hate, and worse.

A key reason Islamists resort to such name-calling is that it allows them to completely dismiss legitimate issues and viewpoints without having to deal with the truthfulness or falsity of the ideas themselves. This tactic is perfectly consistent with what Muslims call *taqiyya,* which "refers to the practice of deception in order to keep Muslims safe."[12] It permits Muslims to suspend their religious convictions and lie—or even deny their faith—when they fear threat or injury.

This concept of *taqiyya* is taught in the Quran: "Let not the Believers take for friends or helpers Unbelievers rather than Believers: if any do that, in nothing will there be help from Allah, except by way of precaution, that ye may guard yourselves from them" (3:28). One Muslim commentator said this about *taqiyya*: "It is lawful for a believer... to keep his faith concealed and to behave in such a manner as to create the impression that he is on the same side as his enemies...he may even state that he is not a believer."[13]

How should we as Christians respond if we become the targets of false accusations? Jesus answers that question for us: "Blessed are you when people insult you, persecute you and falsely say all kinds of evil against you because of me. Rejoice and be glad, because great is your reward in heaven, for in the same way they persecuted the prophets who were before you" (Matthew 5:11-12). And again, "If the world hates you, keep in mind that it hated me first" (John 15:18). If we love Jesus more than our reputations and life itself, we will have nothing to fear.

THE KEYS TO REMAINING FAITHFUL

What kind of a church do we need to be in order to withstand the growing pressure that will be exerted upon us to tone down the gospel and remain silent about the Muslim agenda? What might faithfulness require?

Being a Repentant Church

Many years ago at a retreat I asked the elders at The Moody Church to read the seven letters to the churches of Revelation and see if they could determine which church was most characteristic of our own so that we would know the sins of which we needed to repent. We came up with a variety of answers, and our study made us all the more aware that Jesus is evaluating The Moody Church, just as He did the seven churches of Revelation. And we as Christians should always be asking God to point out the sins from which we need to repent. Martin Luther was right when he said, in the first of his 95 Theses, that "the entire life of believers [is] to be one of repentance."

Jehoshaphat, who ruled the southern kingdom of Judah in the ninth century BC, led his people in fasting, repentance, and prayer when enemy nations approached to do battle. He ended his magnificent intercession with these words: "Our God, will you not judge them? For we have no power to face this vast army that is attacking us. We do not know what to do, but our eyes are upon you" (2 Chronicles 20:12). *We don't know what to do, but our eyes are upon You!* In response, the Lord gave Jehoshaphat the victory because his men went into battle singing praises to God.

Repentance is the natural fruit of embracing an ever-growing appreciation and worship of Jesus Christ, of waking up to all that we have been given in Him. In Christ alone we find the answer for how to remain true in a time of deception and darkness. And in Him alone we can summon the courage to walk into the darkness unafraid. "I have told you these things, so that in me you might have peace. In this world you will have trouble. But take heart! I have overcome the world" (John 16:33). At all times, our greatest need is a fresh vision of Jesus.

Being a Witnessing Church

Many Muslims respect Christians who take their faith seriously enough to share it. Given the casual attitude that so many professing Christians show toward their faith, it is natural for Muslims to be attracted to those who clearly believe in what they say they do. Remember that Muslims do not choose their religion, and they are told they have no freedom to leave Islam. As one Muslim woman put it, "We are abused, but what choice do we have?"

Only love can overcome suspicion and hatred. If you ask former Muslims who converted to Christianity what won their hearts, they often repeat the words of Jesus: "Love your enemies." This is so antithetical to Islam that when Muslims encounter Christians who love them, they have no defense.

So that you can learn how to best approach Muslims, take advantage of the many resources available for witnessing to them. One I've found useful is *The Gospel for Islam: Reaching Muslims in North America*, which will help you to understand the Muslim communities of the West and know how to share the gospel with Muslim individuals.[14] I've listed some additional resources in the bibliography on page 233.

In our witness we must avoid arguments about the character of Muhammad, or the origin and teachings of the Quran. Those issues are important at some point, but they are not the matters upon which a friendship will be formed. One way to build bridges with our Muslim friends is to invite them to read a short passage from the Quran, and then we in turn can share a short passage from the Bible. Friendship builds bridges—arguments do not.

Being a Committed Church

When Pastor Terry Jones of Dove World Outreach Center in Florida foolishly burned a copy of the Quran in March 2011, his deed generated an uproar in the Muslim world. A huge mob rioted at the UN compound in Mazar-e Sharif, Afghanistan, setting fire to the building and killing seven foreigners.[15] Further protests in Kandahar, Afghanistan, led to nine more people dead and at least 90 injured,[16] and there were additional demonstrations in other cities such as Kabul. In an interview on MSNBC, Bobby Ghosh, world editor for *Time*, when asked about Terry Jones's actions, explained that "the Koran to Muslims...it is not the same as the Bible to Christians." Ghosh went on to say, "It is acknowledged by Christians that [the Bible] is written by men...But the Koran...is directly the word of God...So the act of burning a Koran is much more...inflammatory than...if you were to burn...a Bible."[17]

Obviously, Ghosh touched a nerve when he made his inaccurate statement. While it is true that Christians believe that men wrote the Bible, they also believe these men wrote under the inspiration of the Holy Spirit. As 2 Peter 1:21 says, "Prophets, though human, spoke from God as they were carried along by the Holy Spirit." And 2 Timothy 3:16 very directly states that "all Scripture is God-breathed [given of inspiration by God]." Thus for Christians, the Bible is the word of God Himself. It is not one holy book among many, but the one and only Holy Book.

In his attempt to explain why Muslims were so enraged over the burning of a Quran, Ghosh stated that Muslims have a higher view of the Quran than Christians do of the Bible. Not only was he inaccurate about what Christians believe, but he also revealed ignorance about why Christians respond differently than Muslims when it comes to the desecration of their holy book. The reason Christians do not riot when a Bible is burned is *not* because they don't believe that the Bible is God's inspired Word, but because they believe vengeance belongs to

God. As the Bible says, "Do not repay anyone evil for evil...If it is possible, as far as it depends on you, live at peace with everyone. Do not take revenge, my dear friends, but leave room for God's wrath, for it is written: 'It is mine to avenge; I will repay,' says the Lord" (Romans 12:17-19). What's more, here in America, we believe in freedom of religion and speech. People are free to choose which religion they follow, and how they express their views.

However, we Christians must confess to our shame that Muslims often show more devotion to their Quran than we give to the Bible. Most Muslim cab drivers that I've caught a ride with here in Chicago have a copy of the Quran with them and read it during their spare time—perhaps more diligently than some Christians read their Bibles.

However much we Christians disagree about the origin of the Quran, we have to admire those Muslims who are committed to carrying out its demands. Even Martin Luther admitted we have much to learn from Muslims because of their devotion to Muhammad and the Quran. He opined that Christians should be brought to shame when they see the extent to which Muslims sacrifice to live up to their religion, no matter how deceived they otherwise might be.[18]

The question for us as Christians is this: Are we as committed to the Bible as Muslims are to the Quran? A thriving church should have a genuine and fervent love for God's Word.

Being a Sacrificial Church

How will we respond when Muslim converts to Christianity come to our churches seeking help amid threats of violence and intimidation from the Muslim community? That depends, of course, on how we regard the body of Christ. If the church is a true family, we will be willing to sacrifice for the sake of one of our members. Under what conditions do we have the right to separate ourselves from a healthy member for the sake of the whole? Should we back down from associating with a member of the body of Christ because to do so could result in serious consequences, such as attacks carried out against the church or even physical harm? Matters like this test the mettle of a church. As the saying goes, "If we do not hang together, we will hang separately."

Which leads us to the difficult topic of martyrdom.

A WILLING MARTYRDOM

What would you do if this notice were delivered to your doorstep?

> To: The Family Of Infidels; *IN THE NAME OF ALLAH, AND OF HIS FINAL PROPHET, MUHAMMAD (PEACE BE UPON HIM)*:
> The true religion of Islam WILL ARISE in your area; you cannot stop Allah's will. We have been watching your family; we have seen you go to church and seen you pray to your false god. We know that you are infidels and we will deal with you as our holy Quran declares; In Sura 9 verse 5, it says *TO SLAY* the idolaters wherever you find them; take them captive and besiege them.
> It also says in Sura 9 verse 29 *to FIGHT* those who have been given the scripture and believe not in Allah or the Last Day or follow not the religion of truth. If you and your entire family do not leave your false religion and follow Islam, you will be killed. Your sons will be slaughtered and your daughters will become Muslim wives, bearing sons who will fight for Allah in this region. Your ONLY other option is to *FLEE TONIGHT.* Leave your home and everything behind.[19]

According to Voice of the Martyrs, an organization that reports on the persecution of Christians worldwide, notices like this have been appearing on the doorsteps of Christian homes and churches in Muslim countries. Space forbids me to describe at length the kinds of persecution Christians are enduring in Muslim-majority countries such as the Sudan, Saudi Arabia, Iran, Pakistan, Egypt, Somalia, and even the "moderate" country of Turkey. In these places, Christians are systematically jailed and killed. Voice of the Martyrs reports, "The scale of persecution of Christians by Muslims...has caused the death of thousands, including pastors, and the destruction of hundreds, even thousands, of churches."[20]

Thankfully, there are some brave souls who are up to the challenge. Listen to the words of Wagdi Iskander, who grew up in the Sudan and converted from Islam to Christianity. He now lives in Canada and tells Canadian church congregations, "We need a martyr to wake up the church…I am willing to be that martyr." As a young student, he was respected among the Muslim Brotherhood, an organization committed to global Islamization. Wagdi was commissioned to kill a fellow student, a Christian who was sharing the gospel with his friends in the Sudan. Wagdi beat the wrong man, and his victim was paralyzed for life. Then through a series of circumstances, Wagdi came to saving faith in Christ in 1982, and for this he was arrested and sentenced to be executed with two other Christians. Miraculously, he escaped—God spared his life, and he now lives in Canada, warning churches about the dangers of the Islamist agenda.

The book *Fearless Love in the Midst of Terror: Rediscovering Jesus' Spirit of Martyrdom* tells the stories of courageous Christians who have died for their faith.[21] Their witness, along with the testimonies of those who live in constant jeopardy, reminds us that Jesus gives grace to those who follow Him in martyrdom. Here is proof that many believers are willing to pour out their lives for others even as Jesus poured out His life for us.

Ready for Whatever Might Come

One day after a pastors' conference, I visited with Sam Solomon, a Muslim convert to Christianity, and I asked him about what the church should be doing in this hour of crisis. Sam, whose expertise is Islamic law, had just given a group of us a lecture on what America would look like under shariah law. Now in private discussion, I asked, "What should the church be doing in light of the continuing growth of Islamic influence in Europe and America?" We discussed various ways Christians could respond. Then I said, "I guess we will also have to prepare the next generation for martyrdom…we will have to teach them how to die for the faith." Sam then pointed his finger at me and said, "That is exactly what God has called you to do. *Train your people to become martyrs!*"

Now, as I bring this up, know that I am not trying to overexaggerate the threat Islam poses to the American church. We will probably never face the kind of persecution now taking place against Christians in Muslim-majority countries. Rather, our fate is far more likely to be that of the churches in Europe, where Islam is being allowed to triumph by default. Through our silence and ignorance, Islam will continue to make inroads into education, the government, the legal system, and so on, making it possible for Muslims to receive special treatment not given to people of other faiths. Western society will continue to offer appeasements supposedly in the name of cultural sensitivity, and in doing so will only end up lending credibility and respectability not just to Muslims in general, but also to the more radical Muslim elements who are eager to see shariah law practiced in America, among other things.

Or perhaps the church will rise to the challenge and show love to the Muslim community and share the gospel with Muslims. If that were to happen, there is no reason to believe that Islam will somehow weaken the church. Indeed if we remember it is the Lord Jesus Christ whom we serve, these could be days in which the church is strengthened even if persecution were to come our way.

Differing Perspectives on Martyrdom

Both Christianity and Islam value martyrdom, or the willingness to give one's life for the faith. However, they have entirely different perspectives on what awaits those who die as martyrs.

There are Islamic authorities who teach that selfish suicide—the act of killing oneself to escape personal pain for suffering—is considered a one-way ticket to hell. However, if a Muslim commits suicide in an act of self-sacrifice, this is a test of loyalty to Allah, and as such is considered a direct ticket to heaven. In fact, to die while killing infidels—whether one is killed by them or one kills himself in order to kill them—is said to be the highest form of sacrifice. To spill one's blood in an act of self-sacrifice merits the forgiveness of sins, the approval of Allah, and a life of luxury and ease. Those who die a martyr's death are accorded great honor.

Those who wish to portray Islam as a religion of peace claim that the Islamic suicide bombers who are almost daily in the news are betraying the Muslim faith. They argue that Islam forbids suicide and that those who commit this act are headed for hell. But this is a smokescreen that attempts to hide the aforementioned fact that Islam recognizes two possible motives for suicide: one selfish, and the other selfless—and therein lies the need for clarification. As Robert Spencer explains, "The prohibitions against suicide do not apply to suicide bombers, because their intention is not to kill themselves but the enemies of Allah." Spencer goes on to quote Islamic scholar Sheikh Yusuf al-Qaradawi, who said of those who die for Allah, "It's not suicide, it is martyrdom in the name of God."[22]

The way in which hijacker Mohamed Atta prepared himself and his colleagues the night before 9/11 gives us insight into his understanding of the Quran and life beyond. That evening he wrote a letter titled "The Last Night," handwritten in Arabic. He prepared himself for his arrival in heaven, and urged his fellow hijackers to do the same. "The time between you and your marriage [in heaven] is very short" he wrote. "Shave excess hair from the body and wear cologne. Shower. Do not leave your apartment unless you have performed ablution...Know that the gardens of Paradise are waiting for you in all of their beauty, and the women of Paradise are waiting, calling out, 'Come hither, friend of God...they have dressed in their most beautiful clothing.'"[23]

Incredibly, Atta's suitcase did not make it onto the airplane he would later commandeer into one of the World Trade Center towers. Later, those who opened his suitcase discovered his Paradise wedding suit. An American Airlines employee said it was laid out "as if Atta were in it, with a sapphire-blue necktie neatly knotted and looped under a crisp dress-shirt collar." We are told that "at the foot of the bag...was a fancy, leather-bound Quran in gold leaf."[24]

And what was Atta expecting? A wonderful entrance into Paradise and marriage to 72 virgins available for his pleasure for all eternity. The Quran describes these virgins as follows:

- "voluptuous women of equal age" (78:31)
- "fair women with beautiful, big, and lustrous eyes" (44:54)

- "maidens, chaste, restraining their glances, whom no man...has touched" (55:56)

Atta and his companions believed they had assurance of heaven because they would be "slain in the way of Allah." According to the Quran, "Those who are slain in the way of Allah—He will never let their deeds be lost. Soon will He guide them and improve their conditions, and admit them into the Garden which He has announced for them" (Sura 47:4).

No doubt Atta and his companions felt they had met the criteria for entering heaven by their act of selfless martyrdom. Regardless of their previous sins, those were atoned for by dying "in the way of Allah." The reward of death for the cause of Allah is greater than the reward for good works or faith.

This explains why, when fathers and mothers give up their sons to be suicide bombers, they are told not to sorrow over their untimely deaths. After all, Allah's martyrs never really die, says the Quran (Sura 3:170). In an English translation of the Quran with extensive explanatory footnotes by Maulana Muhammad Ali, we read these words of comfort in a footnote: "The dear ones have no cause to grieve at the death of the martyrs. Rather, they have cause to rejoice."[25]

Christianity also places a high regard on martyrdom, but as we know, it's not an admission ticket to heaven. Martyrdom does not save anyone; only faith in Christ forgives our sins and readies us for the life beyond. Martyrdom is only a sign of obedience; by contrast, self-inflicted martyrdom is a form of murder. Absolutely never should a Christian attempt to advance his faith by killing himself with the intention of killing others because they are viewed as infidels.

STAYING STRONG IN THE FACE OF DEATH

The pages of church history are filled with the stories of those who did not count their lives dear to themselves but were willing to die for Christ. This is clear evidence that God does not always deliver His church from persecution and death. Stephen, the first Christian martyr, died soon after the church came into being (Acts 7), and countless numbers of believers have died in the ages since, especially during severe periods of persecution. God will continue to allow evil to run its course until the return of Christ, and Scripture even tells us that God has appointed the number of those who will die for their faith. In Revelation 6:9-10, the apostle John describes this scene in heaven:

> I saw under the altar the souls of those who had been slain because of the word of God and the testimony which they had maintained. They called out in a loud voice, saying, "How long, Sovereign Lord, holy and true, until you judge the inhabitants of the earth and avenge our blood?"

The surprising reply? "Then each of them was given a white robe, and they were told to wait a little longer, until the full number of their fellow servants, their brothers and sisters, were killed just as they had been" (verse 11).

God has a purpose for every believer on earth, and for some of us, that purpose will include martyrdom. Indeed, more Christians have been martyred in the last 100 years than in the previous 1900 years of church history.[26] The exact numbers are hard to estimate because many cases of persecution, which take place in countries with highly restrictive governments, go unreported. One estimate is that "the current rate is 159,000 martyrs per year."[27] Another is "somewhere around 150,000" each year.[28]

Where do those who die for their faith in Christ find the strength to be patient and faithful? What enables them to endure as overcomers even as they lie in a pool of their own blood? The answer is given to us in Revelation 12:11: "They triumphed over him by the blood of the Lamb and by the word of their testimony, and they did not love their lives so much as to shrink from death."

They did not love their lives so much as to shrink from death! As Christians, we must face the reality that sometimes God does not protect us from our enemies. Martyrs for Christ are forever heroes in heaven, having valued Christ more than family and life itself. They can say with the apostle Paul, "For me to live is Christ and to die is gain" (Philippians 1:21).

One day while reading Psalm 44, I was struck by the fact there are times when, despite the pleas of God's people, He does not deliver them, but lets them languish in the hands of their foes. Read this plaintive cry: "You have rejected and humbled us; you no longer go out with our armies. You made us retreat before the enemy, and our adversaries have plundered us" (verses 9-10).

You made us retreat before the enemy, and our adversaries have plundered us! No wonder the psalmist struggled. God's chosen people had become a reproach to their neighbors and were disgraced before the face of their enemies. Later in Psalm 44 we read, "For your sake we face death all day long; we are considered as sheep to be slaughtered" (verse 22). That, by the way, is the context for Paul's use of this verse in Romans 8, where he asked whether there is anything that will separate us from the love of Christ: "Shall trouble or hardship or persecution or famine or nakedness or danger or sword?" (verse 35). Then in Romans 8:36 Paul quotes Psalm 44:22, reminding us that we are like sheep ready for the slaughter, and that the Good Shepherd will stand with us to give us strength—but He will not necessarily deliver us from the sword. "A servant is not greater than his master. If they persecuted me, they will persecute you also" (John 15:20).

Perhaps Sam Solomon was right: My responsibility as a pastor is to help my people to be courageous so they can face ostracism in our present society and perhaps even martyrdom in future generations. There are many godly Christians both in the distant and recent past whom God did not deliever from cruelty, torture, humiliation, or death. The question is whether we as affluent Westerners are willing to reorient our lives and values so that we are willing to suffer for "the Name." It always comes down to a simple question: How much does Jesus mean to us?

IN ANTICIPATION OF VICTORY

Here is the list of promises Jesus gave to those who had ears to "hear what the Spirit says to the churches":

Revelation 2:7—"Whoever has ears, let them hear what the Spirit says to the churches. To the one who is victorious, *I will give the right to eat from the tree of life,* which is in the paradise of God."

Revelation 2:11—"Whoever has ears, let them hear what the Spirit says to the churches. The one who is victorious *will not be hurt at all by the second death.*"

Revelation 2:17—"Whoever has ears, let them hear what the Spirit says to the churches. To the one who is victorious, *I will give some of the hidden manna. I will also give that person a white stone with a new name written on it,* known only to the one who receives it."

Revelation 2:26-28—"To the one who is victorious and does my will to the end, *I will give authority over the nations*—that one 'will rule them with an iron scepter and will dash them to pieces like pottery'— just as I have received authority from my Father. *I will also give that one the morning star.*"

Revelation 3:5—"The one who is victorious will, like them, be dressed in white. *I will never blot out the name of that person from the book of life,* but will acknowledge that name before my Father and his angels."

Revelation 3:12—"The one who is victorious *I will make a pillar in the temple of my God.* Never again will they leave it. *I will write on them the name of my God and the name of the city of my God, the new Jerusalem,* which is coming down out of heaven from my God; *and I will also write on them my new name.*"

Revelation 3:21—"To the one who is victorious, *I will give the right to sit with me on my throne,* just as I was victorious and sat down with my Father on his throne."

You've just read the final destination for all who remain true to the gospel no matter what the pressure, no matter what the price. Paul, who died for the gospel, wrote, "I consider that our present sufferings are not worth comparing with the glory that will be revealed in us" (Romans 8:18). Reread the promises of Jesus, and I'm sure you will agree.

LIVING IN LIGHT OF FUTURE VICTORY

Islam's growing influence can either weaken us or strengthen our resolve; we can be either petrified or purified. We should be grateful that we are alive at this hour of history to serve as living evidence that our Savior reigns. "He is before all things, and in him all things hold together. And he is the head of the body, the church; he is the beginning and the firstborn from among the dead, so that in everything he might have the supremacy" (Colossians 1:17-18). *That in everything He might have the supremacy.*

"And God placed all things under his feet and appointed him to be head over everything to the church, which is his body, the fullness of him who fills everything in every way" (Ephesians 1:22-23). He is our head, inviting us to take our cross and follow Him to both death and resurrection, from apparent defeat to glorious victory.

He shall reign, and all His enemies will be placed under His feet.

— The Triumph of the Cross —

A Personal Testimony

I was born in a little town in Western Turkey. Nobody in my family was a practicing Muslim. I never went to a mosque, even though our house was surrounded by three of them.

In the 1970s, I joined the youth organization of the Turkish Communist Party. Thanks to it, I received good grades at school because the city was controlled by Communists, and the teachers were afraid of what would happen to them if they gave bad marks to a Communist student. In college I got involved in Islamic studies, and in my second semester I became a fundamentalist Muslim and then a fanatical supporter of the Ayatollah Khomeini. Later I left this line of Islam and joined a militant Sunni group.

I then went to Baghdad to continue my study of Muslim theology there. Eventually I ended up becoming a nominal Muslim, though I gave others the impression I was still devout. After I returned to Turkey I was appointed as an imam of a small mosque. I preached hate-filled sermons against Christians, Jews, and Europeans, yet there was no conviction at all behind my words. Secretly I was drinking alcohol, watching the worst sort of Western films, and eating pork.

During a hot phase of the first Gulf War, I frequently visited with some Iraqi friends who studied in Turkey. Our main hobby was listening to the war news together. One day the reception was extremely bad, and we couldn't receive the broadcasts we normally listened to. Suddenly we heard an Arab preacher telling a story in Arabic about an adulterous woman arrested by some Jews. "This sounds interesting," my friends said. "Forget the news—let's listen to this program!" We knew this story was from the "corrupted book of Christians," or the Bible. The Jewish religious leaders had demanded that Jesus pronounce a verdict against this sinful woman, and we knew that Jesus, as a prophet of Allah, had to impose the death penalty on her.

But the Arab preacher's next words shocked me: "Let any one of you who is without sin be the first to throw a stone at her" (John 8:7). This one simple statement made me suddenly realize the ugly hypocrisy in my own life. I was a sinner, and I deserved the same punishment as this poor woman. The Lord had pulled the mask off my face.

In the days that followed, I looked for a Bible in the bookstores of my city. I couldn't find one. Eventually I decided to write to the radio station on which I'd heard the broadcast, and ask if they could send me a Bible. It took me several days to find the station. I then wrote, and they sent me many Christian booklets, including one with the Gospel of John. I read it several times, then knelt and prayed to the Lord. I thanked Him for waiting patiently for my repentance, and asked that Jesus become my Savior.

All that happened because of the words I heard on one radio broadcast. God used His Word to convict me, and I knew what was wrong in my life and that I needed Jesus.

—Ishak

Part III:
A Right Response

The Shadow of the Crescent

"[Our] work in America is a kind of grand jihad
in eliminating and destroying
the Western civilization from within."

Mohamed Akram, The Muslim Brotherhood, 1991[1]

Chapter Nine

What Is Happening in America Today?

We will use the freedoms of the Constitution
to destroy the Constitution!

—Sign carried by a Muslim demonstrator

Those were the words on a sign I saw carried by a Muslim demonstrator on a TV newscast from Detroit, Michigan. Yes, there are Muslims among us who will insist on their freedoms to agitate and scheme to replace our US Constitution with shariah law. Unlike other religions, Islam embodies a detailed system of laws that "regulate all manner of behavior in the secular sphere—economic, social, military, legal and political."[2] It governs "all aspects of civil society and human life, both public and private."[3]

Because shariah is based on the Quran and other sacred writings, and because the Quran is "the letter-perfect revelation of Allah's guidance to humanity,"[4] observant Muslims view shariah as superseding all other forms of law. They consider shariah absolutely supreme, "the final and universal moral code for all humanity until the end of time."[5] Thus they desire to establish shariah worldwide, including in the United States. In fact, Islamists seek to impose shariah in the West because, in their view, "it is impossible...for alternative legal systems and forms of governments to peacefully coexist with the end-state they seek."[6] To them, every Muslim is under obligation to obey the laws of Allah, or shariah—even in non-Muslim countries.

Of course, not all Muslims are on board with this agenda. I have a friend in Turkey who calls himself a secular Muslim. He told me that he is just as opposed to the forced imposition of shariah law as I am, and I have good reason to believe him. Millions of nominal Muslims believe that shariah law should not be the rule of the land in their countries or in the West. However, those who argue against the implementation of shariah and advocate the reform of Islam are often targeted with harassment and death threats by shariah adherents because they are said to be contradicting the clear teachings of the Quran.

Again, the Islamists and hardliners who wish to bring shariah law to the West are not representative of the majority of Muslims. But what many Americans do not realize is that even if the extremists are vastly outnumbered, it is they who wield the political and religious authority in Islam, as Paul Marshall and Nina Shea explain in their book *Silenced*:

> In the contemporary struggle of ideas within Islam, those who are empowered by such restrictions are the extremists, who use law and intimidation to determine which ideas are accessible and acceptable in their society. In contrast, Muslim religious and political reformers, who protest the extremists' agenda and work to lift their societies out of stunting, ideological conformity, are the first to be silenced.[7]

And why are they silenced? Because their attempts at reform are viewed as opposing the Quran and Allah. "Criticizing and questioning religious authority is simply forbidden."[8]

So it is the Islamists and extremists who are in control of the agenda, either by direct force or strategic infiltration. And they are succeeding. Lessons from the history and tactics of Muslim expansion should not be lost on us. Our day may be coming, for shariah has already made significant and irreversible inroads into Europe and the

United Kingdom. Bernard Lewis, a preeminent scholar and historian of Islam, "stunned Western readers when he predicted that Europe will be Islamic by the end of the twenty-first century."[9] Other observers believe this transformation will occur much sooner. US national security expert Andrew McCarthy has this to say:

> The United Kingdom may be in even greater crisis. There, the Islamic ascendancy dovetails with the Labour government's transnational progressivism in a campaign against cultural Britishness...Sharia has become a key element of that campaign.[10]

Indeed, there are now at least 85 shariah councils and 5 Muslim Arbitration Tribunals in the United Kingdom.[11] The shariah councils are said to have tried some 7000 cases decided up through 2010. And because the Muslim Arbitration Tribunals operate as tribunals under the United Kingdom's Arbitration Act of 1996, their rulings are binding under UK law—even when their rulings are *contrary* to UK law.[12] What's more, these tribunals do not provide the legal safeguards many Western court systems have. Maryam Namazie, an Iranian exile who lives in Britain, explains it this way:

> Councils call themselves courts and the presiding imams are judges. There is neither control over the appointment of these judges nor an independent monitoring mechanism. People often do not have access to legal advice and representation. Proceedings are not recorded, nor are there any searchable legal judgments. Nor is there any real right to appeal.[13]

The success Islamists have enjoyed in the United Kingdom has emboldened them—to the point extremist clerics were caught on video in 2008 saying, "It may be by pure conversion that Britain will become an Islamic state. We may never need to conquer it from the outside."[14]

And their success in Britain has not gone unnoticed in other countries. For example, a 2011 article in *The Australian* notes that "the push to recognise sharia law in Australia has entered an ambitious new phase that draws on the tactics that have handed success to

Islamists in Britain."[15] Proponents have also attempted to establish shariah law councils in Europe and Canada.

In the United States, a prominent Muslim businessman has battled to get shariah law recognized in the state of Oklahoma. When citizens of the state voted overwhelmingly to pass a law that would prohibit judges from recognizing shariah, the Council on American-Islamic Relations (CAIR) criticized this action as being discriminatory and filed a lawsuit claiming that such a prohibition is unconstitutional.[16] (While CAIR calls itself a civil rights group on behalf of Muslims, it is anything but. Many CAIR figures, including Ghassan Elashi, Randall Royer, Bassem Khafagi, and Rabih Haddad "have been convicted of federal felonies, including terrorism offenses."[17] This organization has terrorist ties and holds to a thoroughly Islamist agenda.)

At the time of this writing, the situation in Oklahoma is still in dispute, but the mere fact it is even happening stands as a testimony to the determination of some Muslim individuals and organizations to make shariah a ruling force in Western society. So it is with legitimate concern that, as of February 2012, three other states have already passed similar prohibitions, and 21 additional states were considering doing it as well.[18]

IS AMERICA VULNERABLE?

In this book we have considered seven lessons we can learn from the churches in Asia Minor—churches that didn't survive the onslaught of Islam. Having done that, it is time for us to ask ourselves this question: Is America vulnerable to the Muslim advance? Are we immune from the pressures that Islam will bring to bear on us as a nation and as churches? The answer should make us both uncomfortable and alert, for ominous signs are on the horizon.

The Objective of Islamists

Those who wish to spread their vision of a global Islamic State are rarely forthright in declaring their intentions. Rather, they are careful to disguise their aims such that their work goes unnoticed. But through a stroke of providence, the agenda and methods of perhaps the most influential Islamist group in the world—the Muslim Brotherhood—has been exposed for all to see. For the sake of context, keep in mind that the Muslim Brotherhood is "the most important entity promoting Islamic supremacism, shariah, and the caliphate through—at least for the moment—nonviolent means."[19] Back in 2004, through a series of events, a trove of documents intended for Brotherhood eyes only was obtained by the FBI in a raid upon a house in Annandale, Virginia. In the archives was a document written by Mohamed Akram, who headed up the Muslim Brotherhood in America at the time. This document is titled "An Explanatory Memorandum on the General Strategic Goal for the Group in North America." This is what Akram wrote:

> [The Brotherhood] must understand that their work in America is a kind of *grand jihad in eliminating and destroying the Western civilization from within* and "sabotaging" its miserable house by their hands and the hands of believers so that it is eliminated and God's religion is made victorious over all other religions.[26]

It doesn't get any clearer than that. Again, in its own words, the Muslim Brotherhood sees its work as "a kind of grand jihad...eliminating and destroying the Western civilization from within."

What is the Muslim Brotherhood? The organization was founded in Egypt in 1928 by Hassan al-Banna, an educator who believed in global Islamic domination. The Muslim Brotherhood's express purpose is twofold: to implement shariah worldwide, and to reestablish the global Islamic State (caliphate). Thus, ultimately, the Brotherhood has the same objectives as the terrorist groups al-Qaeda and Hamas.

The motto of the Muslim Brotherhood is explicit as well: "Allah is our objective, the Prophet is our leader, the Quran is our law, jihad is our way, and dying in the way of Allah is our highest hope."

That the Brotherhood has a vision for a different America is clear. In 1996, Abdurahman Alamoudi, a top agent of the Muslim Brotherhood in the United States, declared, "I have no doubt in my mind,

Muslims sooner or later will be the moral leadership of America. It depends on me and you, either we do it now or we do it after a hundred years, but this country will become a Muslim country."[21]

FAITH, NOT FEAR

Though it is sobering to consider the mind-set of such Islamists in our midst, my intent in quoting them is not to frighten us, but to instruct us.

We should not automatically assume every Muslim shares these views, because thankfully, the majority do not—and that majority is massive. The difficulty is that those Muslims "who do practice sharia have the grounds for arguing that their version of Islam is the authoritative one."[22] They are committed to a literal reading of the Quran and believe they are fulfilling the vision of their founder, Muhammad. Because they are the spokespersons for Islam by virtue of their control of the political and religious bodies within Islam, they have the most ready access to the media and know how to mobilize their constituencies as needed.

But again, the vast majority of Muslims are not conspirators in all this. As one expert observes, "There are enormous numbers of Muslims in the United States and around the world who want nothing to do with today's global jihad."[23]

I approach this chapter in the spirit of the apostle Paul, who wrote wise and encouraging advice to the Christians in Rome, who found themselves in conflict with a pagan empire:

> Do this [properly relate to the culture] understanding the present time. The hour has come for you to wake up from your slumber, because our salvation is nearer now than when we first believed...So let us put aside the deeds of darkness and put on the armor of light (Romans 13:11-12).

This applies to us today as well. We too should "understand the present time...wake up from [our] slumber...and put on the armor of light."

We should be grateful for the privilege of being alive during this hour of American history. Yes, we have reason to be concerned about the challenges that are arising. But we can either wilt under the pressure or rise in strength and optimism, confident that God is in full control of what's happening today. Nothing happens without His permission. With such assurance we can move forward, refusing to be intimidated and being grateful for the opportunity to have our faith and courage tested. And we can exhibit Christlike love and compassion to our Muslim neighbors, seeing them not as our enemy, but as people in need of a Savior.

THE BROTHERHOOD'S STRATEGY

So how are we to "understand the present time"? What do we need to be aware of?

Though the Muslim Brotherhood is only one aspect of the Islamist movement in America today, it is by far the most influential. So we can consider it fairly representative of all that is happening in our midst. As we noted a moment ago, the archives discovered in the FBI raid in 2004 reveal the Brotherhood's commitment to what some people call civilizational jihad. In those archives was a master plan identified as The Project. Patrick Poole, an anti-terrorism consultant and a leading analyst with regard to the Muslim Brotherhood, reported on this master plan, which was written in 1982. It lays out a 12-point strategy designed to "establish an Islamic government on earth."

Poole describes The Project this way:

> [The Project] represents a flexible, multi-phased, long-term approach to the "cultural invasion" of the West. Calling for the utilization of various tactics, ranging from immigration, infiltration, surveillance, propaganda, protest, deception, political legitimacy and terrorism, The Project has served for more than two decades as the Muslim Brotherhood "master plan."[24]

In America, the Muslim Brotherhood has dozens of front organizations through which they operate. We've already referred to one of the best known, which is CAIR. Other prominent groups are the

Islamic Society of North America (ISNA) and the Muslim Student Association (MSA). These and other such organizations enable the Brotherhood to work through a variety of channels to accomplish their purpose.

The hope of the Brotherhood is that the West will be so focused on halting terrorism that it will turn a blind eye to all the other ways Islam is altering America, as Andrew McCarthy observes:

> Because [our nation's] policymakers won't come to grips with what Islamists are trying to accomplish, they can't even see that there are far more Islamists than terrorists. Focused myopically on only one of the jihadist's means, violence, they mistakenly assume that ending the violence would perforce end Islamism's threat to our way of life.[25]

In 2010, a team of national security, intelligence, and terrorism experts published a book titled *Shariah: The Threat to America*.[26] The book details the successes of the Brotherhood in America, and warns that "stealth jihad" has successfully penetrated the highest levels of the American government, national security, and even the military.

In this 300-page report, they quote Omar Ahmad, cofounder of CAIR, who said, "Islam isn't in America to be equal to any other faith, but to become dominant. The Koran should be the highest authority in America, and Islam the only accepted religion on earth."[27] No wonder the Brotherhood's publication in London, in 2001, featured this slogan on the cover page: "Our Mission: World Domination."[28] What should arrest our attention is how far they have come in achieving their grand plan.

A key reason the Brotherhood has been so successful is they've been able to capitalize on our ignorance and naiveté. They have also used the democratic process to their advantage. They are quick to take advantage of their constitutional liberties in order to insist upon preferential treatment for practicing their religion—at the expense of other people's rights and freedoms. When their demands to exercise certain religious practices are not granted, they allege discrimination and file lawsuits to get their way. And they wield enormous influence over what the education system and media can and cannot say about Islam.

As stated earlier, the Brotherhood sees their work as "a kind of grand jihad...eliminating and destroying the Western civilization from within."[29] And their bylaws mention the means for achieving this:

> D) Make every effort for the establishment of educational, social, economic, and scientific institutions and the establishment of mosques, schools, clinics, shelters, clubs, as well as the formation of committees to regulate zakat affairs and alms;
>
> E) The Islamic nation must be fully prepared to fight the tyrants and the enemies of Allah as a prelude to establishing the Islamic state.[30]

THE IMPOSITION OF SHARIAH LAW

In their investigation of the Muslim Brotherhood archives, seized in 2004, the FBI was able to determine that "the groups' sole objectives are to implement Islamic law in America in furtherance of re-establishing the global caliphate."[31] Such goals, of course, would require the replacement of the US Constitution with shariah.

To get a sense of what life might look like under shariah, consider that it permits the killing of Muslims who leave Islam (Sura 16:106), views women as inferior to men (Sura 2:282; 4:11; 2:223; 4:3; 2:221), gives husbands permission to beat their wives (Sura 4:34), allows parents to kill a child or grandchild for dishonoring Islam or Allah (popularly known as honor killings—see *'Umdat al-Salik*, o1.1-2), permits the marriage of girls as young as eight or nine (Sura 65:4), and asserts Islam is superior to every other culture, faith, government, and society and is ordained by Allah to conquer and dominate them (Sura 3:85; 3:110; 98:6; 48:29).[32]

That sample list of dictates should clue us to the fact that "Islam and western-style democracy can never co-exist in harmony."[33] That's why, from the Islamists' perspective, the ideal would be for shariah to supersede all Western laws. As Muslim Brotherhood spiritual leader Yusuf al-Qaradawi said, "The shariah cannot be amended to conform to changing human values and standards. Rather, it is the absolute norm to which all human values and conduct must conform."[34]

Unfortunately, the assumption of many in the Western world has been that, given time, Islamists would be open to Westernization and social progress. For example, the recent uprisings in Iran, Libya, Egypt, and Syria led many voices in Western media and government to proclaim that an Arab Spring was underway and that these nations were headed toward democracy-style reforms and freedoms. But quite the opposite has occurred. In both Libya and Egypt, the Muslim Brotherhood has more political power than ever before, and the governments are becoming more Islamist, more restrictive. As Mark Steyn observes, the young people who voted in Egypt's 2012 presidential election "are more fiercely Islamic than their grandparents who backed Nasser's revolution in 1952."[35] Why is this the case? Because groups like the Muslim Brotherhood are urging the general Muslim populace to return toward a purer Islamic ideology.

For example, one of the top Brotherhood leaders in Egypt, Khairat al-Shater, said this in a speech in 2011: "The mission is clear: restoring Islam in its all-encompassing conception, subjugating people to God, instituting the religion of God, the Islamization of life...Every aspect of life is to be Islamized."[36]

That represents the mind-set that is significantly prevalent today— a mind-set that explains why the trend among Islamists worldwide is *away* from Westernization, not toward it.

THE METHODS OF THE BROTHERHOOD

There are a number of different resources that provide details about the methodology that groups like the Muslim Brotherhood are using to achieve civilization jihad.[37]

As stated in *Shariah: The Threat to America*, the Brotherhood archives obtained in 2004 reveal their key tactics include the following:

- expand the Muslim presence by birth rate, immigration, and refusal to assimilate
- occupy and expand domination of physical spaces

- ensure the "Muslim Community" knows and follows Muslim Brotherhood doctrine
- control the language [non-Muslims are permitted to] use in describing the enemy
- ensure [non-Muslims] do not study their doctrine (shariah)
- co-opt key leadership
- force compliance with shariah at local levels
- fight all counterterrorism efforts
- subvert religious organizations
- employ "lawfare"—the offensive use of lawsuits and threats of lawsuits
- claim victimization/demanding accommodations
- condemn "slander" against Islam
- subvert the US education system and in particular infiltrate and dominate US Middle East and religious studies programs
- demand the right to practice shariah in segregated Muslim enclaves
- demand recognition of shariah in non-Muslim spheres
- confront and denounce Western society, laws, and traditions
- demand that shariah replace Western law[38]

How successful has the Muslim Brotherhood been? Let's look at just a few examples of what they've achieved.

The Infiltration of the Intelligence Community

Robert Spencer, a recognized expert on Islam, documents in his book *Stealth Jihad* how, on account of political correctness, the FBI turns away competent Arabic-speaking Jews and Christians who apply for jobs as Arabic translators, and favors Muslims to fill such positions. What's more, those who do the hiring are unwilling to probe the political and religious sentiments of the recruits to determine whether they might pose a risk in government or national security positions.[39]

Because no one wants to appear anti-Muslim or discriminatory, Islamists are currently working in security-sensitive positions in the US government. Journalist Paul Sperry, in his book *Infiltration: How Muslim Spies and Subversives Have Penetrated Washington*, traces the extent to which Islamists have infiltrated the FBI, the Pentagon, and other security agencies. Sperry cites John M. Cole, a former FBI program manager for foreign intelligence investigations, who says there have been "serious security lapses involving the screening and hiring of translators."[40]

"We have serious problems with the hiring of language specialists," said Cole. "Background investigations are not being conducted properly, and we're giving people TS/SCI (top secret/sensitive compartmented information) clearance who shouldn't have it." He added that some of the translators have red flags in their files, "and we have espionage cases because of it."[41]

Sperry also reveals a dilemma that makes it difficult for FBI agents to do counterterrorism work. Since 9/11, at the behest of Arab-rights groups, agents have been required to take part in a Muslim-sensitivity training program. Muslim clerics and scholars provide the instruction, which focuses on how not to offend Muslims.

Former and active agents say the Muslim leaders "all have an agenda of making sure FBI agents don't discriminate against Muslims and Arabs."[42] Agents say this puts them in a bind.

On one hand, they are under pressure to aggressively flush out terrorist cells inside the Muslim community. But on the other hand, they are told to bend over backwards to avoid offending individuals in that clearly hard target group. They say headquarters' obsession with minority politics is handcuffing field agents trying to work the Muslim community for leads—particularly when they try to question worshippers at American mosques, a shocking number of which have been discovered to be sanctuaries for terrorist activities.[43]

To get some idea of the extent of the paralysis at the FBI, retired special agent Donald Lavey, who worked for 20 years on counterterrorism efforts, said, "There's a continued reluctance on the part of the entire FBI to ever use Islamic and terrorism in the same sentence."[44]

Clare Lopez, who provides intelligence and counterintelligence training to the Department of Defense for military intelligence personnel and has 30 years of experience working in Middle East-related intelligence, observes that the National Counterterrorism Center, the Department of Homeland Security, and the FBI "all published official lexicons within the last 2 years for dealing with Islamic terrorism, and...they each and every one excised any mention of Islam, jihad, Caliphate, or the linkage between Islamic doctrine and Islamic terrorism."[45]

This is not a recent phenomenon. Prior to 9/11, an FBI agent in Arizona wrote what is known as the Phoenix Memo—a proposal to check on "Middle Eastern students in flight school." The proposal "was shelved at headquarters partly because it would have violated bureau guidelines against racial profiling."[46] If more attention had been paid to the Phoenix Memo, might it have averted 9/11? One can only wonder.

In 2009, Lopez wrote a policy paper entitled "The Iran Lobby," which "details the systematic appointment of Sharia-friendly advocates within the State Department and other government agencies."[47] She states that Islamists "have achieved unprecedented access to the Department of Defense and even the White House."[48]

One particularly powerful example of infiltration is Abdurahman Alamoudi, a leading figure in the Muslim Brotherhood who became a naturalized US citizen in 1996. He founded the American Muslim Council (AMC) and, as its executive director, cultivated working relationships with the White House and other high-level entities in the US government. The US Department of Defense granted him the authority to approve Muslim chaplains for the US military via another organization Alamoudi founded, the American Muslim Armed Forces and Veteran Affairs Council (AMAFVAC).

With his connections, Alamoudi was able to exert great influence at the highest levels of US policy making. For example, in 1995, he helped then-president Bill Clinton and the ACLU to "develop a presidential guideline entitled 'Religious Expression in Public School,'" and in February of 1996, "Hillary Clinton penned a newspaper column based on talking points provided by Alamoudi."[49]

In 2000, Alamoudi and other Brotherhood associates persuaded then-presidential candidate George Bush to "prohibit the use of classified intelligence in deportation proceedings against foreigners suspected of terrorist ties."[50] Such a policy, of course, would make the work of counterterrorism investigators more difficult.

But the facade could last only so long. Alamoudi was later caught on video asserting he was a supporter of Hamas and Hezbollah—both officially recognized by the US government as terrorist organizations. Alamoudi was arrested in 2003 at Heathrow Airport in London when caught with $340,000 obtained from Libyan president Muammar Qaddafi, which was to be laundered through Saudi banks and into US accounts for use by terror-support groups.

Extradited to the United States, Alamoudi was later convicted of being a senior al-Qaeda financier and Hamas operative. He was also involved in a plot to kill then-crown prince Abdullah of Saudi Arabia. As well, recordings surfaced that revealed his "objective of making America a Muslim nation."

This raises important questions: How many other Alamoudis are there? And how have they managed to obtain such high-level access within the US government? This is the conclusion that the authors of the security report *Shariah: The Threat to America* make:

Multiculturalism, political correctness, misguided notions of tolerance and sheer willful blindness have combined to create an atmosphere of confusion and denial in America about the current threat confronting the nation. Of particular concern is the fact that political and military leaders of the United States find it difficult and/or distasteful to explain the true nature of the enemy to the public, and even to discuss it among themselves.[51]

Though at the time of this writing we have not been the victim of bombs in recent years, we have been infiltrated by Islamists who have hostile designs against America.

The Infiltration of the Education System

In an effort to portray Islam favorably, there are Muslim activists who engage in distributing positive literature and establishing centers of peace with invitations to the local community for dialogue. And they're particularly aggressive on college and university campuses, with several hundred chapters of the Muslim Student Association (MSA) in North American schools. The MSA, which was started with the help of Egyptian-based Muslim Brotherhood leaders, hands out free literature, hosts an Islamic Awareness Week, and holds both regional and national conferences throughout the country.

But the MSA isn't merely a student support group or religious organization. According to Steven Emerson, who wrote an extensive investigative report on the MSA, the "MSA promotes the Islamist ideology inspired by the Muslim Brotherhood, seeing itself as part of the global Islamic movement."[52] And what does this movement involve? Emerson cites Ahmed Shama, a former member of MSA at UCLA, who at an MSA West Conference in 2005 stated, "We want to restore Islam to the leadership of society...The goal of everything that we're talking about is the reestablishment of the Islamic form of government..."[53]

In that same speech, Shama described the ideal activist as being committed to "enforcing the shariah sent down by Allah...supporting Allah's friends and fighting Allah's foes, liberating Muslim territories from all aggression or non-Muslim control..."[54]

Throughout his report, Emerson provides detailed evidence of MSA members voicing support for terrorist groups such as Hamas and Hezbollah, and documents MSA presidents who have spoken in favor of jihad.[55] In fact, Abdurahman Alamoudi, the convicted terrorist operative and financier who had White House access, was president of MSA National from 1982 to 1983.

The attempt on the part of Islamists to shape young minds goes even further, reaching into public schools all across America. In 2008,

The American Textbook Council, an independent national research organization, issued a report finding that ten of the most widely used middle school and high school social studies textbooks "present an incomplete and confected view of Islam that misrepresents its foundations and challenges to international security."[56] The bottom line is that these textbooks whitewash the history and teachings of Islam and denigrate Western history and values. This is what the council noted:

> While seventh-grade textbooks describe Islam in glowing language, they portray Christianity in harsh light. Students encounter a startling contrast. Islam is featured as a model of interfaith tolerance; Christians wage wars of aggression and kill Jews. Islam provides models of harmony and civilization. Anti-Semitism, the Inquisition and wars of religion bespot the Christian record.[57]

Not surprisingly, according to these textbooks, America is to be blamed for the world's woes.

The American Textbook Council report further states that the Council on Islamic Education now enjoys "virtually unchecked power over publishers" and is an "agent of contemporary censorship." It exercises authority over publishers, asserting that it may "decline requests for reviewing published materials, unless a substantial and substantive revision is planned by the publisher."[58] The taboo about teaching religion in schools, so zealously promoted by the ACLU and our courts, is conveniently set aside in deference to Muslim demands.

Turning back to higher education, the Saudi royal family and other wealthy Saudi individuals have generously donated many millions of dollars to establish centers for Islamic studies at some of the most prestigious Western universities. For example, in 2005, Georgetown University and Harvard each received $20 million "for the study of Islam and the Muslim world."[59]

Such study centers, however, have received criticism for their "widespread anti-Israel, anti-American bias in scholarship and teaching on the Arab-Israeli conflict."[60] According to Asaf Romirowsky, an adjunct scholar for Campus Watch, a project of the Middle East

Forum, "Students today are subjected to radical views of the Middle East by professors who seldom brook dissent."[61]

A little background is in order here: The Saudi royal family supports Wahhabism, which is Saudi Arabia's official religion. The Quran is the country's constitution, and shariah is strictly enforced. Because Islam's two holiest shrines, Mecca and Medina, reside in Saudi Arabia, the Saudi government "assert[s] that its Wahhabi interpretation of the faith is the authoritative one."[62] What's more, "Saudi Wahhabism fuels a fiery hatred for the West's religious tolerance. It views attempts by the West to promote democratic reforms within its medieval Arab monarchy as an affront to Islam."[63] In short, from the Wahhabist perspective, there is no room for moderation.

What's disconcerting is that the same Saudi government has funded "'charitable' fronts like the Muslim World League, the Al-Haramain Foundation, the International Islamic Relief Organization (IIRO), and others that raised money for al-Qaeda, Hamas and Islamic jihad."[64] One example of "terrorist-tainted infiltration" is the Center for Middle East Studies at University of California at Berkeley. The center was given "a $5 million dollar grant courtesy of Sultan bin Abdulaziz Al-Saud and Sheikh Salahudin Yusef Hamza Abdeljawad. Both are linked to Islamic charities the U.S. government lists as front groups providing funding for al-Qaeda."[65]

Because these study centers are on university campuses, one might get the impression they provide neutral ground for dialogue. Yet "the head of the Muslim American Society, W. Deen Muhammed, has stated that Saudi gifts require the receiver to prefer the Saudi 'school of thought.'"[66] That, of course, explains their anti-Western, anti-Christian, and anti-Jewish bias.

The Infiltration Through Propaganda

Claiming to Be a Religion of Peace

Islamic centers are promoted as places where interfaith dialogue can occur. When some of us visited a mosque in Chicago, we were treated in a respectful, hospitable manner. But in the course of the discussion it soon became apparent that the picture given to us of

Islam could, at best, be described as skewed. Our hosts disregarded the many texts in the Quran about jihad, infidels, and the treatment of women, and never commented on Islam's history of using violence to impose its religion on others. Instead, Islam was spoken of in glowing terms. We were told that it grants freedom of religion, honors women's rights, and seeks to live peacefully in America under the US Constitution.

Americans are generally at a disadvantage in such discussions if they do not know that certain words or phrases, as used by Muslims, are interpreted differently than the way in which we understand them. For example, when we are told that Islam is a religion of peace, we must realize what they mean by this. From their perspective, Muslim countries are considered countries of peace because Islam has prevailed, and non-Muslim countries are countries of war because they stand in opposition to Allah. Given this clarification, we realize that Muslims believe they can bring peace to the world by forcing countries to convert to Islam. As Paul Sperry observes, "Islam *is* a peaceful religion—for devout Muslims. Everyone else is marked for punishment, or 'severe penalty,' as the Quran puts it. Peace exists only insofar as non-Muslims submit to the word, or sword, of Islam. Until then, there is no peace."[67]

Playing the Victim Card

Muhammad himself emphasized the victimhood of Muslims in order to justify his aggression. As Mark Durie explains, "To sustain the theological position that conquest is liberation, it became necessary [for Muslims] to seek grounds to find the infidel enemy [non-Muslims] guilty and deserving of attack."[68] In other words, to justify Muslim aggression, it was argued that the suffering Muslims had received from others was greater than any harm Muslims had poured out upon non-Muslims, as Durie goes on to say:

Since, by divine decree Muslims' sufferings were "worse than slaughter," it became obligatory for Muslims to regard their victimhood as greater than whatever they inflicted upon their enemies...It is this theological root, grounded in the Quran and the

Sunna of Muhammad, which explains why, again and again, some Muslims have insisted that their victimhood is greater than that of those they have attacked.[69]

That explains why, when the translators of Salman Rushdie's book *The Satanic Verses* were assassinated by extremists and Muslims died in the riots that followed, Lord Ahmed of the Labour Party in Britain said it was not the *killers* who should be held accountable for these deaths, but the *author*, who provided "a pretext for their aggression."[70] Allegedly, Muslims suffer more when Islam is dishonored than non-Muslims suffer when they are killed.

By this same logic, the train bombings in London and Italy were the fault of the respective countries that allegedly refused to give Muslims the rights they "deserve." When Theo van Gogh was murdered on an Amsterdam street in 2004, it was actually *his* fault he ended up getting killed because he had produced a movie that depicted the suppression of women in Islam.

This explains why, no matter how radical the actions of those who riot, protest, or kill in the name of Islam, the perpetrators of these acts are frequently exonerated. Rather than hold the instigators or killers to account, the blame is shifted.

During the Danish cartoon controversy, "mob attacks and assassinations...claimed the lives of over 200 people utterly uninvolved with the 'blasphemous' drawings."[71] Yet the widespread violent reaction was said to be justified because Islam had been insulted. The blame for all the deaths was laid at the doorstep of the cartoonist who "inflicted" this suffering on Islam; he was responsible for the killing of these innocent people. The riots were intended to teach the West a lesson: Don't ever criticize Islam, or we will riot and a *fatwa* (Islamic ruling) will be issued against you. This, of course, instills fear in non-Muslims, and where there is fear, there is silence.

Let's take the victimization principle to its logical conclusion. No doubt when King Herod killed all the infant boys in the environs of Bethlehem in an attempt to kill the Christ child, this crime was not his fault. The guilt for the gruesome deed lay with the wise men from the East, who had the audacity to refer to the baby as the King of the

Jews. The wise men should have known Herod would be insulted by this perceived threat to his own throne. What should we expect when a king is offended by a child who dares to take the title of king for himself?

By playing the victim card, Islamists have achieved their desired result. The Western media has censored itself, refusing to make comments critical of Islam—no matter how legitimate. Victimhood is a powerful means of generating sympathy and shifting blame. And it never fails to silence people.

Muslim advocacy groups in America complain that discrimination, intolerance, and harassment against Muslims are on the rise. But The Center for Security Policy released an extensive long-term study, based on FBI statistics, that revealed religious bias crimes against Muslims have "remained relatively low with a downward trend since 2001, and are significantly less than the numbers of bias crimes against Jewish victims."[72] In fact, in 2009, "Jewish victims of hate crimes outnumbered Muslim victims by more than 8 to 1."[73]

Frank Gaffney, the president of Center for Security Policy, makes this observation:

> This report is important because it exposes a false belief perpetuated by a few vocal groups that religious bias crimes against Muslims are on the upswing. The truth is quite the opposite. These arguments, unsubstantiated by hard factual data, are corrosive to community relationships at every level of American society, and a potential threat to national security.[74]

The Infiltration Through Deception

Meanwhile, in the war of words, Islamist organizations and lobbyists cleverly win victories, veiling their true designs and nature. One is to redefine *jihad* as nothing more than "personal struggle." But for hundreds of millions of Muslims, *jihad* is not about the individual person but the *umma*—that is, the Muslim community. Historically, *jihad* has meant to promote Islamic dominance in this world. Historian Bernard Lewis states that "the overwhelming majority of early authorities...discuss *jihad* in military terms."[75] "Shariah scholars typically cite as authority for *jihad* from the Quran any of the 164 verses that specifically refer to jihad against non-Muslims in terms that include military expeditions, fighting enemies, for distributing the spoils of war."[76] The *Dictionary of Islam* elaborates that *jihad* was established as "a religious war with those who are unbelievers in the mission of Muhammad."[77]

This is what Abu Ala Maududi, a leading scholar of Islam who wrote the book *Jihad in the Cause of Allah,* said:

> Islam is a revolutionary ideology, a revolutionary program (agenda) to alter the social order of the whole world, and rebuild it in conformity with its own tenets and the ideals...Islam wished to destroy all states and governments anywhere on the face of the earth, which are opposed to the ideology and program of Islam, regardless of the country or the nation which rules it. The purpose of Islam is to set up a state on the basis of its own ideology and program regardless of which nation assumes the role of the standard bearer of Islam...[78]

Yet Islamist apologists and revisionists have claimed *jihad* isn't necessarily violent, portraying it as more of a reference to an inner struggle. But their attempts to whitewash the meaning of *jihad* aren't very convincing when one reads statements like these on Muslim websites: "Instead of using 'Holy War' to translate the word Jihad, use a more comprehensive and proper term like, 'struggle' or 'striving'...Try to use language that is more appealing to North Americans."[79]

In their attempt to portray Islam as a religion of peace and not war, some Muslims point to Sura 2:256, which says there is "no compulsion in religion." In other words, Islam is not imposed by force. Non-Muslims are free to take it or leave it.

What you aren't told is that Sura 2:256 dates from Muhammad's early Meccan period. At that time, he was still trying to attract followers, of which he had few. Islam teaches that this earlier expression of tolerance to other religions is superseded by Sura 9, which Allah revealed later and includes what is known as the "verse of the sword" (Sura 9:29). Because Sura 9 came later, it in effect "cancels out" anything in Sura 2. In fact, Sura 9 calls for "virtually unlimited war against unbelievers...[and has] abrogated more than a hundred earlier verses which commanded Muslims to deal peacefully with unbelievers."[80]

If it's true there is "no compulsion in religion," then why do the laws of Saudi Arabia prescribe the death penalty for any Muslim who converts to another religion? And why, here in America, do converts from Islam have to flee their families, often hiding in undisclosed locations?

Those are just a few examples of the ways Islamists have infiltrated American society and shaped the dialogue about Islam.

WILL APPEASEMENT WORK?

In Western society, there is a widespread assumption that if we would just be willing enough to accommodate certain Islamist demands, Muslims will return the favor by accepting our values or, at minimum, coexisting peacefully with us. We think that if we grant them their wishes, they will no longer have reason to be offended. But that's not what the evidence says. In actuality, the more we acquiesce, the more insistent they become. In other words, appeasement back-fires and serves only to embolden Islamists.

In an article titled, "Moderate Muslims Turning Radical?" William Federer states that "multiculturalism has alienated an entire generation of young Muslims and made them increasingly radical."[81] As they see the West cave in to their demands and give them special preferences, they interpret this as a sign of weakness and "proof that the world is submitting to Allah—not in the distant future—but right now before their eyes!"[82] Federer asks, "Could it be the more the West exhibits hyper-tolerance, the more it turns some moderate Muslims, who believe the world will submit to Allah in the distant future, into fundamental violent Muslims, who view this tolerance as evidence the world is submitting to Allah now?"[83] The article ends with this observation: "No man can tame a tiger into a kitten by stroking it."[84]

Though we may try to derive comfort from the fact that the

majority of the world's 1.5 billion Muslims would prefer to live in peace with their neighbors, we must remember once again that it is the radicals who set the agenda. "Moderate Muslims are hesitant to speak out against fundamental violent Muslims, as occasionally one does and they are threatened, intimidated, forced to change their names for protection, have fatwas put on them and even killed."[85]

IT WASN'T THE VIDEO

When the US consulate in Benghazi, Libya, was attacked on September 11, 2012 and US ambassador Chris Stevens was slain along with three other Americans, initially the blame was directed at an obscure video that allegedly incited the riot and killings. This, in turn, led to a renewed outcry by Muslim leaders for the United Nations to pass a resolution on blasphemy laws.

But subsequent investigations—and even testimony from the president of Libya himself—revealed the attack was not a spontaneous response to a video, but a carefully orchestrated anti-American strike carried out by radical Islamists, and that the video was but a pretext for the crimes. This is yet another example of how Westerners have assumed that silencing all criticism of Islam (via blasphemy laws) is the solution to ending Islamist hostilities, when in reality the problem is Islamists who are committed to furthering their cause by whatever means necessary, including violence.

Our worst possible response to Islamist violence would be to adopt some form of censorship. Doing so (1) will not stop Islamists from pursuing global Islamic dominion, and (2) will end up allowing them to carry out their agenda without fear of accountability. Instead, Islamic extremism needs to be addressed directly—a problem the United Nations, many Western leaders, and much of the Western media refuse to acknowledge.

WHO ARE THE MODERATES?

As we saw earlier, the Muslim Brotherhood is not a moderate organization. However, the fact they do not advocate terrorism—at least in a clearly visible way in America—has caused many to view them as moderate. So as long as they aren't caught plotting terrorism, popular culture and a compliant media have viewed the Brotherhood as a moderate group.

Then there are those who genuinely are moderates. They are educated in Islam, yet they are opposed not only to violence but also to imposing an Islamic way of life on others. They are content to live in a pluralistic society and focus on the more positive aspects of Islam and ignore its troubling teachings. They are secular Muslims who are in favor of freedom of conscience and are open to Western ideas of democracy and capitalism. For them, Islam is their identity, but it does not control the whole of their lives. Some of these moderates have called for reform in Islam, but they've been greeted by death threats because they dare to challenge Islamic teachings about jihad and shariah, or the texts of the Quran and the Hadith.

Then there are still other Muslims who don't know the Quran or their own history, and might not realize that they have been commanded by their leaders and writings to spread Islam by whatever means necessary. Much as there are some people who call themselves Christians yet know little or nothing about Christianity, there are Muslims who take the name of the religion they grew up in but they know little or nothing of its core teachings.

All that to say, the vast majority of Muslims are not Islamized. They do not share the goals and methods of groups like the Muslim Brotherhood. For the most part, the Muslims who live in our midst desire to live peacefully and to be good neighbors. Many, though not all, assimilate into Western society. We of course welcome them and ask only that they abide by the laws of the US Constitution and refuse to support the implementation of shariah in this country.

RESISTING A GREAT TEMPTATION

I realize that much of what I've written in this chapter gives us reason to be alarmed. And yet as I've said earlier, God has given us an incredible opportunity. Countless Muslims, because they are here in America, have the chance to learn about salvation and eternal life in Jesus Christ. God has brought these people into our lives for a reason. We are called to serve as ambassadors for Christ, to represent Him to others.

The greatest mistake we as Christians can make is to resent Muslims and think they are all the same. They aren't. Just as Christians don't like to be painted with a broad brush, we should not treat all Muslims as if they are at war with the West. It would be a tragedy if we failed to realize we are not only faced with a great challenge, but we have also been given a wonderful opportunity.

We could easily find ourselves tempted to feel overwhelmed and do nothing, or to lash out in a way that turns Muslims off from Christianity. But neither response does any good. I believe every single one of us must ask ourselves what we should be doing, and answer that question as best we can. I'm not saying there is a one-size-fits-all solution. But we can all share in the burden of praying for our Muslim friends and helping them to understand who Christ is. Thankfully, Muslims are turning to Christ in record numbers in the Middle East. We need to pray that that will happen here in the West as well.

So what should the church be doing? To that we now turn.

— The Triumph of the Cross —

A Personal Testimony

Ghulam Masih Naaman was born into a Muslim family in Jammu, Kashmir, India. At the age of five, he began to attend the mosque every Friday and worked on memorizing the Quran. Years later he was sent to the Air Force Academy in Calcutta, where he became part of the Intelligence Corps. There he saw firsthand how the British officers took advantage of their subordinates, with one grand exception, and that was Capitan Baxter, a young officer who showed loving compassion toward all under his charge. He would invite the

Indians to his table, and when there was a bomb attack, instead of going to the trenches for shelter, he would invite all the men to go to "the chapel," which was but a makeshift tent, to pray. He told the men that he would pray in the name of Jesus and, if they wished, they could say "Amen" with him at the end of his prayer. Incredibly, when they would emerge from the tent, they would see that other nearby units had been destroyed, but theirs was spared. Ghulam began to wonder, "Who is this Jesus?"

Sometime later, when Ghulam became wounded, he was nursed back to health by two Christian nurses, Amber and Mary, who sacrificed of themselves to give him good care. When they parted, they explained, "We are not seeking reward; our Master suffered for us and it is our duty to serve others." Their witness left a deep impression on him.

Then Ghulam met a young man named Philip, who was willing to reach out to the most needy and despised of persons. Ghulam wrote, "In the following days, I kept reminiscing over my past experiences: The quiet, Christian life of Baxter, the kindness of Amber and Mary, the practical example of self-sacrifice displayed by Philip..." He wondered about the source of their grace and strength and the Jesus they spoke about.

When Ghulam entered a house intending to kill the only Christian family in a particular village, the daughter of the couple (who was about ten years old) pleaded, "We will not ask you to spare our lives, but just give us a few minutes for prayer, so that we may ask the One who gave us His promise come to our aid." The family knelt to pray and when they said "Amen," a brilliant light rose out of the ground, hiding them from sight. Ghulam was startled and backed away, asking forgiveness for what he had intended to do. He wrote, "Suddenly, I began to detect a pattern in all these experiences. They were like scattered pearls which, when strung together, make a perfect necklace."

In the midst of his despair and depression, Ghulam sought help from Allah, but his conscience would not be silent. He thought of all the people he had killed and knew that if he died he would go to hell. He decided to delve into Islam even more devotedly to seek peace for his soul. In desperation, he awoke early each morning praying for God to give him help.

Then one morning in the waiting room of a railway station, after an intense time of prayer, Ghulam was aware that someone had come up behind him, put a loving hand on his shoulder, and said, "My grace is sufficient for you." The sentence was repeated three times, and it was as if an electric charge had gone through Ghulam's body. His burden was lifted, the guilt was gone. A moment later, a member of the lowest class—an employee, cleaning the floor—witnessed his ecstasy, and when told what Ghulam had just heard, explained that these words were from the New Testament.

Thus Ghulam began his journey by finding Christians and was discipled and began witnessing to others about the grace of God in Jesus Christ. When members of his family plotted to kill him, through a miracle, he was able to escape and eventually became an evangelist, sharing the gospel with Muslim communities. His son, Samuel, now teaches in the World Missions department at Moody Bible Institute in Chicago, and wrote the foreword to this book.

—Excerpts from Ghulam Masih Naaman,
My Grace Is Sufficient for You (Rikon,
Switzerland: The Good Way, 1990)

The Shadow of the Crescent

"If the cross is to triumph over the crescent
it will be not by might or by power but by God's Spirit."

Samuel Zwemer, missionary to Muslims[1]

Chapter Ten

What the Church
Should Be Doing Now

What is the role of the church in the world?
The answer to this question is still debated among church
leaders. At what point do we engage the culture, and when is it best
to remain neutral about religious and political issues in the interest
of maintaining a pure gospel witness? Frequently we are told that
we should be known for what we are *for* rather than for what we are
against. Indeed, the church is often criticized for being judgmental,
culturally repressive, and too closely identified with a political party.
The role of the church, some say, is to preach and live the gospel in a
world filled with strife and hate without being critical of other religions or taking sides in social or political issues.

Strong arguments can be made that churches should stay completely removed from the cultural currents that swirl around us so
that the gospel message is not hitched to a political, cultural, or religious agenda. Whether the issue is same-sex marriage, abortion, or
creeping shariah, some say Christians should remain publicly neutral and silent on such issues and stay focused on love, good deeds,
and sharing the gospel, which alone can bring forgiveness and freedom to the human heart.

We can appropriately call this the "Thou Shalt Not Offend" Approach.

Then at the opposite end of the spectrum is the "We Must Expose the Worst About Islam" Approach. Here we have those who zealously expose all of Islam's faults as if a thorough knowledge of the facts had the power to prompt Muslims to become Christians or spur Christians toward a right response to Islam. But the fear factor ends up obscuring any call to compassion, and the gospel—which alone has the power to transform lives—remains vaguely in the backdrop, a distant secondary element, if at all mentioned.

Both approaches, I believe, are detrimental. After we take a closer look at why that is the case, my intention is to outline a third approach—one of engagement, one that encourages us as Christians to be well-informed about what is taking place around us and, at the same time, remain true to Christ's calling for us to proclaim and live the gospel with clarity, compassion, and integrity.

THE "THOU SHALT NOT OFFEND" APPROACH

Many pastors and church leaders argue that we should not be publicly critical of Islam's history, its sacred texts, or Islamists' intentions for the West for at least two reasons:

First, we are told that our primary purpose is to win people to Christ. Therefore, if we expose the truth about the teachings and history of Islam, we will not be able to build the bridges that enable us to reach out to the Muslim community. If Muslims discover that we are critical of their religion—even legitimately so—they are less likely to be our friends, and therefore we will lose the opportunity to share the gospel with them. We cannot expect to lead Muslims to faith in Christ if we say anything that might prompt them to view us as enemies, even if their conclusion is unwarranted. To be critical of Islam is to build walls, not bridges.

Second, we are told that if we would just be willing to make concessions to Islam, we will reduce the risk of violent protests, death threats, and potential terrorism. Muslims will be grateful that we are accommodating them and therefore will live contentedly among us.

This sort of appeasement is alleged to be better than drawing clear lines of distinction and risking antagonism or confrontation.

These Christian leaders say there is no reason for us to be concerned about our public posture of yielding to Islam in the interest of religious tolerance and harmony. Such leaders have chosen to censor themselves, agreeing that they will speak about Islam only in positive terms and never utter a word of criticism. They are content to selectively view Islam through the lens of a handful of positive verses from the Quran and ignore the many radical teachings within the pages of that very same text. Matters such as Islam's violence against Christians, whether past or present, are overlooked in the name of cooperation and accommodation. Pastors who take this stance refrain from educating their congregations about the dangers of shariah's growing influence and what it has already accomplished in Europe; instead, these pastors speak with deference to and in praise of Islam.[2]

Many of these leaders show no concern when hospitals compliantly remove crucifixes and crosses because Muslims complain that these symbols are offensive; public tax dollars are used to build prayer rooms for Muslim students in our schools; airports and other public spaces build separate washrooms to accommodate Muslims (especially prevalent in European airports and meeting halls); and special exceptions are granted to Muslims in the workplace for times for prayer, Ramadan, the hajji pilgrimage. They are also indifferent to the fact that there are now many Muslim enclaves in Europe and the United Kingdom where civil cases can be tried under shariah councils (with no opportunity to appeal decisions at a higher, outside court), and that in major cities such as New York and Paris, busy streets are blocked off on Friday afternoons to accommodate Muslims en route to their prayer times. This is just a sampling of the many concessions granted to Muslims but not to people of other religious persuasions.

Some church leaders have even invited Muslims to speak in their congregations, evidently unaware that Islamists favor this personal approach because those who are granted authority to speak on behalf of Islam can present a positive and whitewashed picture of their religion and remain silent about the more sordid details of their history.

Then there are those Christians who believe that Muslims can come to faith in Christ without leaving Islam, as the so-called Insider Movement teaches. They can invest the Muslim feasts and teachings with Christian meanings. They advocate that the gospel presentation to Muslims should be based on the Quran not simply as a starting point, but as the primary source for teaching about Jesus. Some churches have even gone so far as to place the Quran in the pews along with the Bible as a show of mutual friendship and tolerance.[3]

What is most interesting is that Muslims themselves do not believe that Christianity and Islam are compatible. Rather, Christianity and Islam, properly understood, are entirely incompatible. Thus while Westerners are generally eager to make concessions as found in the growing Chrislam movement (the notion that Christianity and Islam share enough in common to unite the two), Muslims are well aware that such syncretism is to be accepted only if it is among the means of moving the West from Christianity toward Islam. Tragically, some Christians are overly eager to concede Christian doctrine and turn a blind eye to Islamic views in the interest of unity and religious survival.[4]

I've written the above paragraphs fully aware that some Christian leaders will agree to certain accommodations to Islam, but not to others. But no matter where these leaders may attempt to draw the line, in general, the problem with the "Thou Shalt Not Offend" Approach is that we as Westerners are misunderstanding Islam. Muslims see our many concessions as entering into a covenant of submission with them and an acknowledgment of our inferiority. When we concede to their demands, we are confirming the Quran's statement about Muslims, "Ye are the best of peoples" (Sura 3:110), and thereby we who are not Muslims are second-class citizens.

Even more critical for us is the fact we are standing by and watching the demands of Muslims expand while our freedoms as Christians are being marginalized. Many don't realize that these demands are ultimately part of a larger supremacist agenda with ever-increasing consequences. For example, in the United Kingdom, where the government has very actively engaged in a concerted effort to appease

Islam, according to police statistics, there were over 2800 cases of "honor violence" in 2011, with likely hundreds more going unreported.[5] This, of course, includes honor killings. The fact the United Kingdom has permitted Muslims to resolve civil cases in their own shariah tribunal councils has undoubtedly emboldened many of them to carry out their own form of justice in accord with shariah, even though honor violence is prohibited by British law. The lesson to be learned is that what we call tolerance is interpreted by Muslim advocacy groups as weakness, which only inspires them to call for even more concessions as Islam's influence expands.

What many Westerners don't realize is that if we yield to the demands of Muslims who insist that we make positive statements only about Islam, praising its contributions to civilization while ignoring the explicitly radical teaching of its sacred texts, and insist on receiving special exemptions, including those related to the practice of shariah even though it stands in opposition to our Constitution and its freedoms, then we are in effect entering into a covenant with Islam, confessing that we are *dhimmis* who have acquiesced to Islam's authority.

While we who live in the West can attempt to justify the "Thou Shalt Not Offend" Approach, the Christians who live in Nigeria, Egypt, the Sudan, and dozens of other Muslim-majority countries do not have that luxury. I am convinced they would tell us that we in the West who submit to Islam's demands do so to our peril. We are only pushing "crunch time" to our children and grandchildren. As Martin Niemöller, a German Lutheran pastor, learned in Hitler's Germany, if we don't speak up now, it might be too late later on. Denial leads to bitter regret and unanticipated sorrow.

The covenant that the West has unknowingly adopted with Islam must be broken. We cannot take refuge in silence and justify it as humility, and we cannot submit to Islam's demands for special exemptions and label it tolerance. The aura of fear that Westerners have about speaking the truth with regard to Islam must come to an end. And, at the same time, Christians must be delivered from the fear of befriending Muslims and witnessing to them.

THE "WE MUST EXPOSE THE WORST ABOUT ISLAM" APPROACH

On the opposite extreme are those who say that we must aggressively expose the evils of Islam, warning people about both its errors and dangers and its attempts to destroy freedom of religion and our way of life. Some have even gone so far as to advocate the public burning of the Quran. All of this instills people with fear rather than compassionate concern.

This approach has some serious problems. First, it paints all Muslims with the same broad brush. That is, it assumes that all Muslims are in favor of shariah for Western society. However, the majority of Muslims in the West are opposed to the imposition of shariah in spite of the fact it lies at the heart of their religion. What's more, this approach makes its point by comparing the worst about Islam with the best of Christianity, and either ignores or is unwilling to acknowledge the fact there are many who have done wrong or evil in the name of Christ. And, finally, this approach is at odds with displaying Christian love, fairness, and compassion for Muslims, who are also created in the image of God. Very simply, this approach is un-Christian and counterproductive.

ENGAGEMENT: A BETTER WAY OF MOVING FORWARD

If the two extremes are unacceptable, as I believe they are, is there a better way of moving forward? A way that both speaks to our concerns about Islam's teachings and intentions and yet is consistent with love and compassion? I believe that we must engage Islam in many different ways. We must both oppose Islamic claims to superiority and dominance and, at the same time, build bridges to Islamic communities and individuals.

We must show that truth and love are not fighting against each other. A common misconception is that if we tell the truth and expose Islam, people will fear Muslims and will not love them as they should. But the opposite should be the case: The more we know about Islam and, for example, its treatment of women and how it holds its adherents in the grip of fear of apostasy, the more we should be driven to compassion for Muslims. We should not just love those who are in agreement with our values, but also those who disagree with us, and even those who consider themselves our enemies. In short, we must willingly befriend those whose fundamental beliefs stand in direct opposition to our own. As a friend of mine who works with Muslims says, "We must face the facts without fueling the fear."

Following are eight steps we can take that I believe will provide both a witness to our Muslim communities and give opportunity for us to stand firm for our constitutional freedoms and deny special concessions to Islam. Hopefully these steps will help all of us face Islam's growing influence with compassion and without fear.

1. We Must Build a Community of Mutual Respect

We must treat Muslims (and all people, for that matter) with mutual respect. We dare not demonize them or make generalized personal accusations against them. We must affirm that all people are created in the image of God and have value conferred upon them by the Lord, our Creator. As Jesus admonished, you are to "love your neighbor as yourself" (Matthew 22:39).

Unfortunately, we as Christians are often woefully ignorant of how to share the gospel with Muslims, not realizing that they might be interested in what we have to say if we took the time to gain their respect and trust. And in the rare cases when we do talk with Muslims, we tend to assume the best approach is to explain why the Quran is wrong and the Bible is right. But we must ask ourselves: How would we respond if a Muslim came to us and explained why the Quran is right and the Bible has been corrupted? Respect is the key to cultivating meaningful relationships—not just with Muslims, but with all people regardless of their religion or ethnicity. What's more, though we may disagree when it comes to our faiths, we share enough common ground with Muslims that honest relationships can be built without resorting to antagonism. When it comes to reaching out to them, we must follow the Golden Rule: "Do to others as you would have them do to you" (Luke 6:31).

2. We Must Become an Informed Community

We must educate ourselves (and leaders must enlighten their congregations) about Islam and gain some familiarity with its teachings and history. We must awaken to the reality of what is happening around us. It is a scandal that the evangelical community is, by and large, ignorant of the basic teachings of Islam and assumes all Muslims will eventually assimilate into the Western way of life, along with its freedoms and the principles rooted in the US Constitution. No doubt many Muslims have already adopted Western values to greater or lesser extents, and others wish they could do so, but they recognize their religion will not let them. We must understand that inherently there is an unavoidable clash between the unyielding dictates of Islam and the Western value of tolerance.

Back in the 1970s, Montgomery Watt, writing in Britain, said, "It is hardly too much to say that the intellectual challenge to Christianity from Islam at the present time is greater than any challenge Christians have had to meet for fifteen centuries, not excluding that from natural science."[6] If this was true almost four decades ago, imagine how much more it is true today in Britain and now in the United States. Every Bible college and seminary should make Islamic studies a part of their curriculum. The day has come when it is not enough for Islam to be studied by scholars; it must now be understood by everyone who is concerned about our freedoms and the future of the West as we know it.

All Christians should consider it both a privilege and a duty to know about Islam as well as be aware of the strategies Islamists have for fulfilling their goals in America. This will enable them to share Christ more effectively with Muslims, and it will also equip them to be informed citizens who can help shape the policy debates for our schools, the workplace, the government, the legal arena, and all the other strata of our culture.

Resources such as *Voice of the Martyrs* magazine should be widely distributed so that as many Christians as possible are kept up to date with the face of Islam in other countries. The value of such literature is that it not only provides accounts of what our brothers and sisters in other countries endure, but it also inspires us to be as strong in our faith as they are in theirs.

3. Recognize the Spiritual Nature of the Conflict

Because Islam denies the very heart of the Christian faith, namely the divinity of Jesus as well as His death on the cross and His resurrection, and because Islam has been so successful in overpowering Christianity in so many different countries, we must recognize it is a spiritual battle we're in. As the apostle Paul said in 2 Corinthians 10:4, "The weapons we fight with are not the weapons of the world." Rather, we are to respond to this conflict with the spiritual weapons of Scripture and prayer. For it is the gospel alone that "is the power of God that brings salvation to everyone" (Romans 1:16). And we must become a praying community, praying for ourselves and for others. When King Jehoshaphat of Judah was confronted with an enemy that was too much for him, he proclaimed a fast and said, "Our God... we do not know what to do, but our eyes are on you" (2 Chronicles 20:12).

This is what Samuel Zwemer, the great missionary pioneer who ministered to Muslims, wrote:

> The student of Islam will never understand the common people unless he knows the reasons for their curious beliefs and practices...all of which still blind and oppress the mind and heart with constant fear of the unseen...Witchcraft, sorcery, spells, and charms are the background of the native Muslim psychology to an extent that is realised only by those who have penetrated most deeply into the life of the people.[7]

We must understand the nature of the spiritual battle that holds Muslims in its grip. Therefore, only spiritual resources can break such bondage, and that includes prayer—desperate prayer.

A pastor from Uganda, who had witnessed great persecution at the hands of Muslims, said this to a panel of leading revivalists at Moody Bible Institute:

In Uganda we experienced a nationwide revival as a result of severe persecution. The suffering of the people was beyond description, and no one came to our rescue. But God used the opportunity to wake a nation from its spiritual coma. What we learned is that revival will come either through devastation or desperation. So my question for you in America is, What are you doing to make sure the revival comes through *desperation* and not *devastation*?

So we must ask ourselves: Do we want to become a praying community through *desperation*, or *devastation*? That is the choice we face. I suspect, to our shame, we are not yet desperate, and God might use the growth of Islam to make us so.

Recently I met a Christian leader from England who told me that he and a group of others had met every week for two years to pray for the Muslim community, without apparent results. But they persisted in prayer, and now through building friendships and developing mutual trust, about 75 Muslims have come to trust Christ as their Savior. This leader and his friends are evidence that fervent prayer, combined with fervent love, is the only way to build the kind of openness and trust needed to see attitudes change so that the gospel can get a hearing. Prayer is the key that unlocks closed doors. And he reminds us that "love never fails" (1 Corinthians 13:8).

4. Empower Parents to Refuse to Have Their Children Indoctirinated

In a previous chapter, I gave some details about a report issued by the American Textbook Council. This organization noted that many middle school and high school textbooks in the United States present a whitewashed perspective of Islam, while Christianity is portrayed in a harsh light.

The key perpetrator in all this is the Council on Islamic Education, which "presents itself as a mainstream Muslim organization... [and] claims to act as Islam's liaison to the nation's public schools."[8] The American Textbook Council's report observes, "Islamic organizations, willing to sow misinformation, are active in curriculum politics.

These activists are eager to expunge any critical thought about Islam from textbooks and all public discourse."[9]

The American Textbook Council concluded that the Council on Islamic Education is "a content gatekeeper with virtually unchecked power over publishers."[10] And so it is that "for more than a decade, history textbook editors have done the Council's [Council on Islamic Education] bidding, and as a result, history textbooks accommodate Islam on terms that Islamists demand."[11]

The impact of this misinformation in the lives of school students is huge and growing. We must empower parents to successfully object to such indoctrination and historical revisionism.

5. We Must Oppose the Practice of Shariah

We must graciously explain to Muslims—and all others who care to listen—that we are not opposed to Muslims practicing their religion. The right of religious freedom is guaranteed under the US Constitution, and we gladly recognize this right of all American citizens regardless of their religion. We are, however, opposed to the imposition of shariah in any form whatsoever, even in Muslim enclaves. We also oppose Islamists' attempts to completely shield Islam from any kind of criticism, whether through officially mandated blasphemy laws or simply as a result of the West's self-imposed censorship and concessions to Islam.

When a court in New Jersey had determined that a Moroccan husband had repeatedly abused his wife physically, verbally, and sexually (all of which is permitted under shariah), the court permitted an imam to offer expert testimony on behalf of the Moroccan husband. The imam said that under Islam, a wife must comply with her husband's sexual demands because the husband is prohibited from obtaining sexual satisfaction elsewhere. Although the judge credited the wife's testimony as valid and found that the husband had in fact "harassed and assaulted her," he held that the husband was acting in a manner "consistent with his practices [as a Muslim]." Therefore the judge ruled that the husband did not have "criminal desire to or intent to sexually assault" his wife.[12]

Fortunately, an appellate court recognized this was a case in which "religious custom clashed with the law,"[13] and the trial judge's erroneous decision was overturned. However, this incident reveals how willing some judges are to allow shariah, and not the Constitution, govern Muslims in America. If ever we were to get to the point that American courts were willing to permit shariah to be practiced in the Muslim community, would we descend down a slippery slope to the point that eventually, the Islamic custom of honor killings—which is allowed under shariah—would be tolerated? There are so many points at which shariah violates the human rights recognized by US laws that it immediately becomes clear it would be impossible to permit the two different legal systems to coexist side by side.

As we observed earlier, the state of Oklahoma has already been embroiled in a battle over whether Muslims should be permitted to observe shariah. This debate has already spread to two dozen other states.

THE VIEW OF ISLAMIC SCHOLARS

As explained in *Sharia Law for Non-Muslims*, "Islamic law is perfect, universal and eternal. The laws of the United States are temporary, limited, and will pass away. It is the duty of every Muslim to obey the laws of Allah, the Sharia. US laws are man-made; while Sharia law is sacred and comes from the only legitimate God, Allah."[14]

As stated earlier, there are already 85 official shariah councils in the United Kingdom, and the parliament approved five official Muslim Arbitration Tribunals. Currently, they are limited to trying civil cases, but there is increasing pressure from Islamists for the tribunals to be allowed to try criminal cases as well. Among the arguments for this is that doing so will help reduce terrorism. Islamists also pose the question, "Does not freedom of religion mean that adherents are free to practice their religion according to their own laws and customs?"

The fact shariah is already enacted for civil cases has led Islamists to exert great pressure on the British government to further legitimize the practice of shariah. In 2008, none other than the Archbishop of Canterbury, Dr. Rowan Williams, said it "seems unavoidable" that the United Kingdom would soon need to permit at least certain aspects of shariah.[15]

In 2011, Islamic extremists "launched a poster campaign across the UK proclaiming areas where Sharia law enforcement zones have been set up." The posters read, "You are entering a Sharia-controlled zone—Islamic rules enforced." Those who put up the posters said their goal was to "put the seeds down for an Islamic Emirate in the long term."[16]

"Show me your laws and I will show you your god!"[17] These words by late R.J. Rushdoony have often rung in my ears as I have observed the transitions taking place in the West. The direction in which a country goes is often dependent on the laws of the land. We can gladly invite Muslims to join with us in the political process as permitted by the Constitution, but we must fully oppose the establishment of shariah in any way, shape, or form, lest we find ourselves descending down the same path Europe and the United Kingdom have taken.

Read Robert Spencer's words carefully:

> American pluralism cannot absorb a supremacist creed that demands the subjugation of others under its rule, and allows for deception even under oath. But so effective has been the stealth jihadist campaign to marginalize or vilify anyone who asks uncomfortable questions about Islam that no one in the public square even dares to raise such questions—if they even know that the Quran contains such material.[18]

We must be prepared to insist that American laws, and not shariah, remain the standard for all Americans, no matter what their religion. As a side note, we must encourage those who are entering the law profession to be aware of the kind of impact shariah would have in influencing the direction of our nation.

6. Befriend and Stand with Muslims Who Want Reform

We must remember that many Muslims are strongly opposed to the imposition of shariah here in the West, although it is difficult for them to speak out because doing so is viewed as a serious offense against the Quran and Allah.

Here is a sad story with a happy ending: In 2004, the attorney general of Ontario, Canada issued a report "recommending that Muslims in Canada should have the right to seek arbitration based on their religious laws."[19] Muslim delegates at a conference went ahead and elected a 30-member council to establish the Islamic Institute of Civil Justice. One leader observed that if the practice of shariah were permitted, Canadian Muslims would have to follow both shariah and Canadian laws. He said, "You don't have to be the wisest man to see that there will be conflicts."[20]

The news was greeted with strong protests. The greatest outcry, understandably, came from Muslim women. "They are helping the Islamic groups to legalise violence against women," said Shiva Mahbobi. "It is racism to put people in different categories and define their rights based on where they came from."[21]

Homa Arjomand, born in Iran and a counselor for battered women, has this to say:

> Here in Canada, girls are segregated from boys at private Islamic elementary schools, then forced into arranged marriages through Sharia at the age of 13, 14 or 15 to men over twice their age. How much choice do these women have?... What [Ontario Premier] Mr. McGuinty is doing is simply flirting with political Islam. And that dangerous game is putting the lives and safety of women and children in danger. Shame."[22]

Arjomand went on to say, "The rise of Sharia in Canada is not a coincidence. It is part of a global movement and it is a threat."[23]

Mahmound Ahmadi, a spokesman for the Federation of Iranian Refuges, said, "Don't talk to us about Sharia law, Mr. McGuinty. I am coming from a country [Iran] where marital rape is protected by Sharia law."[24]

In the end, Premier McGuinty declared shariah would not be permitted in Ontario.

The lesson learned in Ontario was not lost on the province of Quebec. In May 2005, Fatima Houda-Pepin, a Muslim born in Morocco, put forth a legislative motion to reject shariah tribunals in Quebec. "The victims of Sharia have a human face…they are Muslim women."[25] She warned that permitting the practice of shariah would "isolate the Muslim community" and force it to "submit to an archaic vision of Islam." She also said that "any move to allow Islamic family law would lead to similar demands in criminal and civil legal areas"[26] (as is currently happening in Europe and the United Kingdom).

In the end, the legislative assembly voted unanimously to prohibit the use of shariah tribunals in Quebec—making it the first province to enact such a law. "They did so to preserve equality, rights, and liberty for all, irrespective of race or religion, in accordance with Canada's Constitution."[27] And who welcomed this decision with great enthusiasm? The Canadian Council of Muslim Women.

Let us seek out and stand with those Muslims who are willing to oppose efforts to impose shariah on Western nations and encourage them to withstand the pressure of Islamic conformity. And, let us courageously stand with converts from Islam to Christianity who find themselves unwelcomed in churches because of the fear that their presence might spark retaliation to the converts or the church. We must welcome and affirm them as members of the body of Christ, and take time to befriend and nurture them in the Christian faith.

7. We Must Form Coalitions that Help Inform and Influence Public Policymakers

A friend of mine was present at a meeting hosted by a prominent politician when the Muslims in the room pressured him about how they wanted him to vote on a particular item of legislation. They reminded him that they represented a large voting bloc, and they said that if he did not accept their demands, he would be denied their support. Now, Muslims have every right to apply such pressure to politicians. But at the same time, we as non-Muslims also have the right to persuade public policymakers as well. When we see politicians granting special rights and preferential treatment to Muslims with disregard for the rights of non-Muslims, we must point out the inconsistency and explain that to do such is to go against the accepted Western value of equal rights.

At this point it's necessary for me to make a clear distinction: Ultimately, the answer to resisting the demands of Islam cannot be found in the political arena. You cannot change people's minds until they have first had a change of heart, and that can only happen when they hear the gospel and receive Jesus Christ as their Savior. But as citizens granted the privilege of participating in the political process, we can definitely exert our influence in the political forum. We must speak up for the sake of our children and grandchildren, and urge government leaders to be informed about the agenda and strategy of the Islamists in our midst.

8. We Must Not Fear Islam or Muslims

As Christians, we have no reason to fear Islam or Muslims. It is fear that keeps people silent about Islamists' worldwide agenda, and it is fear that keeps Christians from witnessing to their Muslim neighbors. Fear makes us refuse to expose error and stand for what is right and proper.

When Jesus commissioned Paul to minister to the Gentiles and preach the gospel to them, He said Paul would "open their eyes and turn them from darkness to light, and from the power of Satan to God" (Acts 26:18). In other words, Paul's ministry would involve spiritual conflict, and thus he could expect resistance. Today, we can expect the same. Sharing the gospel with Muslims won't be easy. Yet Jesus has conquered the evil one, and we who have been made alive in Christ (Ephesians 2:5) can participate in His victory.

Mark Durie says it well:

> Our focus here...is with Islam, and in this case a key point of spiritual engagement must be to challenge the spiritual and territorial claims of the *dhimma* and *shahada* pacts, which on the one hand have enslaved Muslims in a false sense of superiority and schooled them to become oppressors of others, and on the other hand has enslaved Christians and other non-Muslims

in humiliation, false gratitude and silence, placing them under a curse of death (Ephesians 6:11-17).[28]

We have no reason to be fearful. Rather, we can face the future with optimism because God is sovereign. He is in control. And we are in His hands, not the hands of Islam and its threats.

"If you are fear-based, you are not worshipping Jesus,"[29] says Eric Metaxas, author of the widely acclaimed biography *Bonhoeffer: Pastor, Martyr, Prophet, Spy.* And certainly, Bonhoeffer learned early on that too many German Christians had cowered in fear during Hitler's rise to power. They were afraid to speak up, and as we've observed earlier, where there is fear, there is silence. In contrast, we should follow the example of the young people in Egypt who, in the uprisings in 2011, marched the streets of Cairo with T-shirts bearing the slogan "Martyr by Request." That is the kind of courage we need in this and future generations.

Read these challenging words from Ian Freestone, a pastor who serves in the Ruach Neighborhood Churches in Sydney, Australia. He gives a passionate call to arms, but it is arms folded in prayerful service to Christ and our Islamic neighbors.

If we as Christians had half the outrage of Islamic extremists and expressed it, not in violence but in earnest prayer to God and practical support for our suffering brothers and sisters, then perhaps the world would see our love for one another. So I suggest that whilst we should on the one hand be concerned at the rise of Islamic extremism, the answer is to get a bit extreme ourselves. I'm talking about being an extreme follower of Jesus Christ, consumed with love for our brothers and sisters, consumed with love for those who do not know the Lord and consumed with love for those who would persecute the name of Christ. Forget "terrorist cells." How about cells of Christian communities, terrorizing the Kingdom darkness with the love of God?[30]

Thabiti Anyabwile, who himself is a convert from Islam to Christianity, says that the greatest need of the church today is to regain its confidence in the power of the gospel to save people of any religion from their sins. He laments, "We sometimes seem to think that certain people are beyond the saving reach of the gospel."[31] He asks, in effect, "Why should we think that Muslims are outside of God's ability to regenerate a human heart?" The fact is that more Muslims are trusting Christ as Savior and Lord today than at any other period of history. He agrees that we must be delivered from any fear of befriending and witnessing to Muslims.

Estimates vary on how many Muslims reside in the United States. The Pew Research Center estimated in 2010 that there were 2.6 million.[32] Think of what might happen if every Muslim in America knew just one Christian who would shatter the stereotype that many Muslims have of Christians. After all, they frequently hear that America is a "Christian nation," and thus they all too readily associate Christianity with the values of Hollywood, the violence in our streets, and other unbiblical aspects of secular culture. We cannot tremble in fear or stand aloof; we must engage Muslims, many of whom are open to friendship and mutual interaction.

On a news program I was asked, "What is the greatest obstacle that the church faces today?" I had to confess that the greatest challenge we face might be *within* the church itself—the dimness of our light is just as much a problem as the depth of the world's darkness. We cannot be the church God has called us to be unless we allow the message of the gospel to shine forth, no matter how threatening the darkness might be. Given the promises of God, there is no reason for us to be paralyzed by fear and uncertainty.

Three times Jesus said, "Fear not" in the context of persecution. Only when we refuse to succumb to fear can we go forth and live effectively for Christ. With that in mind, at the end of chapter11, I've included a prayer through which we can offer up to the Lord any fears we might have.

WAYS WE CAN TAKE ACTION

We must realize the possibility that despite our prayerful efforts, we at best might be able to slow but not stop shariah's growing influence from eroding away the religious freedom we enjoy in the West.

Given the West's current posture of submission, a posture that all too quickly caves to the demands of Islamist activist organizations, we are conceding more and more ground to the Islamic agenda. If Europe is instructive, we can expect an onslaught of restrictions that will be imposed upon us non-Muslims as we seek to accommodate a religion whose stated goal is to conquer the world, peacefully if possible, but by force and terrorism if necessary.

This calls for all of us to get involved, yet not necessarily in the same ways. Each of us possesses varying skills, connections, and concerns that will help define the role we take. Some of us are able to focus on education, others on politics or law. Some of us can get involved with organizations that are active in taking a stand for our constitutional freedoms. And as Christians, all of us can do our part in helping fellow believers to grow in their awareness of what is taking place today and learn how they can share the love of Christ with their Muslim neighbor.

Keeping in mind the eight steps we reviewed in this chapter, we can prayerfully and humbly commit ourselves to doing the following:

1. We will make information available about Islam within our churches, as well as to the wider community, including our local politicians and policymakers.

2. We will keep our churches informed about the persecution of Christians in Muslim countries and commit ourselves to praying for our brothers and sisters who are undergoing the loss of their properties, their livelihood, and even their lives.

3. We will support freedom of religion for the Muslims among us, but will uphold the importance of and respect for the laws of the land as affirmed by the US Constitution. We oppose reprisals against those who convert from one religion to another and stand against threats and blasphemy laws that keep Muslims bound to their religion out of fear.

4. We will welcome Muslim converts to Christianity into our churches and nurture them in the faith as members of the body of Christ.

5. We will stand with parents who do not wish for their children to be indoctrinated by a whitewashed version of Islam in our schools through revisionist textbooks, pageants, and interfaith studies.

6. We will oppose attempts to introduce the partial implementation of shariah as a concession to Islam. This would include, for example, refusing to concede to demands for the Islamizing of public spaces through Muslim-only prayer rooms in schools, workplaces, prisons, and educational institutions. We oppose the removal of crosses and crucifixes as a further concession to the Islamist agenda.

7. We will stand against the passage of blasphemy laws that would make the legitimate criticism of Islam a crime. We believe people should have the freedom to scrutinize and critically evaluate Islam just as they are free to scrutinize and evaluate other religions or political ideologies.

8. We will work toward giving dignity to all women, and thus we oppose Islam's practice of relegating women to an inferior status in society, the practice of forced marriages (often to underaged girls), and the violence permitted against women per the Quran (Sura 4:34).

9. We will reject concessions intended to appease Islamists in the hopes that this will win greater cooperation and goodwill from Muslims.

10. Finally, and most importantly, we will extend friendship to our Muslim neighbors, assuring them of our respect, personal availability, and love. We will uphold the gospel of Christ without coercion or rancor.

Within one of Jesus' letters to the seven churches in Revelation is an urgent plea that could very well serve as His call to us today:

Wake up! Strengthen what remains and is about to die... Remember, therefore what you have received and heard; hold it fast, and repent. But if you do not wake up, I will come like a thief, and you will not know at what time I will come to you (3:2-3).

If we heed Jesus' words, this could be our finest hour.

— The Triumph of the Cross —

A Personal Testimony

I was born into a devout Muslim family. I believed that Muhammad was a prophet of God, and each day, along with Muslims all over the world, I prayed five times a day, facing toward the city of Mecca. Every year, during the month of Ramadan, I fasted for 30 days, hoping my sins from that year would be forgiven. When I was 18, I moved from Indonesia to Germany to attend fashion design school. While living there, a Christian invited me to read the Bible. At first I was appalled by the idea because I had always been told it was a sin for Muslims to read the Bible. However, my friend knew a lot about Islam, so I began reading the Bible. He told me to begin with the Gospel of John.

I was very impressed whenever Jesus talked, and noticed that He often began by saying, "I tell you the truth." Truth was very important to me, and this showed He spoke with authority. Unlike Christians, we Muslims could never say for sure whether we were going to go to heaven when we died. We could only say, "If God wills, I will go to heaven." So I lived with this burden of fear that when I stood before God on the day of judgment, my bad deeds would end up outweighing my good deeds. However, the Bible said Jesus took my sins upon Himself and died for me. And that by trusting in Him, I could go to heaven. I really wanted to accept Him as Savior, but was afraid to because I knew doing so would upset my family and I could either be killed or forever banned from them.

One night I had a dream and the Lord Jesus appeared to me and said, "Widia, I am the way, the truth, and the life. Follow me."[33] I couldn't resist the Holy Spirit anymore and decided to trust in Christ, alone in my college dorm room. It wasn't until after I became a Christian that I read John 14:6 and saw the same words that the Lord Jesus spoke to me in my dream. Not long after that, God brought some Christians into my life who have helped me grow in my faith. I have since led some of my friends to Christ, including another Muslim from Turkey. I am now married, have two boys, and am still sharing my faith as often as I can.

—Widia

Chapter Eleven

A Final Plea:
The Church Standing Alone

These are the words of him who has the sharp, double-
edged sword. I know where you live—where Satan has
his throne. Yet you remain true to my name. You did not
renounce your faith (Revelation 2:12-13).

—JESUS, TO THE CHURCH IN PERGAMUM

I've just read the book *Allah: A Christian Response* by Miroslav Volf,[1] in which he explores the similarities that exist in the Christian and Islamic understandings of God. He points out a number of perspectives both faiths share, and concludes that there is enough overlap that both Christians and Muslims worship the same God. Therefore, we should be able to coexist peacefully on this planet.

I will not review the book here because that has already been done by many others, except to say that it was interesting for me to see how this author believes Christianity and Islam intersect. However, we have already learned that Islam denies the Trinity and rejects the incarnation (the fact that Jesus was God in human flesh)—two doctrines at the very heart of the Christian faith. On that basis alone we can profoundly disagree with Volf's suggestion that it's possible for a person to be a practicing Muslim and 100 percent Christian without denying certain core convictions of one's beliefs and practice.[2]

Be that as it may, Volf's book and others like it will continue to inspire the push toward interfaith dialogue with the intention of minimizing the irreconcilable differences between Islam and Christianity. Muslim leaders gravitate to positions of responsibility in those forums that aim at minimizing the gap between the two religions. For example, after 9/11, American Muslim Council (AMC) board member Madhi Bray "became the first Muslim named to the Interfaith Alliance, a leading Washington voice for religious pluralism."[3] Take note of Paul Sperry's words:

> There is no doubt that many Islamists secretly want to Islamize America, turning everyone, including Uncle Sam, into a Muslim. But that requires first infiltrating the religious establishment. To do that, they must be recognized and accepted by the national clergy. And critics point out that the only way they can do that is by posing as moderates and pluralists. *Posing* is the right word. A closer look at Esposito's book on Islam shows he lionizes Palestinian terrorists as leaders of a "political movement," and the late PLO chief Yasir Arafat as a "statesman." And he urges Washington to distance itself from Israel.[4]

Yet tolerance of different points of view often goes in only one direction. In the years that I have served as pastor of The Moody Church, we have had former Muslims give their testimony of conversion from Islam to Christianity. In each case we were asked by the person to not advertise their coming beyond our own membership lest Muslims attend to disrupt the services, as frequently happens when such a witness is given. These converts tell stories of how their families seek their death, and how they have been harassed and threatened because of their conversion. And *where there is fear, there is silence*.

There indeed may be value in so-called interfaith dialogue if issues are honestly faced and if the interaction brings both insight and understanding. In a discussion I had with an imam, some of my misconceptions of Islam were clarified, as were some of his misconceptions of Christianity. But such dialogue must be undertaken with a great deal of respect, forethought, and especially clarity because the issues involved touch sensitive nerves in Islam, Judaism, and Christianity. To "lay all the cards on the table," as the saying goes, can sometimes end up producing more heat than light.

Most assuredly, we should listen to what Muslims say about their religion, but we must also study their texts and their history, and pay careful attention to what their own scholars teach about Islam. And of course, they should be invited to have the same posture toward us, our texts and our history—both good and bad.

The bottom line is that we can expect increasing pressure to find unity between the two religions. As mentioned earlier, what is taking place in Europe now might be an indicator of things to come in North America. I've had the privilege of leading tours to the sites of the Protestant Reformation in Europe, giving lectures at the various places related to Martin Luther's life and ministry. On one occasion, when the tour group was about to enter the famous Castle Church in Wittenberg, where Luther posted his 95 theses, a service was in progress. I decided to stay and watch. Though my German is limited, I am able to comprehend it when it's spoken. Incredibly, the pastor read from the Old Testament, the New Testament, and the Quran, explaining that "this church honors all three of the major religions." He said this standing at a lectern about 15 feet from Luther's grave!

Liberal churches in Europe are doing what liberal churches have always done—namely, trade the gospel in exchange for whatever political or cultural benefits appear immediately before them. Of course there are some churches in Europe that still preach the gospel and have not bowed to the pressure to blend their understanding of Christianity with Islam. But by and large, the European church has done little to withstand the growing acceptance of Islam as a dominant or even future religion of Europe.

Although we can expect to come under increasing pressure to compromise the gospel by minimizing its uniqueness to Christianity alone, we must stand strong, explaining why Jesus Christ, of necessity, is the only way to God the Father. The apostle Paul, writing from prison, prayed that believers would be found standing firm "in one

Spirit, striving together as one for the faith of the gospel without being frightened in any way by those who oppose you. This is a sign to them that they will be destroyed, but that you will be saved—and that by God" (Philippians 1:27-28).

A LESSON FROM GERMANY

Ask the average Christian about what happened in Germany as World War II approached, and he will tell you that the church in that country, for the most part, failed to withstand the onslaught of the Nazi agenda. We can certainly voice criticism over the failure to speak up against the Nazi regime, but we must be careful to not indict the *whole* church.

You might be surprised at the identity of one very famous individual who commended the church in Germany—the Jewish physicist Albert Einstein. He is reported as saying that as Nazism was rising to power, he looked to the country's universities, those supposed bastions of free thought, and expected them to oppose Nazism, but *the universities were silent.*

Then he looked to the newspapers, which had carried inspiring editorials defending freedom and the liberties of an educated country. But when Nazism came, *the newspapers were silent.*

Einstein then went on to say that only the church had shown the courage to stand in Hitler's path.[5]

True, while most of the churches did not withstand the onslaught, some did so heroically. More than 700 pastors and priests were thrown into concentration camps, where they died horrid deaths. At least there were some Christians who proved that there are things in life worth dying for. *But they had to stand alone. No one else in their society stood with them.*

I expect—and I pray I am wrong—that for a variety of reasons, true evangelical Christians will become increasingly ostracized and isolated here in North America. There may come a time when we will not be able to depend on our courts to defend our freedoms or give us a fair hearing. As Christianity is painted as the villain, we can expect lawsuits that will attempt to render us without a voice. New laws purporting to be based on the US Constitution will be enacted, attempting to force us to remain silent; our right to express our views will be restricted to within the confines of a church or the privacy of our own homes.

Consider our universities, which are not as much the bastions of free thought as they used to be. They have become increasingly secularized, and we can expect Christian students to be more and more marginalized, pressured to bow before the god of modernity if they wish to graduate. Free thought will be limited to variations of the liberal agenda with its insistence on political correctness and humanistic values, along with a heightened respect for Islam.

Just as homosexuality has been gaining a privileged status in America, growing more and more immune from criticism, just so Islam is being given a similar special exemption. One of our cable television networks here in America boasts that its reports are "fair and balanced." But make no mistake: When such news organizations are threatened for reporting honor killings or exposing Islam's killing of Christians in Muslim-dominated countries, these news organizations will become silent. When truth falls out of favor as a cultural norm, it will either be turned into a lie, or, more likely, silence will prevail. Self-censorship, as was the case in Germany, will be the norm.

Is the church in the West strong enough to stand alone without any support from the state, the media, our schools, our courts? That was the question the church faced in Nazi Germany, and the answer was, at best, mixed. Most Germans were swept away by the powerful cultural stream of Nazism. And others who knew better ended up cowering under the pressure of threats, ostracism, and persecution. Will we respond any differently?

Will the levees hold?

THE DIALOGUE WE MUST HAVE

I deeply believe that we who are part of the evangelical church in the West have the responsibility of beginning our own dialogue about Islam and the Christian church in America. We are hearing more and more about how Europe must wake up to the Muslim agenda that is engulfing it. Can we not learn from what is happening overseas and wake up while there is still time for us to provide some answers for the advance of Islam's stealth jihad to subvert the West?

The previous chapter of this book was written to spur us toward national dialogue that will raise the fundamental issues about our future and what we should do in light of the religious and cultural challenges facing the church. As evangelicals, we need one another's support and the collective wisdom of all believers as we discuss and pray about our uncertain future.

And, in the midst of these challenges, we cannot lose sight of the fact that we are called to proclaim the gospel of Christ to this world. We should not see a dichotomy between a realistic view of our challenges and continuing to be a loving witness to those around us. We must learn from our Christian brothers and sisters in Muslim-dominated countries, who have learned to do both. Our best example, of course, is Jesus, who witnessed to the forgiving grace of His Father even as He went to the cross.

This is why I believe the story of Dietrich Bonhoeffer is so relevant for us today. As a pastor faced with the evils of Nazism, he had to think through a Christian response to the fierce winds of anti-Semitism and the lust for power that were blowing through Germany like a hurricane. The question was, who would stand with him in that hour of dire need? Those who stood with him numbered in the hundreds, rather than the tens or hundreds of thousands. It takes courage to stand against a culture's willing blindness.

In such a dialogue, the topics for discussion should include the legal, moral, and political aspects of the Muslim challenge to the West. We should discuss, for example, shariah versus the US Constitution and why they cannot coexist side by side. More importantly, there should be instruction on sharing Christ with Muslims and the great inroads Christianity is making even in Muslim-dominated nations. Finally, we should discuss how to grow strong Christians at a time of increasing adversity.

And yes, of course the church can stand alone if she has to! As the apostle Paul correctly determined, "If God is for us, who can be against us?" (Romans 8:31). In standing, she will honor our Lord and prove to all that there are some things more important than life itself. We should all be able to say with Paul, "To me, to live is Christ, and to die is gain" (Philippians 1:21).

May we look to Revelation 3:2-3 as a final plea from Jesus to us: "Wake up! Strengthen what remains and is about to die...Remember, therefore, what you have received and heard; hold it fast, and repent. But if you do not wake up, I will come like a thief, and you will not know at what time I will come to you."

Let us consider it an honor to rise to the challenge.

— A Prayer —

Father, we pray for Your church at this critical hour. We have been purchased by the blood of Your Son, who gave Himself up for us that we might be Yours forever. Yet, Father, we often feel weak and helpless in the presence of opposition, persecution, and those who would seek our destruction.

So we earnestly pray for these things:

We pray that we might fully repent of those sins that stand in the way of Your unhindered blessing. We humbly ask that You might reveal to us the compromises and the rationalizations that have made us so much *like* the world that we can no longer be a powerful witness *to* the world.

We repent of our love of possessions, sensuality, personal prestige, and the so-called "good life" that overshadows our love for You and our witness to our neighbors and friends. We repent of being more concerned about our own personal peace and security than we are about reflecting Your glory through personal and corporate suffering. Scripture tells us the early believers "*joyfully accepted the plundering of [their] goods, knowing that [they] have a better and an enduring possession for [themselves] in heaven*" (Hebrews 10:34 NKJV). May we share in that same joy.

We seek to heed the words of Jesus to the churches in Revelation, and repent of our lack of love, false teaching, immorality, and lukewarmness. Help us to capture the vision of a powerful, repentant, Spirit-filled church that is a credit to our Lord regardless of the opposition it faces in the world.

Deliver us from the fear of Islam. We pray that You will help us realize that You have brought Muslims to our shores that they might have a better opportunity to hear the good news of the gospel, and You intend that we would befriend them and introduce them to Jesus, not just as a prophet, but as a Savior. Help us to live before them as Christ followers, as those who truly know and live like Jesus.

Deliver us from the fear of persecution, threats, false accusations, or even martyrdom. Help us to remember that ultimately, there is nothing that can harm those whose faith is in the Prince of Life.

We affirm that Christ is Lord over the entire world; He is Lord over all the countries and religions of this world. He is Lord over all false gods and false prophets who lead others astray. He is Lord over circumstances and relationships. He is Lord over our finances, our health, and every aspect of our lives and witness. We submit ourselves to the total Lordship of Christ.

Today, we offer ourselves up to be Your witnesses in this world. We do not ask for comfort or for safety, but for a loving boldness that affirms the truths that we profess to believe. We pray that with confidence and hope we might live in this world as those who are "*looking forward to the city with foundations, whose architect and builder is God*" (Hebrews 11:10).

Let the vision of Christ, who gave Himself up for us, motivate us to follow in His footsteps that we might show His love and glory to a world that has lost its way. May we suffer as He suffered, love as He loved, and forgive as He forgave. To that end we submit ourselves.

All for Your glory—in Jesus' name,
Amen.

Select Bibliography

Anyabwile, Thabiti. *The Gospel for Muslims: An Encouragement to Share Christ with Confidence.* Chicago: Moody Publishers, 2010.

Claydon, David, ed. *Islam: Human Rights and Public Policy.* Victoria, Australia: Acorn Press, Ltd., 2009.

Caner, Emir Fethi, and H. Edward Pruitt. *The Costly Call: Modern-Day Stories of Muslims Who Found Jesus.* Grand Rapids: Kregel Publications, 2005.

Daniel, Robin. *This Holy Seed: Faith, Hope and Love in the Early Churches of North Africa.* Harpenden, Herts, England: Tamarisk Publications, 1993.

This self-published book by a longtime missionary in the Muslim world sheds light on the demise of the church in North Africa at the hands of Muslim conquerors. Though once a thriving center of Christianity, the church succumbed to the Muslim invaders soon after the death of Muhammad.

DeYoung, Kevin, and Greg Gilbert. *What Is the Mission of the Church? Making Sense of Social Justice, Shalom, and the Great Commission.* Wheaton: Crossway, 2011.

Durie, Mark. *Liberty to the Captives: Freedom from Islam & Dhimmitude Through the Cross.* Deror Books, 2010.

This book clarifies what life is like for non-Muslim subjects in Muslim-majority countries and shares how Muslims can attain spiritual freedom from Islam and follow Christ.

Durie, Mark. *Revelation? Do We Worship the Same God? Jesus, Holy Spirit, God in Christianity and Islam: Guidance for the Perplexed.* Upper Mt. Gravatt, Australia: City-Harvest Publications, 2006.

Durie, Mark. *The Third Choice: Islam, Dhimmitude and Freedom.* N.p.: Deror Books, 2010.

Dyer, Charles H., Mark Bailey, Erwin W. Lutzer, Larry Mercer, Samuel Naaman, and Michael Rydelnik. *Prophecy in Light of Today.* Chicago: Moody Publishers, 2002.

Extreme Devotion: The Voice of the Martyrs. Nashville: Thomas Nelson, 2002.

Federer, William J. *What Every American Needs to Know About the Qur'an: A History of Islam & the United States.* St. Louis: Amerisearch, Inc., 2010.

Gabriel, Brigitte. *They Must Be Stopped: Why We Must Defeat Radical Islam and How We Can Do It.* New York: St. Martin's Press, 2008.

Geisler, Norman L., and Abdul Saleeb. *Answering Islam: The Crescent in Light of the Cross.* Grand Rapids: Baker Books, 1996.

Greear, J.D. *Breaking the Islam Code.* Eugene, OR: Harvest House Publishers, 2010.

Horowitz, David. *Unholy Alliance: Radical Islam and the American Left.* Washington, DC: Regnery Publishing, Inc., 2004.

Jenkins, Philip. *The Lost History of Christianity: The Thousand-Year Golden Age of the Church in the Middle East, Africa, and Asia—and How It Died.* New York: Harper-One, 2008.

Karsh, Efraim. *Islamic Imperialism: A History.* New Haven, CT: Yale University Press, 2007.

Lewis, Bernard. *Islam and the West.* New York: Oxford University Press, 1993.

Lingel, Joshua, Jeff Morton, and Bill Nikides. *Chrislam: How Missionaries Are Promoting an Islamized Gospel.* Garden Grove, CA: i2 Ministries Publishing, 2011.

Madden, Thomas F. *A Concise History of the Crusades.* Lanham, MD: Rowman & Littlefield Publishers, 1999.

Marshall, Paul, and Nina Shea. *Silenced: How Apostasy & Blasphemy Codes Are Choking Freedom Worldwide.* New York: Oxford University Press, 2011.

The first major survey of the political effects of blasphemy and apostasy laws in Muslim countries, this outstanding volume documents how Islamists are attempting to impose such laws in the West to stifle discussion and debate about Islam. The authors report on the many victims of such laws, and how such laws empower extremist forces in the Muslim world whose agenda is to Islamize the West.

McCarthy, Andrew C. *The Grand Jihad: How Islam and the Left Sabotage America.* New York: Encounter Books, 2010.

Medearis, Carl. *Speaking of Jesus: The Art of Not-Evangelism.* Colorado Springs: David C. Cook, 2011.

Milton, Giles. *Paradise Lost—Smyrna 1922: The Destruction of Islam's City of Tolerance.* London: Sceptre, 2009.

Moeller, Dr. Carl A., and David W. Hegg with Craig Hodgkins. *The Privilege of Persecution (And Other Things the Global Church Knows That We Don't).* Chicago: Moody Publishers, 2011.

Oksnevad, Roy, and Dotsey Welliver, eds. *The Gospel for Islam: Reaching Muslims in North America.* Wheaton, IL: Evangelism and Missions Information Service (EMIS), 2001.

Richardson, Don. *Secrets of the Koran: Revealing Insights into Islam's Holy Book.* Ventura: Regal Books, 2003.

Shariah: The Threat to America—An Exercise in Competitive Analysis—Report of Team BII. Washington, DC: The Center for Security Policy, 2010.

Compiled by a team of government officials and national security policy experts, this extensive analysis is based on documents and resources that reveal the aspirations and intents of Islamists in America. It provides well-documented evidence of the threat of the legal-political-military doctrine known as shariah.

Solomon S. and E. Alamaqdisi. *The Mosque Exposed*. Charlottesville, VA: ANM Press, 2007.

Sookhdeo, Patrick. *A Christian's Pocket Guide to Islam*. Ross-shire, Scotland: Christian Focus Publications, 2010.

Sookhdeo, Patrick. *Faith, Power and Territory: A Handbook of British Islam*. McLean, VA: Isaac Publishing, 2008.

A detailed and informative survey of Islam in Britain that provides insight into the ways British authorities are yielding more and more to the process of Islamization.

Spencer, Robert. *The Complete Infidel's Guide to the Koran*. Washington, DC: Regnery Publishing, Inc., 2009.

Spencer, Robert. *Stealth Jihad: How Radical Islam Is Subverting America Without Guns or Bombs*. Washington, DC: Regnery Publishing, Inc., 2008.

Spencer, Robert. *The Truth About Muhammad: Founder of the World's Most Intolerant Religion*. Washington, DC: Regnery Publishing, Inc., 2006.

Sperry, Paul. *Infiltration: How Muslim Spies and Subversives Have Penetrated Washington*. Nashville, TN: Nelson Current, 2005.

Volf, Miroslav. *Allah: A Christian Response*. New York: HarperOne, 2011.

This book attempts to demonstrate that the Allah and the biblical God share enough attributes in common to say that Muslims and Christians worship the same God. It discusses the question of whether it is possible to be both a Muslim and a Christian based on such similarities. Though widely hailed as a breakthrough in Muslim/Christian relations, it minimizes the deep—and irreconcilable—differences that exist between the two religions.

Wagner, William. *How Islam Plans to Change the World*. Grand Rapids, MI: Kregel Publications, 2004.

Warner, Bill, Center for the Study of Political Islam. *Sharia Law for the Non-Muslim*. CSPI, LLC, 2010.

Witt, David and Mujahid El Masih. *Fearless Love in the Midst of Terror: Rediscovering Jesus' Spirit of Martyrdom*. Greenville, TX: Casscom Media, 2009.

Ye'or, Bat. *The Decline of Eastern Christianity Under Islam: From Jihad to Dhimmitude: Seventh–Twentieth Century*. Madison, NJ: Fairleigh Dickinson University Press, 1996.

Ye'or, Bat. *Europe, Globalization, and the Coming Universal Caliphate*. Madison, NJ: Fairleigh Dickinson University Press, 2011.

Zwemer, Samuel M. *Islam and the Cross: Selections from "The Apostle to Islam,"* ed. Roger S. Greenway. Phillipsburg, NJ: Presbyterian & Reformed, 2002.

Notes

INTRODUCTION—THE DAY THE LEVEES BROKE

1. The idea for this imagery regarding Hurricane Katrina and the levees breaking in New Orleans was inspired by Tony Evans, as found in Tony Evans, *Oneness Embraced* (Chicago: Moody, 2011), p. 253.

2. Abdurrahman Wahid as quoted in Andrew C. McCarthy, *The Grand Jihad* (New York: Encounter Books, 2010), p. 32.

3. Tony Evans, *Oneness Embraced* (Chicago: Moody, 2011), p. 252.

4. Evans, *Oneness Embraced*, p. 253.

CHAPTER ONE—THE CHURCH OF THE CLOSED DOOR

1. Soeren Kern, "Muslims Converting Empty European Churches into Mosques" (January 16, 2012), http://www.gatestoneinstitute.org/2761/converting-churches-into-mosques, accessed May 13, 2012.

2. Frank Wright, during a message given on September 23, 2009 at the National Religious Broadcasters convention in Washington, DC.

3. Kern, "Muslims Converting Empty European Churches into Mosques."

4. Kern, "Muslims Converting Empty European Churches into Mosques."

5. Philip Jenkins, *The Lost History of Christianity* (New York: HarperOne, 2008), pp. 4, 30.

6. Bernard Lewis, *Islam and the West* (New York: Oxford University Press, 1993), p. 41.

7. Paul Marshall and Nina Shea, *Silenced: How Apostasy & Blasphemy Codes Are Choking Freedom Worldwide* (New York: Oxford University Press, 2011), p. 127.

8. Marshall and Shea, *Silenced: How Apostasy & Blasphemy Codes Are Choking Freedom Worldwide*, p. 129.

9. Jenkins, *The Lost History of Christianity*, pp. 23-24.

10. Leonard Ralph Holme, *The Extinction of the Christian Churches in North Africa* (New York: B. Franklin, 1969, originally published 1898), p. 244.

11. Holme, *The Extinction of the Christian Churches in North Africa*, p. 3.

12. *Shariah: The Threat to America—An Exercise in Competitive Analysis, Report of Team B II* (Washington, DC: The Center for Security Policy, 2010), 18; citing Steven Merley, "The Muslim Brotherhood in the United States," *Research Monographs on the Muslim World,* Series No. 2, Paper No. 3 (Washington, DC: Hudson Institute, April 2009), Appendix II, p. 52.

13. Investigative Project on Terrorism, document archive at http://www.investigativeproject.org/document/id/20, accessed on May 6, 2012.

14. See "About OIC" at http://www.oic-oci.org/page_detail.asp?p_id=52, accessed June 7, 2012.

15. "Criticism of Islam Could Soon Be a Crime in America" (December 11, 2011), http://creepingsharia.wordpress.com/2011/12/11/criticism-of-islam-could-soon-be-a-crime-in-america/, accessed June 7, 2012.

16. Marshall and Shea, *Silenced: How Apostasy & Blasphemy Codes Are Choking Freedom Worldwide*, p. 208.

17. Marshall and Shea, *Silenced: How Apostasy & Blasphemy Codes Are Choking Freedom Worldwide*, p. 16.

18. "Ten-year Programme of Action to Meet the Challenges Facing the Muslim Ummah in the 21st Century," from the Third Extraordinary Session of the Islamic Summit Conference, Article VII, number 3, "Combating Islamophobia," http://www.oic-oci.org/ex-summit/english/10-years-plan.htm, accessed June 7, 2012.

19. Marshall and Shea, *Silenced: How Apostasy & Blasphemy Codes Are Choking Freedom Worldwide*, p. 17.

20. *Shariah: The Threat to America*, p. 2.

21. *Shariah: The Threat to America*, pp. 4-5.

22. Abdallah Bahri, "Aspects of Sharia Introduced into Non-Islamic States," in *Islam: Human Rights and Public Policy,* ed. David Claydon (Victoria, Australia: Acorn Press, 2009), pp. 185-86.

23. *Shariah: The Threat to America*, p. 3.

24. Yusuf Al-Qaradawi, "Why is secularism incompatible with Islam?" from *The Saudi Gazette*, cited by Andrew C. McCarthy, "Inventing Moderate Islam," National Review Online (August 24, 2010), http://www.nationalreview.com/articles/244545/inventing-moderate-islam-andrew-c-mccarthy, accessed June 18, 2012.

25. Lewis, *Islam and the West*, p. 41.

26. Joseph Myers, "Homeland Security Implications of the Holy Land Foundation Trial," *American Thinker* (September 18, 2007), http://www.americanthinker.com/2007/09/homeland_security_implications_1.html, accessed May 6, 2012.

27. George Santayana, *The Life of Reason, Reason in Common Sense,* vol. 1 (New York: Schribner's 1905), p. 284.

CHAPTER TWO—LESSON #1: WE CANNOT TAKE THE CONTINUED EXISTENCE OF THE CHURCH FOR GRANTED

1. As cited in S. Solomon and E. Almaqdisi, *The Mosque Exposed* (Charlottesville, VA: ANMPress, 2007), p. 49.

2. Dionysios Hatzopoulos, "The Fall of Constantinople, 1453," http://agios vasileiospeiraiws.blogspot.com/2010/05/fall-of-constantinople-1453-by .html, accessed May 12, 2012.

3. Hatzopoulos, "The Fall of Constantinople."

4. David Nicolle, *The Janissaries* (London: Osprey Publishing, 1995), p. 7.

5. Hatzopoulos, "The Fall of Constantinople."

6. "Christians and Muslims: From the Editor—the Cover's Story," *Christian History,* Issue 74, http://www.christianitytoday.com/ch/2002/issue74/may24. html, accessed May 12, 2012.

7. Philip Jenkins, *The Lost History of Christianity* (New York: HarperOne, 2008), p. 102.

8. Jenkins, *The Lost History of Christianity*, p. 34.

9. Jenkins, *The Lost History of Christianity*, p. 130.

10. Jenkins, *The Lost History of Christianity*, p. 100.

11. S. Solomon and E. Alamaqdisi, *The Mosque Exposed* (Charlottesville, VA: ANM Press, 2006), p. 29.

12. Solomon and Alamaqdisi, *The Mosque Exposed*, p. 37.

13. Sarah Hassan, "Preachers of separatism at work inside Britain's mosques," *The Telegraph* (August 31, 2008), http://www.telegraph.co.uk/news/ uknews/2653266/Preachers-of-separatism-at-work-inside-Britains-mosques. html, accessed May 6, 2012.

14. Jamie Glazov, "Shari'a and Violence in American Mosques," *FrontPage Magazine* (June 10, 2011), http://frontpagemag.com/2011/06/10/sharia-and-violence-in-american-mosques/, accessed May 6, 2012.

15. Glazov, "Shari'a and Violence in American Mosques."

16. Glazov, "Shari'a and Violence in American Mosques."

17. Glazov, "Shari'a and Violence in American Mosques."

18. Clare M. Lopez, "Palestinians Petition for 'Sacred Space'" (October 6, 2011), http://obsfotrans.wordpress.com/2011/10/06/palestinians-peti tion-for-sacred-space/, accessed August 15, 2012.

19. Patrick Sookhdeo, *Faith, Power and Territory: A Handbook of British Islam* (McLean, VA: Isaac Publishing, 2008), p. 45.

20. *Shariah: The Threat to America—An Exercise in Competitive Analysis Report of Team BII* (Washington DC: Center for Security Policy, 2010), p. 92.

21. *Shariah: The Threat to America*, p. 92.

22. *Shariah: The Threat to America*, p. 93.

23. Staff writers, "Anger over mosque plan for Ground Zero," *Herald Sun* (Melbourne, May 14, 2010), http://www.heraldsun.com.au/news/breaking-news/

anger-over-mosque-plan-for-ground-zero/story-e6frf7jx-1225866534163, accessed August 15, 2012.

24. Solomon and Almaqdisi, *The Mosque Exposed*, p. 41.

25. Solomon and Almaqdisi, *The Mosque Exposed*, p. 49.

26. Solomon and Almaqdisi, *The Mosque Exposed*, p. 50.

27. Jenkins, *The Lost History of Christianity*, p. 42.

28. Jenkins, *The Lost History of Christianity*, p. 41.

29. For an outstanding and thoughtful study of the transformation that has been taking place in Europe in recent decades, read Bat Ye'or's book *Europe, Globalization, and the Coming Universal Caliphate* (Madison, NJ: Fairleigh Dickinson University Press, 2011).

30. Assad Elepty, "Islamic Suppression and Humiliation of Egypt's Coptic Community Continues," *Free Copts* (December 8, 2010), http://english.freecopts.net/english/index.php?option=com_content&task=view&id=1152&Itemid=1, accessed May 12, 2012.

31. Mary Abdelmassih, "Egyptian Christians Clash With State Security Forces Over Church Construction," *Free Copts* (November 26, 2010), http://www.assistnews.net/Stories/2010/s10110185.htm, accessed June 18, 2012.

32. Reza Sayah, "Egypt's military begins rebuilding burned Coptic church," *CNNWorld* (March 13, 2011), http://www.cnn.com/2011/WORLD/meast/03/13/egypt.church/index.html, accessed May 12, 2012.

33. Larry Poston, "The Current State of Islam in America," in Roy Oksnevad and Dotsey Welliver, eds., *The Gospel for Islam: Reaching Muslims in North America* (Wheaton, IL: Evangelism and Missions Information Service, 2001), p. 17.

CHAPTER THREE—LESSON #2: FAITHFULNESS TO CHRIST REQUIRES AN ACCEPTANCE OF PERSECUTION

1. The Quran.

2. Philip Jenkins, *The Lost History of Christianity* (New York: HarperOne, 2008), pp. 23-24.

3. Jenkins, *The Lost History of Christianity*, p. 117.

4. Jenkins, *The Lost History of Christianity*, p. 118.

5. Jenkins, *The Lost History of Christianity*, p. 23.

6. Efraim Karsh, *Islamic Imperialism* (New Haven, CT: Yale University Press, 2007), p. 62.

7. Mark Durie, *The Third Choice: Islam, Dhimmitude and Freedom* (n.p.: Deror Books, 2010), pp. 122-23.

8. Karsh, *Islamic Imperialism: A History*, p. 63.

9. As cited in Mark Durie, *The Third Choice*, p. 129.

10. Professor A.R. Momin, "Istanbul: European Capital of Culture (2010)," http://iosminaret.org/vol-5/issue4/Istanbul.php.

11. Jenkins, *The Lost History of Christianity*, p. 104.

12. Jenkins, *The Lost History of Christianity*, p. 100.
13. Bernard Lewis, *Islam and the West* (New York: Oxford University Press, 1993), p. 6.
14. Lewis, *Islam and the West*, p. 7.
15. Bat Ye'or, *The Decline of Eastern Christianity Under Islam* (Madison, NJ: Fairleigh Dickinson University Press, 1996), p. 69.
16. Ye'or, *The Decline of Eastern Christianity Under Islam*, p. 69.
17. Karsh, *Islamic Imperialism: A History*, p. 26.
18. Durie, *The Third Choice*, p. 109.
19. "Over 23 million Christians in China, official survey shows," *Christianity Today* (August 12, 2010), http://www.christianitytoday.com/article/over.23.million.christians.in.china.official.survey.shows/26488.htm, accessed May 12, 2012.
20. Durie, *The Third Choice*, p. 131.
21. As cited by Durie, *The Third Choice*, p. 133.
22. Ye'or, *The Decline of Eastern Christianity Under Islam*, p 74; see also p. 78.
23. As cited by Durie, *The Third Choice*, 3; "Tougher law for Malaysia converts," AlJazeera.net, June 27, 2007, http://english.aljazeera.net/NR/exeres/BC3FDD7B-66C9-467D-AD7D-F77EAB74B27D.htm, accessed August 15, 2012.
24. Art Moore, "Punishment Includes Islam Indoctrination," *WorldNetDaily* (October 31, 2002), www.wnd.com/2002/10/15738/, accessed August 15, 2012.
25. Moore, "Punishment Includes Islam Indoctrination."
26. Paul Marshall, "Blasphemy and Free Speech," *Imprimis* (February 2012), p. 1.
27. Marshall, "Blasphemy and Free Speech," p. 5.
28. Paul Marshall and Nina Shea, *Silenced: How Apostasy and Blasphemy Codes Are Choking Freedom Worldwide* (New York: Oxford University Press, 2011), p. 273.
29. Marshall and Shea, *Silenced*, p. 237.
30. Marshall and Shea, *Silenced*, p. 234.
31. Marshall and Shea, *Silenced*, p. 230.
32. *Shariah: The Threat to America—An Exercise in Competitive Analysis Report of Team BII* (Washington DC: Center for Security Policy, 2010), p. 239.
33. William J. Federer, "Moderate Muslims Turning Radical?" WND, February 15, 2008, http://www.wnd.com/2008/02/56286/, accessed June 16, 2012.
34. Federer, "Moderate Muslims Turning Radical?"

CHAPTER FOUR—LESSON #3: EVEN WHEN A CHURCH IS IN THE DEVIL'S HANDS, IT IS STILL IN GOD'S HANDS

1. As cited in Andrew Bostom, "Sharia in America: Will Imam Feisal Rauf Denounce These 'Fatwas' by Muslim Jurists of America?" Gatestone Institute

(August 16, 2010), http://www.gatestoneinstitute.org/1483/sharia-in-america, accessed May 13, 2012.

2. Philip Jenkins, *The Lost History of Christianity* (New York: HarperOne, 2008), p. 138.

3. Giles Milton, *Paradise Lost—Smyrna 1922: The Destruction of Islam's City of Tolerance* (London: Sceptre, 2009), p. 6.

4. Stylianos T. Ayanogou, *Far Above Rubies* (self-published, 1970), p. 37.

5. James Bryce, as cited in Joseph Naayem, preface to *Shall This Nation Die?* (New York: Chaldean Rescue, 1921), http://www.lulu.com/items/volume_2/140000 /140495/2/preview/Naayem__Preview.pdf, accessed May 8, 2012.

6. Jenkins, *The Lost History of Christianity*, p. 140.

7. Giles Milton, *Paradise Lost*. This chapter's description of what happened in Smyrna is based on the accounts provided in this excellent book.

8. Sir Valentine Chirol, *The Occident and the Orient* (Chicago: University of Chicago, 1924), p. 58.

9. Milton, *Paradise Lost*, p. 316.

10. Milton, *Paradise Lost*, p. 317.

11. Milton, *Paradise Lost*, p. 315.

12. See John F. Walvoord and Roy B. Zuck, eds., *The Bible Knowledge Commentary—New Testament* (Wheaton, IL: Victor Books, 1983), pp. 57-58: "Jews would understand hade's gate to refer to physical death. Jesus was thus telling the disciples His death would not prevent His work of building the church…He was therefore anticipating His death and victory over death through the resurrection."

CHAPTER FIVE—LESSON #4: THE CRESCENT CANNOT DESTROY THE CROSS

1. See Michael Yon, "Christian Cross Is Seen as the 'Mark of the Beast' by Islamists: Crosses on unarmed Army MEDEVAC helicopters make them a target for extremists," PJ Media (November 21, 2011), http://pjmedia.com/blog/ christian-cross-is-seen-as-the-mark-of-the-beast-by-islamists/?singlepage=true, accessed May 13, 2012.

2. Thomas F. Madden, *A Concise History of the Crusades* (Lanham, MD: Rowman & Littlefield, 1999), pp. 181-82.

3. There are several variations of this view. One says, "Allah transformed Judas so that he looked like Jesus, and then Judas was nailed to the cross to die." Others say that when the Roman soldiers arrested Jesus, "it was dark, and in the commotion the soldiers mistakenly arrested Judas instead of Jesus." For more on these theories, see Ron Rhodes, *Reasoning from the Scriptures with Muslims* (Eugene, OR: Harvest House Publishers, 2002), pp. 136-38.

4. Chawkat Moucarry, *The Prophet and the Messiah—an Arab Christian's Perspective on Islam and Christianity* (Downer's Grove: InterVarsity, 2001), p. 127.

5. Bruce A. McDowell and Anees Zaka, *Muslims and Christians at the Table* (Phillipsburg, NJ: Presbyterian & Reformed, 1999), p. 108.

6. Moucarry, *The Prophet and the Messiah,* p. 156.

7. Robert Spencer, "The Guardian of Islamic Extremism," Frontpagemag.com (September 21, 2006), http://archive.frontpagemag.com/readArticle .aspx?ARTID=2475, accessed May 9, 2012.

8. Thomas F. Madden, "Crusade Propaganda," *National Review Online* (November 2, 2001), http://www.nationalreview.com/blogs/print/220747, accessed May 9, 2012.

9. Madden, "Crusade Propaganda" (emphasis in original).

10. Thomas F. Madden, gen. ed., *Crusades: The Illustrated History* (London: Duncan Baird Publishers, 2004), p. 36.

11. In his book *On War Against the Turk* (1528), Martin Luther wrote, "But what moved me most of all was this. They undertook to fight against the Turk under the name of Christ...and this is straight against Christ's doctrine and name. It is against His doctrine, because He says that Christians shall not resist evil, shall not fight or quarrel, not take revenge or insist on rights. It is against His name, because in such an army there are scarcely five Christians, and perhaps worse people in the eyes of God than are the Turks; and yet they would all bear the name of Christ."

12. Samuel Zwemer, *Islam and the Cross: Selections from "The Apostle to Islam,"* ed. Roger S. Greenway (Phillipsburg, NJ: Presbyterian & Reformed, 2002), p. 29.

13. Daniel Pipes, "Away with Crucifixes, Crosses, and Christmas" (December 6, 2005; updated May 28, 2011), http://www.danielpipes.org/blog/2005/12/ away-with-crucifixes-crosses-and-christmas, accessed June 18, 2012.

14. Pipes, "Away with Crucifixes, Crosses, and Christmas."

15. "Hospital Chapel Crosses Removed," *CathNews* (April 9, 2009), http://www. cathnews.com/article.aspx?aeid=12898, accessed May 9, 2012.

16. "Frankfurt: Hospital Removes Crosses," http://islamineurope.blogspot .com/2010/02/frankfurt-hospital-removes-crosses.html.

17. John Piper, *The Passion of Jesus Christ* (Wheaton: Crossway, 2004), p. 21.

18. Piper, *The Passion of Jesus Christ,* p. 20.

19. Ron Rhodes, *Reasoning from the Scriptures with Muslims* (Eugene: Harvest House, 2002), p. 235.

20. Muhammad Asad, "The Spirit in Islam," in *Islam—Its Meaning and Message,* ed. Khurshid Ahmad (Leicester, UK: The Islamic Foundation, 1993), p. 53.

21. Unfortunately, I have long since forgotten the title of the book, but its description of Christianity in England has remained with me.

22. *Today in the Word,* February 1989 (Chicago: Moody Bible Institute, 1989), p. 17.

CHAPTER SIX—LESSON #5: COMPROMISE WEAKENS THE CHURCH

1. Philip Jenkins, *The Lost History of Christianity* (New York: HarperCollins, 2008), p. 130.

2. Christopher Atamian, "April 24th: Remembering the Armenian Dead," Huffingtonpost.com (April 24, 2012), http://www.huffingtonpost.com/christopher-atamian/april-24th-remembering-th_b_1447345.html, accessed August 15, 2012.

3. "Iraq: Muslims Attack Church," *The Voice of the Martyrs* (November 5, 2010), http://www.persecution.com/public/newsroom.aspx?story_ID=MzE1, accessed August 15, 2012.

4. Khalil Ullah, "The 'Insider Movement': A Brief Overview and Analysis," BiblicalMissiology.org (March 20, 2011), http://biblicalmissiology.org/2011/03/20/the-insider-movement-a-brief-overview-and-analysis/, accessed August 15, 2012.

5. Joshua Lingel, Jeff Morton, and Bill Nikides, eds., *Chrislam: How Missionaries Are Promoting an Islamized Gospel* (Garden Grove,CA: i2 Ministries Publishing, 2011).

6. Robin Daniel, *This Holy Seed: Faith, Hope and Love in the Early Churches of North Africa* (Harpenden, Herts, England: Tamarisk Publications, 1993), p. 404. This book, written by a missionary to North Africa, describes the history of the region and the impact of Islam's takeover of these Christian lands. Although written from the standpoint of North Africa, it also gives a rather accurate summation of the state of the church in other Middle Eastern nations conquered by Islam.

7. Alan Hirsch, *The Forgotten Ways: Reactivating the Missional Church* (Grand Rapids: The Brazos Press, 2006), p. 83.

8. For more on this BBC broadcast, see http://www.bbc.co.uk/programmes/b010n3qr, accessed August 15, 2012.

9. This blog comment was saved in the author's files, but it unfortunately appears to no longer be available on the Internet.

10. See "The Secret of the Bristlecone Pine" in the July 2002 issue of *Homiletics*, pp. 21-23. More information about the bristlecone pine can be found online.

11. "The Secret of the Bristlecone Pine," p. 23.

CHAPTER SEVEN—LESSON #6: THINGS ARE NOT WHAT THEY APPEAR TO BE

1. "The Twelfth Imam" at http://www.shia.org/mehdi.html, accessed May 12, 2012.

2. See Mark Durie, *The Third Choice* (n.p.: Deror Books, 2010), pp. 31-32.

3. *Sahih Muslim.* Book of Prayers (*Kitab al-Salat*). 1:4:1062.

4. Alphonse Mingana, *The Book of Religion and Empire* (Manchester: University Press, 1922), p. 14; as cited in Mark Durie, *The Third Choice*, p. 20.

5. Ayaan Hirsi Ali, "The Rise of Christophobia," *Newsweek* (February 13, 2012), p. 30.

6. Hirsi Ali, "The Rise of Christophobia."

7. Dan Wooding, "Convert from Islam to Christianity beheaded, video shown on

Egyptian TV," Godreports.com (July 10, 2012), http://blog
.godreports.com/2012/07/convert-from-islam-to-christianity-beheaded
-video-shown-on-egyptian-tv/, accessed July 18, 2012.

8. Hirsi Ali, "The Rise of Christophobia."

9. In 2007, Ayaan Hirsi Ali published her memoir, *Infidel*, which tells her life story (New York: Free Press).

10. Thomas F. Madden, *A Concise History of the Crusades* (Lanham, MD: Rowman & Littlefield, 1999), p. 208.

11. Luther's Works 25:22 Genesis [W, XLIII, 392-93].

12. Luther's Works 25:22 Genesis [W, XLIII, 392-93].

13. Mark Durie, *Revelation? Guidance for the Perplexed* (Australia: CityHarvest Publications, 2006), p. 25.

14. "The Twelfth Imam" at http://www.shia.org/mehdi.html, accessed May 12, 2012.

CHAPTER EIGHT—LESSON #7: THE REMNANT WILL TRIUMPH

1. *Shariah: The Threat to America—An Exercise in Competitive Analysis Report of Team BII* (Washington, DC: The Center for Security Policy, 2010), p. 26.

2. Rosemary Sookhdeo, *Breaking Through the Barriers: Leading Muslims to Christ* (McLean, VA: Isaac Publishing, 2010), p. 15.

3. Thabiti Anyabwile, *The Gospel for Muslims* (Chicago: Moody, 2010), p. 15.

4. J.D. Greear, *Breaking the Islam Code* (Eugene, OR: Harvest House, 2010), p. 36.

5. Andrew C. McCarthy, *The Grand Jihad* (New York: Encounter Books, 2011), p. 64.

6. See, for example, Chris Hedges, *American Fascists: The Christian Right and War on America* (New York: Free Press, 2007); Michael Goldberg, *Kingdom Coming: The Rise of Christian Nationalism* (New York: Norton, 2006); James Rudlin, *The Baptizing of America: The Religious Right's Plans for the Rest of Us* (New York: Thunder's Mouth, 2006); Kevin Phillips, *American Theocracy: The Peril and Politics of Radical Religion, Oil, and Borrowed Money in the 21st Century* (New York: Viking, 2006).

7. "Christians under attack again in Pakistan," http://www.cms-uk.org/tabid/151/articleType/ArticleView/articleId/3538/Christians-under-attack-again-in-Pakistan.aspx, accessed June 18, 2012.

8. Paul Marshall and Nina Shea, *Silenced: How Apostasy and Blasphemy Codes Are Choking Freedom Worldwide* (New York: Oxford University Press, 2011), p. 186.

9. Marshall and Shea, *Silenced*, p. 187.

10. Marshall and Shea, *Silenced*, p. 187.

11. For more details about these and other examples of Islamist lawfare, see Pamela

Geller's book *Stop the Islamization of America* (Washington, DC: WND Books, 2011), pp. 96-101.

12. Mark Durie, *The Third Choice* (n.p.: Deror Books, 2010), p. 57.

13. Mawdudi, *Towards Understanding the Qur'an*, p. 130. Commentary on Q3:28.

14. Roy Oksnevad and Dotsey Welliver, eds., *The Gospel for Islam: Reaching Muslims in North America* (Wheaton, IL: Evangelism and Missions Information Service, 2001). Other resources include Thabiti Anyabwile, *The Gospel for Muslims* (Chicago: Moody, 2010), and J.D. Greear, *Breaking the Islam Code* (Eugene, OR: Harvest House, 2010).

15. Joshua Partlow and Ernesto Londono, "At least seven foreigners killed in attack on U.N. compound in northern Afghanistan," *The Washington Post* (April 1, 2011), http://www.washingtonpost.com/world/12-killed-in-attack-on-un-compound-in-northern-afghanistan/2011/04/01/AFrb5iHC_story.html, accessed August 15, 2012.

16. Joshua Partlow, "Protests over Koran burning spread in Afghanistan, with 9 dead in Kandahar," *The Washington Post* (April 2, 2011), http://www.washingtonpost.com/world/taliban-attack-nato-base-in-kabul-koran-protests-spread/2011/04/02/AFTC9rMC_story.html, accessed August 15, 2012.

17. "MSNBC's *Hardball* Guest Tries To Explain Why Burning The Koran is Worse Than Burning The Bible," as quoted from a transcript that appears on http://www.mediaite.com/tv/msnbcs-hardball-guest-explains-why-burning-the-koran-is-worse-than-burning-the-bible/, accessed August 15, 2012.

18. Miroslav Volf, *Allah: A Christian Response* (New York: HarperOne, 2011), pp. 66-67.

19. Quoted from the August 2010 *Voice of the Martyrs* newsletter, as cited by the Christian Coalition of America at http://www.cc.org/blog/outrage_ground_zero_mosque_open_911_anniversary, accessed May 12, 2012.

20. "Nigeria," *The Voice of the Martyrs*, http://www.persecution.net/nigeria.htm, accessed May 12, 2012.

21. David Witt and Dr. Mujahid el Masih, *Fearless Love in the Midst of Terror: Rediscovering Jesus' Spirit of Martyrdom* (Greenville, TX: Casscom Media, 2009).

22. Robert Spencer, *The Politically Incorrect Guide to Islam (and the Crusades)* (Washington, DC: Regnery Publishing, 2005), p. 102.

23. Paul Sperry, *Infiltration: How Muslim Spies and Subversives Have Penetrated Washington* (Nashville, TN: Nelson Current, 2005), p. 49.

24. Sperry, *Infiltration*, p. 49.

25. Quran footnote #478, p. 172.

26. Justin D. Long, "More Martyrs Now Than Then?" http://jmm.aaa.net.au/articles/2904.htm. In this article, Long states, "During this century, we have documented cases in excess of 26 million martyrs. From AD 33 to 1900, we have documented 14 million martyrs," accessed May 12, 2012.

27. Long, "More Martyrs Now Than Then?"

28. Ron Csillag, "Christians arguably the most persecuted religion in the world," TheStar.com, http://www.thestar.com/news/insight/article/901492—christi-anity-arguably-the-most-persecuted-religion-in-the-world, accessed May 12, 2012.

CHAPTER NINE—WHAT IS HAPPENING IN AMERICA TODAY?

1. Andrew C. McCarthy, *The Grand Jihad* (New York: Encounter Books, 2010), p. 58.

2. *Shariah: The Threat to America*, p. 2.

3. *Shariah: The Threat to America*, p. 5.

4. Mark Durie, *The Third Choice* (n.p.: Deror Books, 2010), p. 32.

5. Bill Warner, *Sharia Law for the Non-Muslim* (n.p.: Center for the Study of Political Islam, 2010), p. 9.

6. *Shariah: The Threat to America*, p. 3.

7. Paul Marshall and Nina Shea, *Silenced: How Apostasy and Blasphemy Codes Are Choking Freedom Worldwide* (New York: Oxford University Press, 2011), p. 6.

8. Marshall and Shea, *Silenced*, p. 314.

9. Christopher Caldwell, "Islamic Europe?—When Bernard Lewis Speaks...," *Weekly Standard* (October 4, 2004), as cited in Andrew C. McCarthy, *The Grand Jihad* (New York: Encounter Books, 2010), p. 96.

10. McCarthy, *The Grand Jihad*, p. 97.

11. Maryam Namazie, "Sharia Law in Britain: A Threat to One Law for All and Equal Rights" (London: One Law for All, 2010), p. 9, http://www.onelawforall.org.uk/wp-content/uploads/New-Report-Sharia-Law-in-Britain.pdf, accessed June 7, 2012.

12. Maryam Namazie, "Sharia Law in Britain: A Threat to One Law for All and Equal Rights." See also Arbitration Act 1996 (UK): http://www.opsi.gov.uk/acts/acts1996/ukpga_19960023_en_1.

13. Namazie, "What Isn't Wrong with Sharia Law?"

14. A. Millar, "From Magna Carta to Sharia Law—Britain's Decline," *The Brussels Journal* (September 15, 2008), http://www.brusselsjournal.com/node/3522, accessed May 12, 2012.

15. Chris Merritt, "Local Islamists draw on British success in bid for sharia law," *The Australian* (October 7, 2011), http://www.theaustralian.com.au/business/legal-affairs/local-islamists-draw-on-british-success-in-bid-for-sharia-law/story-e6frg97x-1226160671193, accessed May 12, 2012.

16. Oklahoma "Sharia Law Amendment," State Question 755 (2010), Ballotpedia, http://ballotpedia.org/wiki/index.php/Oklahoma_%22Sharia_Law_Amendment%22,_State_Question_755_(2010), accessed May 12, 2012.

17. McCarthy, *The Grand Jihad*, p. 153.

18. Ashby Jones and Joe Palazzolo, "States Target Foreign Law," *The Wall Street*

Journal (February 7, 2012), http://online.wsj.com/article/SB10001424052970 2046622045771993726860774 12.html, accessed May 12, 2012.

19. *Shariah: The Threat to America*, pp. 16-17.

20. McCarthy, *The Grand Jihad*, p. 58.

21. *Shariah: The Threat to America*, p. 26.

22. *Shariah: The Threat to America*, p. 58.

23. Robert Spencer, *The Politically Incorrect Guide to Islam (and the Crusades)* (Washington, DC: Regnery, 2005), p. 45.

24. Patrick Poole, "The Muslim Brotherhood 'Project,'" *Frontpage Magazine* (May 11, 2006), http://archive.frontpagemag.com/readarticle.aspx?artid =4476, accessed August 15, 2012.

25. McCarthy, *Grand Jihad*, p. 51.

26. *Shariah: The Threat to America*.

27. *Shariah: The Threat to America*, p. 47.

28. According to Lt. Col. (ret.) Jonathan D. Halevi, "Even in recent years the Muslim Brotherhood's publication in London, *Risalat al-Ikhwan*, maintained its *jihadist* orientation; it featured at the top of its cover page in 2001 the slogan, 'Our mission: world domination' (*siyadat al-dunya*). This header was changed after 9/11, but the publication still carried the Muslim Brotherhood's motto which includes: '*jihad* is our path; martyrdom is our aspiration.'" See "The Muslim Brotherhood: A Moderate Islamic Alternative to al-Qaeda or a Partner in Global Jihad?" Jerusalem Center for Public Affairs (November 1, 2007, http://jcpa.org/article/the-muslim-brother hood-a-moderate-islamic-alternative-to-al-qaeda-or-a-partner-in-global -jihad/, accessed August 15, 2012.

29. McCarthy, *The Grand Jihad*, p. 58.

30. Excerpted from "Missing Bylaws of the International Muslim Brotherhood" (March 1, 2011), http://islamthreat.com/brotherhood/Muslim_Brotherhood_ Bylaws.pdf, accessed April 29, 2012. These same objectives were reported in *Shariah: The Threat to America* (pp. 110-11), which accessed the official Muslim Brotherhood website on September 7, 2010 at http://www.ikhwanweb. com/article.php?=22687. But in early 2011, according to *The Jerusalem Post*, the Muslim Brotherhood "removed its explicitly worded bylaws from its English-language website. The bylaws are still available via an archived version of the Web page. The bylaws have long been a source of discussion and debate on the Internet because of the group's stated intention to create an Islamic state, uniting Muslims around the world, while 'building a new basis of human civilization.'" See Steven Emerson, "Brotherhood changes English website to appear moderate" (3/2/2011), http://www.jpost.com/MiddleEast/Article. aspx?id=210426, accessed May 9, 2012.

31. *Shariah: The Threat to America*, p. 119.

32. This vastly abbreviated list is based on information provided in *Shariah: The Threat to America*, see pp. 41-54.

33. *Shariah: The Threat to America*, p. 43.

34. *Shariah: The Threat to America*, p. 43.

35. Mark Steyn, "Islamist Generation," *National Review Online* (July 14, 2012), http://www.nationalreview.com/articles/309398/islamist-generation-mark-steyn, accessed July 17, 2102.

36. Oren Kessler, "Every aspect of life is to be Islamized," *The Jerusalem Post* (April 10, 2012), http://www.jpost.com/MiddleEast/Article.aspx?id=265583, accessed July 17, 2012.

37. Among the resources are *Shariah the Threat to America: An Exercise in Competitive Analysis Report of Team BII* (Washington, DC: The Center for Security Policy, 2010); Robert Spencer, *The Politically Incorrect Guide to Islam (and the Crusades)* (Washington, DC: Regnery, 2005); Paul Sperry, *Infiltration: How Muslim Spies and Subversives Have Penetrated Washington* (Nashville, TN: Nelson Current, 2005); and Paul Marshall and Nina Shea, *Silenced: How Apostasy and Blasphemy Codes Are Choking Freedom Worldwide* (New York: Oxford University Press, 2011).

38. *Shariah: The Threat to America*, pp. 125-26.

39. Robert Spencer, *Stealth Jihad: How Radical Islam Is Subverting America without Guns or Bombs* (Washington, DC: Regnery, 2008), p. 22.

40. Paul Sperry, *Infiltration: How Muslim Spies and Subversives Have Penetrated Washington* (Nashville, TN: Nelson Current, 2005), p. XXIII.

41. Sperry, *Infiltration,* pp. XXIII-XXIV.

42. Sperry, *Infiltration,* p. 4.

43. Sperry, *Infiltration,* p. 8.

44. Sperry, *Infiltration,* p. 5.

45. Clare Lopez, "The Threat of Islam: Three Things You Need to Know...," Patriot Symposiums, http://www.patriotsymposiums.com/The_Threat_of_Islam.html, accessed May 1, 2012.

46. Transcript of FBI director Robert S. Mueller's testimony before the Senate Judiciary Committee, June 6, 2002, as cited by Sperry, *Infiltration,* p. 8.

47. Lopez in Anthony Martin, "Obama quietly appoints Muslim Brotherhood to key posts" (February 15, 2011), Examiner.com, http://www.examiner.com/article/report-obama-quietly-appoints-muslim-brotherhood-to-key-posts-updates, accessed August 15, 2012.

48. Spencer, *Stealth Jihad,* p. 268.

49. *Shariah: The Threat to America*, p. 125.

50. *Shariah: The Threat to America*, p. 128.

51. *Shariah: The Threat to America*, p. 19.

52. Steven Emerson, "Muslim Students Association: The Investigative Project on Terrorism Dossier," The Investigative Project on Terrorism, http://www.investigativeproject.org/documents/misc/84.pdf, accessed May 2, 2012.

53. Emerson, "Muslim Students Association: The Investigative Project on Terrorism Dossier."

54. Emerson, "Muslim Students Association: The Investigative Project on Terrorism Dossier."

55. Emerson, "Muslim Students Association: The Investigative Project on Terrorism Dossier."

56. Spencer, *Stealth Jihad*, p. 195.

57. Spencer, *Stealth Jihad*, p. 195.

58. Spencer, *Stealth Jihad*, p. 206.

59. Caryle Murphy, "Saudi Gives $20 Million to Georgetown," *Washington Post* (December 13, 2005), http://www.washingtonpost.com/wp-dyn/content/article/2005/12/12/AR2005121200591.html, accessed May 3, 2012.

60. Asaf Romirowsky, "Balancing the Bias," *Jerusalem Post* (February 2, 2009), at Middle East Forum, http://www.meforum.org/2058/balancing-the-bias, accessed May 3, 2012.

61. Asaf Romirowsky, "Balancing the Bias."

62. Marshall and Shea, *Silenced*, p. 7.

63. Lee Kaplan, "The Saudi Fifth Column On Our Nation's Campuses," Frontpagemag.com (April 5, 2004), http://archive.frontpagemag.com/readArticle.aspx?ARTID=13551, accessed May 3, 2012.

64. Kaplan, "The Saudi Fifth Column On Our Nation's Campuses." For more on the evidence that the Muslim World League and International Islamic Relief Organization have been linked to financing terrorist fighters, see Alfred B. Prados and Christopher M. Blanchard, "Saudi Arabia: Terrorist Financing Issues," *CRS [Congressional Research Service] Report for Congress*, updated September 14, 2007, http://www.fas.org/sgp/crs/mideast/RL32499.pdf, accessed May 3, 2012.

65. Kaplan, "The Saudi Fifth Column On Our Nation's Campuses."

66. Kaplan, "The Saudi Fifth Column On Our Nation's Campuses."

67. Paul Sperry, *Infiltration*, p. 34.

68. Durie, *The Third Choice*, p. 113.

69. Durie, *The Third Choice*, p. 113.

70. Durie, *The Third Choice*, p. 114.

71. Marshall and Shea, *Silenced*, p. 174.

72. Center for Security Policy, "New Study on Hate Crimes Debunks Muslim Victimization," *Right Side News* (March 29, 2011), http://www.rightside news.com/2011032913155/us/islam-in-america/new-study-on-hate-crimes-debunks-muslim-victimization.html.

73. Center for Security Policy, "New Study on Hate Crimes Debunks Muslim Victimization."

74. Center for Security Policy, "New Study on Hate Crimes Debunks Muslim Victimization."

75. Bernard Lewis, *Islam and the West* (New York: Oxford University Press, 1993), p. 155.

76. *Shariah: The Threat to America*, p. 72.

77. McCarthy, *The Grand Jihad*, p. 46.

78. Abu Ala Maududi, as cited in S. Solomon and E. Alamaqdisi, *The Mosque Exposed* (Charlottesville, VA: ANM Press, 2006), pp. 48-50.

79. "Dawa: Time to Come Out of Our Boxes!" Muslim Student Association National website, as cited by Steven Emerson, "Muslim Students Association: The Investigative Project on Terrorism Dossier," The Investigative Project on Terrorism, http://www.investigativeproject.org/documents/misc/84.pdf, accessed May 5, 2012.

80. Durie, *The Third Choice*, p. 36.

81. William Federer, "Moderate Muslims Turning Radical?" WorldNetDaily (February 15, 2008), http://www.wnd.com/2008/02/56286/.

82. Federer, "Moderate Muslims Turning Radical?"

83. Federer, "Moderate Muslims Turning Radical?"

84. Federer, "Moderate Muslims Turning Radical?"

85. Federer, "Moderate Muslims Turning Radical?"

CHAPTER TEN—WHAT THE CHURCH SHOULD BE DOING NOW

1. Samuel Zwemer, *Islam and the Cross: Selections from "The Apostle to Islam,"* ed. Roger S. Greenway (Phillipsburg, NJ: Presbyterian & Reformed, 2002), p. 29.

2. In 2007, 138 Muslim scholars sent a letter to the scholars of the Christian world titled "A Common Word Between Us and You." In response, a group of Yale theologians wrote a letter that was published on a full page in the *New York Times*. The letter adopted a tone of self-humiliation, apologizing for the Crusades and the War on Terror and praising Islam. It was endorsed by many leading evangelicals, and it represents an example of Christian submission or "dhimmitude" in interfaith dialogue. Interestingly, the Muslim letter contained no parallel expression of gratitude toward Christianity nor guilt over past or current wrongs done against Christians.

3. See, for example, Stefanie Schartel, "'Chrislam' Rising," Charismanews.com (November 22, 2011), http://www.charismanews.com/world/32349 -chrislam-rising; Margaret Minnicks, "What is Chrislam?" Examiner.com (November 27, 2011), http://www.examiner.com/article/what-is-chrislam.

4. See Joshua Lingel, Jeff Morton, and Bill Nikides, eds., *Chrislam: How Missionaries Are Promoting an Islamized Gospel* (Garden Grove, CA: i2 Ministries Publications, 2011).

5. Brittney R. Villalva, "Honor Killings Rise Across Europe and the US," *World* (January 4, 2012), http://www.christianpost.com/news/honor-killings-rise -across-europe-and-the-us-66406/, accessed May 22, 2012.

6. W. Montgomery Watt, *Times Literary Supplement*, insert on Islam (April 30, 1976), p. 513.

7. Samuel Zwemer, "Studies in Popular Islam," quoted by Bill Musk, "Popular Islam: The Hunger of the Heart" in *The Gospel and Islam: A 1978 Compendium,*

ed. Don McCurry (Monrovia, CA: Missions Advanced Research and Communications Center, 1979), p. 209.

8. Gilbert T. Sewall, *Islam and the Textbooks* (New York: American Textbook Council, 2003), p. 41.

9. Sewall, *Islam in the Classroom* (New York: American Textbook Council, 2008), p. 9.

10. Sewall, *Islam and the Textbooks*, p. 25.

11. Sewall, *Islam and the Textbooks*, p. 26.

12. Maxim Lott, "Advocates of Anti-Shariah Measures Alarmed by Judge's Ruling," *Fox News* (August 5, 2010), http://www.foxnews.com/us/2010/08/05/advocates-anti-shariah-measures-alarmed-judges-ruling/, accessed May 23, 2012.

13. Michael Stone, "Court Rejects Religious Rape Defense on Appeal," *Examiner* (July 26, 2010), http://www.examiner.com/article/court-rejects-religious-rape-defense-on-appeal, accessed May 23, 2012.

14. Bill Warner, *Sharia Law for Non-Muslims* (Nashville: Center for the Study of Political Islam, 2010), p. 2.

15. "Sharia law in UK is 'unavoidable,'" *BBC News* (February 7, 2008), http://news.bbc.co.uk/2/hi/7232661.stm, accessed May 23, 2012.

16. Rebecca Camber, "'No Porn or Prostitution': Islamic Extremists Set Up Sharia Controlled Law Zones in British Cities," *Daily Mail* (July 28, 2011), http://www.dailymail.co.uk/news/article-2019547/Anjem-Choudary-Islamic-extremists-set-Sharia-law-zones-UK-cities.html#ixzz1vqQwPu00, accessed May 24, 2012.

17. Rousas John Rushdoony, *Law & Liberty* (Vallecito, CA: Ross House Books, 1984), p. 33.

18. Robert Spencer, *Stealth Jihad* (New York: Regnery, 2008), p. 164.

19. Elizabeth Kendal, "Case Study: Ontario and Quebec, Canada—Muslims Rally Against Islamists to Defeat Sharia," in David Claydon, ed., *Islam, Human Rights, and Public Policy* (Victoria, Australia: Acorn Press, 2009), p. 192.

20. Kendal, "Case Study: Ontario and Quebec, Canada," p. 193.

21. Kendal, "Case Study: Ontario and Quebec, Canada," p. 193.

22. Kendal, "Case Study: Ontario and Quebec, Canada," p. 194.

23. Kendal, "Case Study: Ontario and Quebec, Canada," p. 194.

24. Kendal, "Case Study: Ontario and Quebec, Canada," p. 194.

25. Kendal, "Case Study: Ontario and Quebec, Canada," p. 194.

26. Kendal, "Case Study: Ontario and Quebec, Canada," p. 195.

27. Kendal, "Case Study: Ontario and Quebec, Canada," p. 195.

28. Mark Durie, *Liberty to the Captives* (n.p.: Deror Books, 2010), p. 53.

29. Eric Metaxas, "What Is the Church's Responsibility to the State?" *Truth & Triumph*, volume V, number 1, http://www.alliancedefensefund.org/TruthAndTriumph/5-1/OnTheSquare, accessed June 7, 2012.

30. Samuel Naaman, "The Future of Islamic Fundamentalism," *Insider Report* (November 6, 2001), as cited in Charles Dyer, et al., *Prophecy in Light of Today* (Chicago: Moody, 2002), pp. 68-69.

31. Thabiti Anyabwile, *The Gospel for Muslims: An Encouragement to Share Christ with Confidence* (Chicago: Moody, 2010), p. 18.

32. "The Future of the Global Muslim Population," The Pew Forum on Religion & Public Life, http://features.pewforum.org/muslim-population/, accessed May 24, 2012.

33. In the testimony on page 140, reference is made to the words from John 14:6 as well. Interestingly, it is not unusual to hear of certain Bible verses or truths that surface repeatedly in the conversion experiences of Muslims.

CHAPTER ELEVEN—A FINAL PLEA: THE CHURCH STANDING ALONE

1. Miroslav Volf, *Allah: A Christian Response* (New York: HarperOne, 2011).

2. Volf, *Allah: A Christian Response*, pp. 197-200. In his book, Volf leaves the question of whether one can be 100 percent Muslim and hold to all orthodox Christian teachings up to Muslims to decide. Of course, given what we know about the major doctrinal differences between Christianity and Islam, it would not be possible for a Muslim to say yes to Volf's proposition.

3. Paul Sperry, *Infiltration* (Nashville, TN: Nelson Current, 2005), p. 97.

4. Paul Sperry, *Infiltration* (Nashville, TN: Nelson Current, 2005), p. 98.

5. These statements were attributed to Albert Einstein in the December 23, 1940 issue of *Time* magazine (p. 38).

Other Good Harvest House Reading

LIFE-CHANGING BIBLE VERSES YOU SHOULD KNOW
by Erwin and Rebecca Lutzer

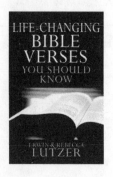

After Erwin Lutzer, senior pastor of The Moody Church, and his wife, Rebecca, realized that memorizing Scripture has nearly become a lost pursuit today, they decided to create this practical, relevant resource filled with powerful verses and insightful explanations to help stimulate a spiritual hunger in your life, which includes more than 35 topics and questions for reflection and further study.

These handpicked verses provide a foundation of wisdom and hope to show you who God is and what He has done for you, as well as who you are and how *you* can successfully live the Christian life.

REASONING FROM THE SCRIPTURES WITH MUSLIMS
by Ron Rhodes

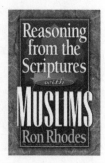

Anyone interested in sharing the gospel with Muslim friends or understanding the doctrines and historical basis of Islam will appreciate this addition to the popular *Reasoning from the Scriptures* series. Using an easy-to-follow question-and-answer format, each chapter examines a Muslim belief and compares it with biblical Christianity.

You'll find this an invaluable tool for discussing and sharing the words and life of Jesus Christ with your Muslim friends and acquaintances.

THE POPULAR ENCYCLOPEDIA OF CHURCH HISTORY
by Ed Hindson and Dan Mitchell

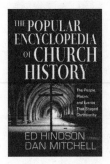

General editors Ed Hindson and Dan Mitchell have extensive experience with producing reference works that combine expert scholarship and popular accessibility. Together with a broad range of well-qualified contributors, they have put together what is sure to become a standard must-have for both Bible teachers and students.

With nearly 300 articles across 400 pages, you will enjoy...

- a comprehensive panorama of church history from Acts 2 to today

- a clear presentation of how the church and its teachings have developed

- concise biographies of major Christian figures and their contributions

- fascinating overviews of key turning points in church history

This valuable resource will enrich your appreciation for the wonderful heritage behind your Christian faith.